Also by Wallace Terry

*Bloods: An Oral History of the Vietnam
War by Black Veterans*

MISSING PAGES

BLACK JOURNALISTS OF MODERN AMERICA: AN ORAL HISTORY

WALLACE TERRY

CARROLL & GRAF PUBLISHERS
NEW YORK

For Noah and Sophia, our grandchildren.

MISSING PAGES
Black Journalists of Modern America:
An Oral History

Carroll & Graf Publishers
An Imprint of Avalon Publishing Group, Inc.
245 West 17th Street
11th Floor
New York, NY 10011

AVALON
publishing group incorporated

Copyright © 2007 by Janice Terry

First Carroll & Graf edition 2007

Library of Congress Cataloging-in-Publication Data

Terry, Wallace.
Missing pages : black journalists of modern America : an oral history / Wallace Terry. — 1st Carroll & Graf ed.
   p. cm.
Includes bibliographical references and index.
ISBN 978-0-7867-1993-8 (trade pbk. original)
1. African American journalists--Biography. I. Title.

PN4871.5.T47 2007
070.92'396073--dc22
[B]

2007005674

ISBN-10: 0-7867-1993-1

9 8 7 6 5 4 3 2 1

Interior book design by Bettina Wilhelm
Printed in the United States of America
Distributed by Publishers Group West

CONTENTS

AUTHOR'S NOTE

ONE DAY WHEN I WAS teaching journalism at Howard University, I picked up an acclaimed book on the history of war correspondents. At first glance, it seemed a perfect selection for a course I was teaching on the role of the foreign correspondent. I was hardly surprised to see that no black correspondents were mentioned, although they had covered World War II, the Korean Conflict, and the Vietnam War. Black journalists were usually missing from historical accounts of war.

What stunned me, however, was the story of a British correspondent who claimed that he had rescued the bodies of four white journalists murdered by Viet Cong sappers in the Vietnam War. I knew this story was a lie because I was there, and he wasn't. In reality, the rescue was made by me and another American correspondent. This was a major and very dangerous event in my life.

Why, I asked, was I left unmentioned? Was it because I was black?

That's when I made up my mind to research and write a book about black journalists, beginning with World War II and taking them through the civil rights movement in America and the Vietnam War. This work would help fill the missing pages in the history of modern American journalism.

I hoped it would serve as a book of instruction for a journalism course, where none existed. But I also wanted it to be of interest to general readers, of whatever race and ethnic background, who would like to hear about major events in American history as seen through the eyes of a special breed of professional observers.

Since I was present at many of the events they described, I could assure readers that it was their own stories and adventures, not someone else's version—and honestly told.

—*Wallace Terry*

CARL ROWAN

Carl Rowan began as a reporter for the Minneapolis Tribune *and evolved into a columnist and TV personality. He became friends with John F. Kennedy and Lyndon Johnson, and served as the director of the United States Information Agency.*[1]

———

I was in Helsinki. My wife Vivien and I had come home from an embassy party. I was in bed with some papers to read, about to fall asleep, when the phone rang.

The voice was familiar.

"Carl, Lyndon. Come home. I need you."

That's all he said.

I got out of bed and said, "Jesus Christ." I called my administrative boss and asked him to book me on the first plane to Washington.

When I arrived in the States, Bill Moyers, Johnson's assistant, met me at the airport.

"Carl, for God's sake, don't let the president know I've told you this," Moyers said. "You know how he is about leaks of his appointments. He intends to name you as director of the U.S. Information Agency. But he doesn't have all of his ducks in line—McClellan and Ellender and a lot of those Southern senators who've got to confirm you. He wants you to go to the Madison Hotel and stay incognito until he tells you he's got everything in line."

Four days later Johnson called and asked if I could come over to the White House to have supper with him and Lady Bird. He had something special to tell me. I would be replacing Edward R. Murrow, who had cancer beyond hope, as the director of USIA.

After dinner, he put on the USIA film Ed Murrow had done on the civil rights march on Washington, and we watched it together.

"I'm getting heat from some of these Southern senators who don't want USIA to show this movie abroad," Johnson said. "If you were director, would you show it overseas?"

"Mr. President," I said, "if I am director, that movie will be shown. And if you don't want it shown, now is the time for you to know that you have to get yourself somebody else as director of USIA."

"That's good enough for me," he said. "It'll be shown."

I found out later what the furor was really about. J. Edgar Hoover had gone before the appropriations committee with salacious tapes and every rumor he could find about Martin Luther King. Congressman John Rooney took me into his confidence and told me what the Southern guys would try to hand me when I went up for appropriations, if we showed the USIA film.

I said, "Well, they'll just have to hand it to me if they can."

After I was confirmed we distributed the film. The guys in the Senate didn't know that I knew how to play a few games, too. Before we went up for the appropriations hearings, I had the embassy in South Africa and fifteen other posts send me telegrams about the remarkable impact of that film, what a great tool it was for U.S. foreign policy.

Ol' Senator Ellender and the boys never said a word. They waited until the last crunch day. Then all of a sudden they sprang all this stuff they got from Hoover about Martin Luther King, and criticized the film because King was in it.

That's when I sprang my messages from abroad. Those senators just sat there. They didn't know what hit them. We got all the money we asked for—and then some!

I first joined the government in the Kennedy Administration. I had worked for the *Minneapolis Tribune* for a number of years. I had gotten a lot of lucky breaks and more than my share of great assignments.

The first great break was to have a publisher with a social conscience, John Cowles Sr. Cowles told his editor, "You cannot tell me that in all these United States you cannot find a Negro reporter who can work across-the-board on your staff. Look hard."

After I was hired, the managing editor asked me what would happen if an interview subject didn't want a Negro reporter writing about him.

"Sir, I think if we get one thing straight right now, we'll never have any problems," I said. "If people know that I represent the *Minneapolis Tribune*, and if they don't want me, and then they find out they are not going to get anybody else, I don't think they will complain. But if they ever find out they can call you and get me replaced with another reporter, you'll receive so many telephone calls that you won't know what to do with them."

He said, "I understand you completely."

I got the idea to go back to my native South to write about what it was like for Negroes there in the wake of World War II. I did a series, which led *Time* magazine to write about me. Alfred Knopf, the publisher, flew to Minneapolis to offer me a contract to write my first book, *South of Freedom*. I won a lot of awards. And I got a lot more breaks.

When Kennedy and Nixon were campaigning for the presidency, I was asked to do a series on them. The guys who ran the Washington *Tribune* bureau weren't pleased worth a damn that the editors had asked somebody from the home boonies to write the story—and especially a black guy. But I came down, did the series, and wrote a piece for *Ebony* magazine.

That year Minnesota had a great football team. The Golden Gophers were riding high, partly because I recruited Sandy Stevens and Bobby Bell, guys who were to become all-pros. So I went to Pasadena to write about them in the Rose Bowl. On the morning of the game, I was awakened by a call from Louie Martin, a black advisor to the White House.

"The president asked me to wake you up and tell you that he wants to talk to you," he said. "He wants you to join his administration."

I was flabbergasted. I had never campaigned for anybody a day in my life.

"What's he got in mind?" I asked.

"He wants you to replace the spokesman at the State Department."

I thought that was interesting. But not knowing what the hell they were talking about, I called Hubert Humphrey,[2] who had been a friend for years.

Humphrey said, "Oh, you don't want to replace the spokesman, you want to be the spokesman's boss. You want to be at least a deputy assistant secretary."

I took Humphrey at his word and came to Washington as deputy assistant secretary of state for public affairs.

Jack Kennedy was a good guy to work for because you could talk to him. But he was a hard one to convince when he had his mind set on something. Probably the most traumatic episode of my days with him occurred when Pierre Salinger, the White House press secretary, and Art Sylvester, the spokesman at the Pentagon, convinced him to send a message to Saigon ordering the embassy to keep newsmen from flying on helicopters and going on missions.

I saw this message on a Saturday morning. I said, "My God, this is outrageous. The president is going to get crucified. He can't get away with this." I called McGeorge Bundy, Kennedy's national security adviser.

"I'll be damned if I'll have anything to do with this," I said. "I won't let anybody think that I am part of this business to muzzle the press in Vietnam."

Bundy said, "Maybe you ought to tell the president."

"Good. Set up an appointment."

Bundy called back a little later and said the president would see me. I walked into his office. Kennedy said, "Now, Carl, isn't this a bunch of shit?" We had a go for an hour and a half.

"Mr. President," I said, "the only thing that you can get away with is the appearance of maximum feasible cooperation with the press."

He had Pierre Salinger on the phone from California. Sylvester was on another line. Both were opposing me. Finally, Kennedy sided with me and changed the message that went out, to ease the restrictions.

After about two years on that job, the *Chicago Daily News* made me an offer to write a column. President Kennedy got word that I might be leaving, and he called me from Florida while I was at a reception. He pleaded with me not to leave.

Then he said, "Hey, maybe this will interest you. I've got a guy in Finland that I want to replace. Would you consider going to Helsinki as ambassador?"

I left the reception and got a State Department country report on Finland. I came home and stayed up all hours talking to Vivien and the kids about it. With their agreement, I decided to go to Finland.

Months later, when I was sitting in Helsinki, I picked up the paper and read that some congressman had said I was responsible for muzzling the press in Vietnam.[3] I hit the ceiling. As it turned out, Bob Manning, who was the assistant secretary of state and knew all about the muzzling business, hit the ceiling, too. We just raised hell.

Finally, the congressman admitted that his staff had gotten it ass-backward. When I came up for confirmation as director of USIA, he sent a glowing statement of recommendation by way of apology for his mistakes. But even today, I can walk on a college campus, and somebody will ask me about muzzling the press in Vietnam.

That shows you, once a lie gets its boots on, the truth has a hell of a time catching up with it.

I had the last meeting with Kennedy before he left Washington for Dallas and his death. We exchanged small talk and gossip, things like who was the girlfriend of the president of Finland. Then we got into some serious talk.

Finally, I said, "One thing I never understood, Mr. President. And that is why you asked me to come to Washington, since I never campaigned for you or anybody else."

"Remember when you did the series of articles on Nixon and me?"

"Yes."

"Well, I had my spies out, and they told me that your publisher, John Cowles, was going to support Nixon. And that Johnny Johnson at *Ebony* was going to support Nixon. I was having troubles with the black community because of my breakfast meeting with the governor of Alabama. My agents said that you were coming down to do a hatchet job on me. But later, I read the articles and said, 'Goddamn, these are eminently fair.' I never forgot your name. That's how I happened to ask you to join my administration."

One thing I quickly learned by working in Washington was that minorities have a devil of a time making progress when they don't have someone in the White House who is sympathetic to their needs and aspirations. You can go through the list of presidents and see the progress flow, or stagnation occur, or the clock rolled back, according to who is in office.

Kennedy's greatest impact on the black community was to articulate what the nation's position ought to be on justice and civil rights. As a result, he had a great moral impact on the country. If he had lived, I doubt that he could have ever gotten through Congress all the civil rights legislation that Lyndon Johnson did. Kennedy didn't have the old friendships, the chips to call in, that Johnson had. And he was not of a personality to twist the guy's arm out of his socket like Johnson was.

Kennedy was devoted to civil rights and the idea of black equality as an intellectual concept. He thought bigotry was vulgar, crass, and beneath his dignity. With Lyndon Johnson, it was something else.

Lyndon Johnson had grown up a segregationist and had voted for Jim Crow. But Johnson, particularly in his fights with the Kennedys, came to understand another kind of bigotry—social snobbery. Lyndon Johnson knew that a lot of people looked down on him.

Many times he said to me, "I don't speak with a Boston accent. I didn't go to Hah-vahd."

I think he really felt in his heart that the Harvard guys were better educated than he was, coming as he did from a little school in Texas. And as he began to understand the pains of discrimination, he wanted to prove that the Kennedys were no more devoted to civil rights and equal justice than he was.

I traveled with LBJ when I was in the State Department. Once we were in Saigon. It was 3:00 A.M. We'd been to a state dinner. I was sitting with Horace Busby,[4] trying to write the speech Johnson would give to South Vietnam's National Assembly next morning.

"Hey, Bus. Hey, Carl. Y'all got any beer?"

"No, Mr. Vice President."

"Can't we get somebody to get some beer?"

He called a servant. The servant said the beer bearer had gone to bed, and acted like it was beneath him to bring us some beer.

I said, "Beer bearer, my ass. Go get us some beer."

He finally did. And Johnson sat there talking.

Busby slipped me a note. It said, "Carl, I've already heard all these stories. He's telling them for your benefit. If you could find an excuse to leave the room for a while, he'll go back to bed, and we can finish this speech."

So I went down to the foyer of the Gia Long Palace, where my secretary had fallen asleep, waiting for a copy of the speech. I woke her up and told her what was going on. I waited a while and went back up. I didn't hear a sound. I thought, *He's gone*.

The moment I opened the door, this voice says, "Mr. Row-wan, this is why our country's going to hell. The vice president of the United States is sitting here waiting for some important advice from you, and you're off somewhere diddling your secretary."

I said, "What advice do you want, Mr. Vice President?"

"I want you to tell me whether I should buy Perle Mesta's house."

"What?" Perle Mesta was a leading socialite in Washington.

"Let me tell you something, Mr. Row-wan. You're gonna discover when you really get to know me that I'm a damn sight more liberal than most of these liberals you've been cottoning to.

"One of them talked me into joining the Chevy Chase Club.[5] First time Lady Bird got ready to give a party for Lynda Bird, they asked for her guest list.

"Lady Bird says, 'How come y'all want my guest list? Y'all don't discriminate, do you?'

"You know, Lady Bird didn't make no million dollars in one dollar bills being stupid.

"And they said to Lady Bird, 'No. We don't discriminate. We just want to be sure you don't invite too many Jews and Negroes.'"

"When Lady Bird told me that, I got so mad I said, 'Lady Bird, I'm gonna buy you a house and when you get ready to give a party, you can give your party at home and don't have to give no damn body your guest list.'

"Now, Mr. Row-wan, do you think I should buy Perle Mesta's house?"

He was, at the time, waiting for a call from the real estate agent back in the States. He bought the house.

I hadn't known Lyndon Johnson at all until one day the secretary of state informed me that Johnson had requested that I be in his party on his trip to the Far East and around the world. He had been having some difficulties with his own press people, and I was supposed to substitute for one of them.

I walked into the planning meeting for the trip, and Lyndon Johnson soon rushed in, ranting and raving about who had been leaking details to the press about his impending trip.

He shouted, "You're all a bunch of little puppy dogs, leaking on every fire hydrant you pass."

When I talked to him a little later, he said, "I gave them all hell, but I know who's doing the leaking. Chester Bowles.[6] You can always tell who's doing it. All you got to do is watch the newspaper. Sooner or later, the reporter who got the leak is gonna write something nice about the fella who leaked it. And this guy just had a good article on Chester Bowles."

We had a stormy beginning in Saigon on that trip. He got mad because Spencer Davis of UPI wrote that he had $50 million in his pocket for President Diem.

"Mr. Row-wan, do I look like I'm wearing glass pants?"

I shook my head "no."

"Well, how in the hell can that Spencer Davis know that I've got $50 million in my pocket?"

He ranted and raved some more. When he met the journalists that night at the press conference, he got up and made a sarcastic remark about me.

I walked over to him.

"Mr. Vice President, I want to whisper a little something to you."

He stopped the press conference and looked at me like I was crazy.

I whispered, "We better get one thing straight right now. Nobody insults me in public. I didn't ask to come to Washington. Kennedy asked me. I didn't ask to come on this trip. *You* asked me. I'll take the next plane back home. But just beware. You call me a sonofabitch in front of these newsmen, and I'll call you a sonofabitch. You treat me with respect, and I'll treat you with respect."

Boy, his face turned red as a beet. But that was the end of that crap. He knew from that day forward that while he could insult George Reedy[7] and all the rest of them on his staff, he couldn't do that to me.

One night we were having dinner on the rooftop of the Caravelle Hotel in Saigon. Liz Carpenter[8] came over and said, "Carl, where's the press, the camera guys?"

"I guess they're doing what we're doing—having dinner."

"The vice president wants you to go get them. He wants his picture taken."

"I'm not going to go get them," I said. "You tell the vice president it would not serve his interest, and it sure won't serve mine for me to tell those guys to leave dinner to come take his picture."

Did he burn over that!

By the time we got to New Delhi, Johnson decided he would cut me out of the major deliberations. I wasn't asked to read, to approve, or to clear anything. I decided that was his problem. I had loads of friends in Delhi from the months I'd spent in India and Southeast Asia lecturing for the State Department at the request of Secretary Dulles when I was with the *Tribune*. So I went off to party with some people.

When I came back, Walter Jenkins, LBJ's chief aide, was waiting for me.

"Carl, I'm glad you came back. The vice president urgently wants you to approve what he's going to give to Nehru for the joint communiqué."

I looked at the paper. It described how the United States believed in India and was willing to gamble money on India. It sounded as though we were talking about a horse race.

"This is ridiculous," I said. "No way can I approve this language."

"Well, I'll put a note under the vice president's door saying that you can't approve the language," Jenkins said. "And I'll put one under Ambassador Galbraith's door, too."

I said, "Fine."

When I briefed the press the next morning, Johnson went to see Nehru. After a while, I saw him return.

"Mr. Row-wan, you were right again, goddammit."

"I beg your pardon?"

"I wanted to go along with you," Johnson said, "but Galbraith didn't. We handed that paper over to Nehru. He looked at it and threw it up in the air. Just like that. We ain't got no damn joint communiqué."

Then he punched me in the chest.

"Let me tell you something, Mr. Row-wan. It don't never hurt to get knocked down a few times for saying what you believe."

He started to walk away, and I went in the other direction.

He hollered back, "Hey, but you would know about that, wouldn't you? 'Cause you been getting knocked down all your life."

One day in 1964, after I became USIA director, I was sitting with LBJ and Humphrey, and he said, "Hubert, this country can't go on with little Negro girls getting their heads busted open because they want a drink of Coca-Cola at the soda fountain at a department store in Atlanta. Hubert, we've got to pass that public accommodations act. But we can't get that act through if we can't break the filibuster. I can get enough votes for cloture if I can get Ev Dirksen[9] to come along and give me two Republican senators from the mountain states.

"Hubert, Ev's only mad at Negroes 'cause he thinks they didn't do right by him in his reelection campaign in Illinois. So you go soothe ol' Ev's feathers. Now, Hubert, don't pull no protocol on him or anything 'cause ol' Ev's a proud man."

Hubert said, "Yes, sir."

Hubert started to walk out of the room.

"Hubert, don't forget," Johnson said, "Ol' Ev loves to bend his elbow. I want you to go there and drink with him until he agrees to vote for cloture and brings me two senators."

Hubert went to Capitol Hill and drank himself damn near blind. But he came back with Dirksen's vote—and three senators!

They broke the filibuster, passed the public accommodations act, and not only took the weight of insult off black Americans, but also removed a big badge of shame from white America.

When Johnson got ready to go up before the joint session of Congress to make his speech for the Voting Rights Act[10] in 1965, he asked if I would sit with Lady Bird. When I listened to that powerful speech, which ended by him saying, "We shall overcome," I couldn't even dream that today there would be a black mayor in Birmingham or black mayors in Atlanta or New Orleans. Or that

Mississippi would lead all states with 433 black elected officials. To think all that flowed from that legislation!

After the speech, I returned to the White House, and we sat in the living quarters having a few scotches. Some of his other aides were there too. He picked up the phone and called one black leader after another. Atlanta. Chicago. Detroit. New York.

He always started the conversation by saying, "How did I do?"

As he talked, I remembered back to a time I was writing part of one of his speeches while he was still vice president. He wanted something in the speech that would make Americans have an emotional commitment to social justice. He recalled going to San Antonio to make a campaign speech.

"You know," he said, "I was standing in the back of a pickup out at the square. An old black man crawled up in the truck and introduced me. Afterward he said, 'Mr. Vice President, I was born about two blocks from where this pickup is standing. And I never thought I'd live to see the day when a black man would get up here and introduce a white vice president, who's going to ask the people to vote for a Mexican.'

"When that fella said that to me, the tears just streamed down my cheeks. You know, Carl, a man ain't worth a good goddamn if he can't cry at the right time."

I believe Johnson really wanted to make Americans cry a little about poverty and the lack of social justice.

In the fall of 1965, *Newsday*, the Long Island newspaper, made me a wonderful offer to leave government to write a column. I felt a moral obligation to give the *Chicago Daily News* a chance to bid against anybody else. When the bidding was over, I went with the *Daily News*. I figured four-and-a-half-years was long enough to ask anyone to go broke for his country.

I told Johnson that I would be leaving. He had Jack Valenti[11] to come by and try to talk me out of it. But my mind was made up.

One day after I had been writing the column for a while, he

called and asked if I would come to the White House to chat with him. After a few pleasantries, Johnson went into a soliloquy.

"Well, I'm glad that I don't have to worry about you joining the Mary McGrorys[12] and that crowd, writing all this less than patriotic stuff about what I'm trying to do in Veet-nam."

He was ticking off every columnist of consequence in America, and telling me which category he placed them in, in terms of their position on the war.

I had to laugh several times, because he could be extremely funny when he was laying it on you verbally. But I knew this was an effort to co-opt me, to stop my criticism of the war. When it didn't work, he really got ticked off and put me on the Don't-Invite-to-the-White-House list.

That went on for many months. Finally, he changed his mind and decided to go back to the technique of wooing and cooing. So I've been on the Don't-Invite list of Democrats as well as Republicans.

We often say that we blacks have known racism for so long that we can smell a racist a mile away. And anytime I was anywhere close to Richard Nixon, I could see, smell, and almost hear his uneasiness. I didn't trust the man.

I'll never forget the year when I first started to learn to play tennis. Vivien and I were on an indoor court out in Montgomery County, Maryland, when the manager walked out and said, "Mr. Rowan, I hate to interrupt your game, but the president wants to talk to you."

I said, "The president of what?"

"Of the United States."

Richard Nixon was on the telephone.

"Hey, Carl, you lucky devil. I wish I could be out playing tennis on a Monday morning."

Then Nixon said, "I called you because they put in my weekend reading file a column of yours that moved me very much."

I had written about J. T., a little black boy in a CBS television special. It told the story of how he had no father, and went around with his radio strapped to his head, and almost lost his life trying to steal food for a hungry cat he loved. I wrote that there were too many J. T.'s in Washington and Philadelphia and Houston, and in the world. Somehow, we had to provide them with a better break, better supervision, better food, better education.

Nixon said, "I just called to let you know that I was so moved that I'm going to dedicate myself to seeing that this kind of support you talk about comes about."

"Well, Mr. President, you obviously know that I did not support you against Hubert Humphrey. But if you support the kinds of bills we're talking about today, you will have my support."

Two weeks later the Congress passed a child care bill. Nixon vetoed it.

Beyond that, Nixon was the first president in my days to try to subtly use racial code words to produce the kind of white backlash he needed to get votes. The law and order campaigning, the screams about welfare cheats and taking crime off the street—all this was antiblack gibberish.

But even Nixon did not go as far as the Reagan Administration turned out to go. For instance, Nixon would have had no part of trying to give tax exempt status to Jim Crow schools, like Bob Jones University. Yet there was a malevolent spirit in the Nixon White House. The Haldemans,[13] the Ehrlichmans,[14] guys around him like that, wouldn't have given a black person the sweat off their eyebrows if it had been left solely to them.

In those days, college students asked me if I wasn't a moderate, compared to Stokely Carmichael[15] and Rap Brown.[16]

I said, "I'll let you figure it out. Richard Nixon has an enemies list that was just revealed. Did you see Stokely Carmichael on there? No. Rap Brown? No. Did you see Carl Rowan on Nixon's list? Yes."

Gerald Ford was a nice guy, but he had no real convictions and not a hell of a lot of knowledge about what the civil rights movement was all about. I went to see him for a one-on-one interview in the midst of the '74-'75 recession, which had been the worst since the Great Depression.

"Mr. President," I asked. "Do you have anything on your mind special, anything that's different to help black Americans who are suffering out of proportion to all others in this recession?"

"The only plan I have, Mr. Rowan," Ford said, "is to follow the old adage that all ships rise with the tide. When we lift the economy, blacks will rise with it."

"Mr. President, if you will get your people to give you a little bit of history, you will discover that all ships don't rise with the tide."

Soon after, a woman in Grand Rapids wrote me a letter, obviously unhappy with me for criticizing Ford. She said, "Dear Mr. Rowan. Life for you must be a terrible burden, being black and stupid at the same time."

I answered, "Dear Madam. Thank you for your letter. Life for you can't possibly be so bad since you obviously have only half my problem."

In his heart, I think, Jimmy Carter was dedicated to the idea of racial equality. But he didn't know how to do anything about it. He came as an outsider, bragged about it, and found out that he would leave as an outsider. He had no power in the Congress. He didn't know where the levers were, and couldn't have pushed them if he could have found them. The result was that for all the things he hoped to do, blacks didn't make much progress during his tenure.

But I did have a close personal relationship with Carter, in the sense that he would call me over for lunch, usually with another columnist, such as Hugh Sidey of *Time*. And sometimes, I would get a call at home from him after he had watched the *Agronsky & Co.*[17] broadcast.

Once, during the hostage period, one of the journalists had said on the show, "If the Iranians want to go back to the Dark Ages, I'd help them back to the Dark Ages. I'd send the planes over and bomb every one of their hydro-electric facilities."

Before the broadcast—which had been taped earlier—was over, the president called me from Camp David and said, "You tell that journalist that when he exchanges places with the hostages, I'll send those planes in and blow up all those facilities."

I tried not to get into a position of being an advisor to the president. I am a columnist. A newsman. But once when I was taping a show I was producing about Mrs. Carter, she said, "You've been mighty hard on Jimmy lately."

I said, "If he wants to know why I am writing what I am writing, I'll tell him." Then I told her four or five problems troubling blacks and the poor.

"I wish Jimmy could hear that."

And she went over and hauled him out of a meeting. She didn't tell someone else to get him. She went into the meeting, and when she came out, she had him with her.

I repeated to him what I told her. He said, "I'm just doing everything I can from the White House. But I'm not getting much cooperation from Congress."

The Reagan Administration was clearly the most racist administration since Woodrow Wilson and his wife went around Jim Crowing the White House, putting black and white signs on water fountains.

Ronald Reagan told the press that the only programs he had cut were for those who were not morally deserving. How in hell can you tell a five-year-old school kid, whose food you've taken away, that he or she is not morally deserving?

Nixon had me on his enemies list, Johnson had me on his no-invite list. But I'm proud to say that the Reagan gang hated me more than any other. That was when they were so eager to curb the powers of the press. It galled the hell out of them that I could write the things I did about the Reagan Administration, and they couldn't feel free to send a gumshoe around to lock me up.

One thing I've learned over the years. If you're going to be in the business I'm in, you have to keep your nose clean. My taxes were audited every year that Richard Nixon was in office—and in some years when Lyndon Johnson was there. And I was audited under the Reagan Administration. They never found anything, because I didn't leave them anything to find.

When Reagan sent the marines to Lebanon,[18] I knew they were going on a *Mission Impossible*. To keep a peace that didn't exist. To be sitting ducks. And I knew that as soon as some of them got killed, the cries would go up for the U.S. to bomb somebody. That would guarantee getting the United States in a posture of killing Arabs, which is not in our national interest. All we have done is create the enmity of most of the 800 million Muslims on earth.

More times than not, though, I wrote about the problems of blacks. Few other people in journalism were going to do it. You had no reason to assume that some white columnist was going to care about all of the things black people care about. I know more about what it means when black women head households, in terms of poverty, in terms of day care centers. I know more about the sexual pressures on young black women living in ghetto environments than any white person does. I know more about what it means to be black and poor because I've been poor as hell and I'm still black.

If I have this cherished right to say what I want to in my columns and radio commentary, then I need to use it in a way that enlightens a lot of white Americans to things they don't know about. And sometimes to things they do know about.

Take this small town in Oregon. Probably has only one black family. I didn't even know the local newspaper carried my column, until the editor cancelled it and published a front-page editorial with his explanation for doing it. He said I had written too many columns criticizing the government's economic policies, that I had done too much wailing about the plight of poor blacks.

So, whammo! He was deluged with letters he certainly never expected. People were saying, "What do you mean, wailing about blacks? Rowan ain't just writing about black people. He's writing about us. He's writing about my brother who lost his job at the lumber mill. It got my husband, too."

The editor wrote another front-page editorial. He said he was wrong.

I was back in Oregon.

Ethel Payne, one of the first two black women to cover the White House, worked for the Chicago Defender *and later became a columnist. She was known as the First Lady of the Black Press.*

———

"Mr. President," I said, "the Interstate Commerce Commission[19] has issued an opinion saying it is time to end segregation in interstate travel. When can we expect you to sign an executive order to that effect?"

President Eisenhower got so furious! His face became flushed. He drew himself up. He became the five-star general again. And he chewed me out in front of the White House press corps.

"What makes you think I'm going to do anything for any special interest?" he said. "I'm the president of all the people. I'm going to do what I think is right for all the people."

He was so angry that it stunned the whole press corps. I was astonished. I thought it was a legitimate question.

When I left the meeting that morning, Ed Folliard of the *Washington Post*, who was the dean of the White House press corps, came over to me. He said, "Now don't feel badly, Ethel. Once I asked Franklin Roosevelt a question and he almost leaped out of his wheelchair at me."

But that wasn't the end of it.

It was all over the news. *The Washington Star* had a front-page banner headline: "Negro Woman Reporter Angers Ike." My mother in Chicago called and said, "Now, Sister. You ought not to be down there making the president mad."

Mother always worried about us. My father, who was a Pullman car porter, died when I was ten years old. I was the fifth of six children growing up in Chicago. So my mother, who was a high school Latin teacher, had the six of us to rear. There really wasn't any chance for all of us to think about college.

One day we had a family council and decided that one of us should go away to school. We decided to send Avis, the youngest girl, to West Virginia State University. That meant everybody else had to pitch in and help to keep her in college.

I was one of the strong persons in the family. I was always bold and outgoing. I had one brother, Lem, who was quite sickly. I used to glory in taking up a fight for him—much to his embarrassment. I think that gave me a sense of, well, I just had to defend people who couldn't defend themselves. That's why I always wanted to be a lawyer. But my college education was quite spotty, since I had to go to school at night. And I didn't have the finances.

Nevertheless, I took the examination to go to law school at the University of Chicago. The law school didn't bother to reply.

I worked for the Chicago Public Library. After a while, I found the work boring. This was 1948 and the army was recruiting people to be service club hostesses overseas. I signed on and was sent to the quartermaster depot in Tokyo.

I kept a diary of my experiences in Japan. I took notes about black GIs and their relationships with Japanese women. That's where a lot of the brown babies came from in that period. I noted the segregation that I saw on this huge army post—rigid segregation in every way, blacks on one side, whites on the other.

Despite the fact that President Truman had ordered the armed forces desegregated in 1948, General MacArthur was doing nothing about it on this post. MacArthur, who considered himself above even the emperor of Japan, totally ignored the order. That's how imperial he was.

Many of the things I wrote in my diary were not known in the States. When the Korean Conflict broke out in 1950, the *Chicago*

Defender sent Alex Wilson[20] over. Jimmy Hicks,[21] another reporter working for the black press, came over, too. We all met at the Overseas Club in downtown Tokyo. I told them what I was doing.

"Hey, this is something the folks at home don't know about," Alex said. "Can I see your notes?"

I let him see my notes.

Alex started reading and looked up. "God, this is so great! Do you mind if I take it back and share them with the folks?"

"I might get in trouble," I said.

"No you won't. I'm just going to share them with some folks."

So I let him have the notes. About three weeks later, all hell broke loose!

The *Defender* ran articles based on my notes, with big, bold, red headlines across the top—very inflammatory headlines. I was called to MacArthur's headquarters and dressed down for hurting the morale of the troops—allegedly. They said they were going to ship me home because I had disgraced the whole service.

At the time, Thurgood Marshall was traveling through the area investigating the treatment of black soldiers for the NAACP. What happened to me got included in his report. So the military command held off sending me home immediately. But I was moved to another area, where they thought I could do no damage. Meanwhile, Louie Martin, editor of the *Defender*, called me in Tokyo. He said he was delighted with the articles.

"Hell, if you can write like that, why don't you come on home?" he said. "We've got a job for you."

After a couple of months, I decided to go home. I was still hoping to go to law school. But when I didn't get admitted again to the University of Chicago, I decided to work for the *Defender* until I could get into law school.

One day Louie said, "We need somebody in Washington." Our correspondent had joined the Democratic National Committee. "If you don't like it, Ethel, come back home. But try it for six months."

I went to Washington during the first year of the Eisenhower administration. The first thing I did was apply for White House credentials. They had a rule that precluded people from weekly papers—you had to work for the daily press. So that kept most of the black press out. Only two blacks represented black newspapers at the White House. Louis Lautier worked for the National Newspaper Publishers Association, which included the *Atlanta Daily World*. And Alice Dunnigan, the first black woman accredited to the White House, represented Claude Barnett's Associated Negro Press, which also serviced the *Atlanta Daily World*.

I went to James Haggerty, Eisenhower's press secretary, to see if I could get accredited.

I told him, "I think I have all the qualifications."

He was in a relaxed mood. "Come on aboard, Miss Payne."

He later regretted it.

Eisenhower was the only president that I can remember who held press conferences on a regular basis every week. Other presidents, from Kennedy and Johnson on, held them infrequently, or just when they wanted to influence the news. We met in the Indian Treaty Room in what is now the Executive Office Building. There was no air-conditioning, and we were jammed in tight. There were favored people among us who got the attention. The smaller papers hardly had any opportunity to ask questions.

There was an unwritten gentlemen's agreement that blacks didn't ask questions. Louis Lautier was an excellent court stenographer. He sat there and took all the words down in shorthand. Then after the press conference was over, the lazy white guys would take their notes from Lautier's notes. He was really there in a service capacity. Alice, the other black reporter, didn't assert herself much. She was a placid person

Louis Lautier said to me, "You don't need to ask any questions. If there are any questions you want to ask, I'll do it."

When I got accredited, I read the rules and said to myself, *Now that I'm in the press corps, I want to exercise the same rights and privileges as everybody else.*

I was very aggressive and determined to be accepted like anyone. My opportunity soon came.

The Republican Party had a Lincoln Day celebration at the old Washington Arena. Three choirs were to perform—Emory, Duke, and Howard University. When the Howard University choir came by bus to the entrance of the Arena, they were refused entry. Warner Lawson, the conductor, was so angry that he marched the students back to the bus and returned to the campus. Somebody told me about the incident.

At the next press conference, I decided to be bold. So I jumped up and shouted, "Mr. President! Mr. President!"

Eisenhower looked startled, and then recognized me.

I asked if he knew that the choir from Howard—a black university—had been turned away from the Lincoln Day celebration.

"No," he said. "I didn't know about it. But if, as you imply, there's some discrimination there, I'll be the first to apologize."

What he said was really equal to an apology. And, of course, that made front-page news. Reporters all over town were asking, "Who is Ethel Payne? What is this Negro woman doing asking questions?"

Louis Lautier became very resentful. He thought I was usurping his prestige. But from then on, I got recognized at White House press conferences on a regular basis.

Meanwhile, the McCarthy era was in full swing. It centered on hearings led by Senator Joseph McCarthy on communist subversion in the government. It was a terrible period, many totally innocent people got hurt.

Joe McCarthy became so desperate that Roy Cohn of his subcommittee dug up Annie Lee Moss, a black woman who was a lowly file clerk at the Pentagon. Blacks were so far down in the hierarchy at the Defense Department that they could never get near anything sensitive. Yet she was presented as the number one evidence of communism in the government. Someone had told Cohn that she was a communist because she subscribed to the *Daily Worker*.[22] She probably didn't know anything about the great issues that were burning at the time. But she was promptly fired.

At first none of the major publications picked up her story. I was the first to publicize her plight. When I interviewed her, she explained that someone had sent the subscription to her husband. He had been a janitor in one of the government buildings. He probably never read a single issue. After he died, the subscription kept coming, and Mrs. Moss had piled the papers up on her back porch.

"We didn't pay any attention to them," she told me.

She was a simple woman. They were plain folks. They didn't have any idea what the *Daily Worker* was.

The hearing room was crowded when she was called to testify. Roy Cohn came down so hard on her. He was just obnoxious. And he wouldn't let her attorney, George E. C. Hayes, testify at all. Finally, Senator Stuart Symington, who had been feuding with McCarthy over his reckless tactics, asked her, "Mrs. Moss, do you follow the teaching of Karl Marx?"

The mike was open.

Mrs. Moss turned to Hayes and said, "Who is Karl Marx?"

Then Senator Symington said, "Mrs. Moss, I may be sticking my neck out, but I think that you are innocent."

Everybody applauded.

McCarthy became so angry that he stormed out of the hearing room. And Mrs. Moss was finally reinstated at her job.

It was my first big story.

This was a time, too, when the struggle for civil rights legislation was in full force. So I got to know Clarence Mitchell Jr. very well. He was the Washington lobbyist for the NAACP. We discussed pending legislation, and he helped me develop questions that needed to be asked at the White House. I began to feel that I was a conduit for the civil rights movement because I could get answers at the White House.

Before then, the white people in the press corps didn't relate to civil rights. But after I began asking questions, they decided that they would ask some, too. I really set a precedent. And I'm proud of that.

So when I learned about the ICC opinion on ending segregation in interstate travel, I thought it would be very important to ask

Eisenhower what he planned to do. Blacks were still traveling in Jim Crow cars. But my question obviously hit a raw nerve.

Later, I found that his background probably made him react like that. He was a segregationist at heart. When he sent troops into Little Rock during the school integration crisis, he did it out of the necessity to restore order, not for any other purpose.

Jim Haggerty was furious with me. He called me to his office and said I had violated the White House correspondents' rules, because I had written some freelance pieces for the political action committee of the old CIO.[23] He said they would have to lift my White House press credentials. I found out that they had also asked the IRS to look into my income tax payments.

I went straight to Clarence Mitchell. Clarence hit the ceiling! He wrote a blistering letter to Haggerty. Then Drew Pearson[24] took up the matter, saying this was an abridgement of freedom of the press. It got to be a real war. The White House backed off. The IRS retreated.

It wasn't long after that when segregation in interstate travel was banned. I like to think I had some part in contributing to that.

I was beginning to feel that even though I couldn't get into law school, journalism was an effective way of carrying out the kind of law that I would have liked to practice. So I did not regret being in journalism. I was then, and will continue to be the rest of my life, an advocate journalist. I go back to Frederick Douglass's advice: "Agitate. Agitate. Agitate."

Oddly enough, though there was plenty of prejudice against black reporters, I sometimes felt I was more at a disadvantage because of being a woman than being a black person. Antifeminism was very strong. Sarah McClendon, a white reporter, had to be so strong and had to bore in to get the president's attention. She had to be aggressive to survive. And the white reporters always called her "that pushy bitch." I guess I was "that pushy black bitch."

I caught plenty of flack from my black brothers and sisters, too. The *Pittsburgh Courier*, a black newspaper which was Republican-oriented, published scathing articles about me, saying I was annoying the president. I learned to roll with the punches. After the ICC incident, the White House put me in the deep freeze. I got recognized only one time after that.

My aggressiveness didn't seem to trouble Richard Nixon, however. I was in the press party that traveled with him for the independence celebration in Ghana in 1957. A year later, the reporters in that group decided to hold a reunion. I had moved into a new apartment on Belmont Road, and didn't have a thing but a cot and a table. So Simeon Booker, Washington bureau chief of *Jet* and *Ebony*, suggested that we hold the reunion there.

He said, "We can just boogie-woogie all over the place."

I agreed. Then Simeon said, "Why don't you ask the vice president to come?'

"Oh," I said, "you know he wouldn't come."

"Send a note anyway."

We dutifully sent a note to Nixon's office. And I didn't think any more about it. That was a Tuesday. On Wednesday, I got a call from Nixon's office. "The vice president and Mrs. Nixon will be happy to come to the party on Saturday."

I said to myself, "Oh, Lord God. What am I going to do? I don't have a thing in this house!"

I rushed downtown to the Hecht Company and asked to see the manager.

"I've got a problem," I said.

"Which is?"

"The vice president is coming to my apartment on Saturday, and I don't have any furniture. I don't have any dishes. I don't have anything. And I don't have any money."

"Maybe we can help," he said.

The next day, a Hecht Company van rolled up and unloaded dishes, silverware and everything else. They didn't bill me until a long time later. And I paid for it on time!

All the neighbors got excited. I called my family in Chicago, and they jumped on a plane and came down. Of course a secret service agent checked things out, and on Saturday they cordoned off the street, not letting anyone on my block.

I had to go to the hairdresser that morning. On my way back, when I gave the cab driver—who was black—my address, he said, "You can't get there lady. They got it blocked off. I don't know what's going on. Somebody told me that some colored woman is having the vice president over. But I don't believe it!"

I said, "Let's give it a try."

When we got to the entrance of my block, I whipped out my White House press card, and the secret service man waved us through. The cab driver's mouth flew open. He turned around and looked at me.

"Yes," I said, "I'm that colored lady."

I thought the Nixons would stay about fifteen minutes. But all the neighbors came over. And Nixon shook hands and chatted with everybody. He lingered about two hours. He brought me a bottle of Kentucky bourbon with a label reading, "The President's Choice Richard M. Nixon."

I kidded him. "Does this label mean something, Mr. Vice President?"

He laughed.

I've always been an adventurer, so I welcomed any opportunity to go overseas. It seemed only natural for me to go see how the black soldiers were doing in Vietnam. I landed in Saigon on Christmas Day of 1966. When I walked across the runway, I knew that I was in a war zone. I had second thoughts. "Maybe," I said, "I ought to get back on that plane!"

As soon as I got billeted, they took me to Dian, about twenty miles outside of Saigon, where Bob Hope was entertaining the troops. There were thousands of soldiers. Some were on stretchers. Bob and Phyllis Diller gave a wonderful show. But right in the middle, a commercial plane flew low overhead. A chorus went up saying, "I wish I was going home." It brought tears to my eyes.

As we were returning to our bus, some black soldiers came over and said, "Merry Christmas, sister." I started crying. I couldn't stop. I cried and cried.

After we got back to Saigon, I heard that a land mine had exploded on the road we had taken. We had just missed it, but two of the GIs who helped us were killed.

That was my introduction to the Vietnam War. I was not prepared for that war. I felt so naïve. I didn't grasp the enormity of the situation. I don't even like to talk about it now.

The next year I went to Nigeria. The Nigerian ambassador in Washington had complained that he couldn't get the government's story told in the majority press about the war against the secessionist Biafra.[25] Lillian Wiggins, a reporter for the *Washington Afro-American*, suggested that we cover the federal side. We traveled down the eastern zone, right to the border of the conflict, where we interviewed many refugees.

Our guide was a colonel they called the Black Scorpion because he was so tough, a fierce fighter, and as cruel as he had to be. He was covered with scars from hand-to-hand combat. He brooked no insolence from his troops, and he was largely responsible for carrying the war to its successful finish.

One day he told us, "I don't like to see you in European clothes. Go upstairs, and my women will take care of you."

We went upstairs and Nigerian women came out with bolts of cloth. In thirty minutes, they had whipped up some Nigerian costumes for both of us. And that was something to do! They fastened these big turbans around our heads and said, "You can go downstairs now."

When we came to the top of the stairs, the colonel looked up and said, "Now you are properly attired."

A band was in place when we stepped outside. It struck up a march as we passed by. For the rest of the trip, we had to wear Nigerian clothes. I can't say that I became accustomed to it, but it was okay.

Winston Churchill III[26] was in the area at the time. He had come over for one of the British papers. He followed us around. He was still filled with a colonial mentality and arrogance. When he saw us in Nigerian clothes, he became disgusted. He said, "You are totally corrupt. This is all propaganda."

But as I traveled around, I became more and more convinced that both sides of the story had not been told. When I returned home, I persuaded the publisher of the *Defender* to turn the paper over to me. And that was one of the few breaks the Nigerian federal government got.

I likened the Biafra War to a civil war. There were interests—European powers—anxious to split this huge black country. I called it Balkanizing.[27] And I likened General Gowan, head of the Lagos government, to Abraham Lincoln because his sole purpose was to keep the country together. The war ended when the Ibos[28] were routed. But Gowan really saved that country. He kept it together. And he gave the Ibos help to get their lives started over again. He was a devout Christian in a Muslim world.

A few years later I met Idi Amin[29] in Monrovia, and he invited me to Uganda.

I said, "I don't know if I can make it."

He said, "You will come. And you will see that these are all lies they tell about me. You will be very welcome. I will send you a ticket."

Sure enough, when I got home, there was a telegram from his embassy saying I had been booked on a flight through Paris. They didn't say anything about a return ticket. I said, "Thanks, but no thanks." There had been too many atrocity stories. I thought Amin was a big swaggering bully, a real tyrant.

But my most exciting assignment came in April of 1955 when I covered the Asian-African conference at Bandung. I was a little astonished that my publisher would open up his purse to send me. This was long before most black publications took an interest in international affairs. And over the years, the black press had suffered from the myopia of many black publishers. They had an abominable record of being penurious, afraid to spend money, and being cavalier with the people who worked for them.

I knew many black reporters who would have preferred to stay in the black press, but they couldn't stand the bad treatment and the low pay. I hung in there because I could write my own ticket.

Bandung was the first gathering of what you might call the majority of people of the earth—the darker-skinned people. Burma, Ceylon, Pakistan, India and Indonesia—the Colombo Powers—invited twenty-four nations to join them. They represented two-thirds of the earth's population.

None of the so-called Western powers were invited. And that sent a tremor through them like an earthquake. They were scared to death of the implications of such a meeting.

When I got to Manila, Adam Powell was already there holding a press conference. Since the Western powers were not included, he had not been invited. But being a member of Congress representing Harlem, he signed himself on as an observer. He was such an audacious character. He tried his best to speak to the conference, but he couldn't get permission. He spoke, though, in press conference after press conference.

Carlos Romulo, a former ambassador, had a private plane put at his disposal by the Philippine government. He invited us to join him for the journey to Djakarta. The plane was loaded with politicians—the prime minister of Ceylon, the prime minister of Pakistan. It was my first encounter with important heads of state. I couldn't believe that I was seeing all this with my own eyes!

I sat in the back of the plane respectfully and listened to their conversations. When we got to Djakarta, there was a huge welcome for the dignitaries. As I looked out the window, I saw a crowd of students. They all had pads and pencils. I thought, "Typical autograph seekers."

I waited until everybody filed off the plane. I came off last. The students swarmed around me. They wanted *my* autograph!

I said, "I think you are mistaken."

"No, no. We came to see the American Negro. We heard you were coming. We want to know how you are treated in your country."

They insisted, so naturally I obliged them, signing their pads. Adam Powell stood off to the side. He was something to look at—very fair-skinned, very handsome, very dashing, very daring. The students didn't know who he was.

Finally, Adam could stand it no longer. He walked over, put his arm around me and said, "Me colored, too."

On the opening day, Sukarno, the president of Indonesia, gave a stirring address. He was quite an orator. He quoted Patrick Henry, and talked about George Washington. There were all these great figures of history—Nehru from India, U Nu from Burma, many others.

One evening, the Liberians presented a film. Everyone was ushered in, but a few late-comers arrived after the theatre was darkened. When the lights came up during intermission, I saw Adam Powell sitting next to Zhou Enlai.[30]

Powell boomed out, "How do you do, Mr. Prime Minister? My name is Adam Clayton Powell. I'm the Negro Congressman from New York. I've been trying to see you. What are you going to do about releasing the American flyers?"

Zhou En Lai, who understood English perfectly, said, "No speak English. No speak English." And he hurried out of the theatre.

Richard Wright, who wrote *Native Son*, was there, staying in the same compound. We struck up a friendship. I didn't realize at the time that he was having a lot of personal problems. He said he was trying to find a link for his own identity with what was happening at the conference. I learned later, after he became famous, that he was continually at war with himself. He never quite knew where he fit into things. Africa? America? The Third World?

These were the days when you hard-pressed your hair, long before the Afro style. There was no such thing as going about with nappy hair, you straightened your hair.

Before leaving Chicago, I had packed my straightening comb

and six cans of Sterno, a heating liquid in a small can. When you set a match to it, you could heat anything, like a can of beans—or a straightening comb. My sisters went through my baggage and said, "You don't need all this Sterno." They left me with one can!

Bandung was very humid. I got up early in the morning to press my hair. Pretty soon, I had used all the Sterno. I didn't know what to do. My hair was in tight balls.

I said to Richard Wright, "Richard. I've got a problem."

He said, "What's the matter?"

"The Sterno has run out."

"Well, if there is any Sterno in Bandung, I'll find it for you."

He went his way, and I went mine.

When I came back late that night, I saw a bottle wrapped in white on the table. I was so sleepy and tired that I went right to bed.

About four in the morning, I heard an agonized cry.

"Ethel! Ethel! Ethel Payne! Ethel Payne!"

I said, "Yes?"

I looked out the window.

"It's me. It's Dick. Are you all right? Did you drink that stuff?"

"No."

"I forgot to tell you. That bottle is pure alcohol."

"Pure alcohol?"

"I couldn't find any Sterno, but I found some pure alcohol."

"What do you do with it?"

He came and showed me. We got some cotton and a dish. He poured the alcohol on the cotton and lit it. He held the straightening comb and I'd pull. Richard Wright pressed my hair that day! We got along famously.

One day Chet Huntley of NBC walked with me to the meetings. He seemed to have a mortal fear of that conference. He saw it as a red herring, a communist plot. He kept saying to me, "I hope you won't be influenced by all this propaganda." I just kept smiling.

When we got to the line of Indonesian guards, they allowed me to pass. Then Chet Huntley stepped up and Bam! They pointed their bayonets at him, challenging him to show his credentials. They were being very rough with him.

I was on the other side of the line, trying to see what was happening. And Chet was pointing at me!

Then the strangest feeling hit me, like a bolt of lightning. For the first time in my life, it dawned on me that I was a member of a majority, not a minority. It was a revelation. I started laughing like crazy.

I yelled, "Hey, Chet. Now you know what it means to be a minority!"

I think Bandung was probably the most important conference that ever took place. It brought together such a disparate group of people who had a common link—color. But they also had many problems in common. They were resentful of the Western powers' reluctance to include them in decisions affecting Asia and elsewhere. Bandung was the catalyst for the independence movement among Third World countries. And in many unseen ways, Bandung's effect can still be felt. When, for instance, there are solid votes that go against the big powers in the United Nations, that's Bandung.

I met with a group of Indonesian women, strong feminists. One of them went over to a piano, sat down, and pulled out some sheet music. She said she wanted to play some American songs for me. She began playing. I recognized the piece without any problem.

"Old Black Joe" by Stephen Foster.

When she was finished, I rose and said, "My sisters, I appreciate this very much."

I called them sisters because they were very sweet people.

"But that song represents a period that American blacks would not like to remember. It reminds us of the days when our ancestors were in slavery."

I launched into a discussion of slavery and the impact it had had on black people. They all listened intently. Then a young woman stood up very dramatically.

She took the sheet music and tore it up.

"We will never play that again," she said.

Joel Dreyfus, a Haitian immigrant, was a reporter for the New York Post *and later the* Washington Post, *where he was active on racial issues.*

———

I quickly developed a reputation in the business as a troublemaker because I never condescended to limits that people were trying to impose on me.

Even Ben Bradlee, the *Washington Post's* executive editor, called me "a pain-in-the ass."

That was my whole history in the business from the time I came into it. I just refused to accept the idea that I wasn't supposed to be able to do something, or was ineligible for something, or was not qualified for something because I was a black person. I knew that I was better educated. I had better breeding. And I had a hell of a better background than most of these people who were telling me what I was supposed to be doing.

And that was the initial source of my problem in journalism.

I once had a colleague at the *Washington Post* who got exasperated by my rather outspoken and critical attitude about race relations at the paper. He was annoyed by my lack of tact and reserve. He was black and a rather senior writer.

He said to me, "You act like you discovered discrimination."

I said, "Well, I have."

And that was it, too. I was an immigrant. So my perspective was different because of that.

In America I learned that black was supposed to mean underprivileged, to mean inferiority. There was a whole string of things which, before I came here, were totally meaningless to me. I found that the myth of no class distinctions was exactly that—a myth. I couldn't believe people made such class and racial associations. It didn't make sense to me. And I became outraged.

But later I became absolutely fascinated by it. That is a reason why I became a journalist. I wanted to point out the distinctions of racism, to analyze it, to write about it from my outsider's perspective.

To an outsider, everything about America is fresh. And as an outsider, I could say, "Bullshit."

My family were middle-class immigrants from Haiti. When I came to the United States in 1960, I was fifteen years old. My background was very privileged, not in terms of wealth, but in terms of social background. We had an upper-class family history. We were a very proud people.

We had a traditional Caribbean heritage—a racial mixture of Jews, Italians, Irishmen and Africans. There were presidents and generals, revolutionaries and academicians in my background. I knew that the folks on my mother's side were from Dahomey.[31] The slave ship they were on was intercepted by the Haitians, who freed everybody and settled them in Haiti.

My Jewish grandfather immigrated to Haiti at the height of anti-Semitism in France. That's how I got the name Dreyfus. He was a cousin of *the* Alfred Dreyfus. He went into business with other Frenchmen who came to Haiti, and married into a Haitian family, which had viewed him as an upstart.

But I was always very clear on the fact that I was a black person.

For many years my father worked for UNESCO[32] as an education expert, traveling to underdeveloped countries to help set up public school systems. We lived in France. We lived in Liberia. And because of my father's work, I crossed the Atlantic ten times before I was sixteen years old.

Until I got to college in the United States, I had never known that being black was something to hold you back. Then I started to get into trouble because I was very arrogant. And I was arrogant because I insisted on being treated just like white people.

In 1969 I applied for a job in the Associated Press bureau in New York. They were looking for blacks desperately because they didn't want their white reporters to get hurt covering riots and facing hostile community groups. Although I had graduated from the City College of New York and had a drawer full of clips from three different student newspapers, I had to take an IQ test. I had to take a spelling test. I had to take a vocabulary test. I had to take a writing test. All that to get a job at the AP.

I was a very good test taker. The guy giving the test said, "Gee, I guess we're gonna have to hire you." That set the tone of my whole experience at the AP.

Fifty reporters covered New York for AP. Everybody had beats or assignments. I was a general assignment reporter. I went out and did four stories a day. I did six news conferences a day. I worked day and night. I showed immediately that I was a very competent reporter. Then I got made a state editor, then a rewrite person for the bureau.

I developed one story from a police report about a guy whose seeing-eye dog had been stolen. It was a typical New York story. I wrote it almost tongue-in-cheek, but it was moving and full of imagery. It went on the front page of fifty papers, and people sent in money. It sort of proved to them how awful and horrible New York was.

The AP loved it.

I was a good, smart kid. I knew how to write because I had been writing since I was six or seven years old. I'd always had an interest in writing. But I never thought of it as a way to make a living.

After a while, I told the editors I would like to go overseas. They showed hesitation and trepidation. They said, "Eventually. Eventually." But I saw white kids with my level of experience, and not as much talent, being moved much more quickly than I was.

Then someone told me, "You're *too* ambitious."

I first became aware of the conservative nature of the AP when I complained one day about the use of racial identifications in a story. There was a rule against using race unless it was relevant to the story. I saw an item running on the wire that said three black men had been arrested for robbing an armory in Florida.

I told one of the editors, "I don't understand this. This seems counter to our own rules. I mean, there isn't anything racial about three men robbing an armory. Why are you identifying them as black?"

He said, "Aren't blacks arming themselves?"

Later, the AP got very pissed off at me when I talked to a writer who was doing a story about the FBI for *New York* magazine. I told the writer I really didn't know what was going on between the AP and the FBI, but the relationship was very uncomfortable for me and for a lot of other reporters. I had started getting some funny feelings about the relationship between the AP and the police agencies when I would be called at home and told that the police were going to raid someplace the next day. Go and be there. The police were going to do this and that. They had an inside source.

There was a lot of militant activity at this time, some rioting in the streets. Of course, I knew a lot of Puerto Rican kids because I had grown up in the city. So I was sent to cover the Young Lords, who were a kind of a Puerto Rican version of the Black Panthers. They had invaded a church and were holed-up, making demands. I went in and out of the church at will.

An AP editor asked me to give him a list of the leaders. I wrote down all the heads and their titles. I was very naïve. I thought someone was writing a feature and just wanted some facts. But there was no story. And no plans for a story. I believe now the list was turned over to the cops.

Another time we moved a story on the wire that said three Black Panthers had been arrested for a robbery. I was sent to the police precinct to follow it up. When I got there, I was told there were only two suspects. I'm a reporter. I'm a little suspicious. When I pressed them, they said they had turned the third suspect over to the Feds for a weapons violation.

"He had a sawed-off shotgun."

I said, "Okay."

When I went back to the office, I called the Feds. They had never heard of him. So I wrote my editor a little memo. "There's something a little fishy in this. Here's the original dispatch. Here's the name of this guy. But when I checked him out, I couldn't find anything. He's disappeared. Something's wrong."

I went back to making my calls. Then all of a sudden my editor called me in.

"Just leave that," he said. "Do something else."

He was calling me off the story.

A year later, it turned out that the missing guy was an FBI plant. When the case went to trial, it was revealed that this guy had set up, planned, and led the robbery. It was a landmark entrapment case, which Leonard Boudin[33] won for the defense.

It also came out in the news that there was a very close relationship between the head of the FBI in New York and the New York bureau chief of the AP. And I was very upset to hear it. I had come into the business with the kind of idealism that journalism is about discovering the truth and nothing but the truth. Let the chips fall where they may. I didn't think we should be protecting the police department or the FBI any more than we should be protecting the Young Lords or the Panthers. I was willing to walk the line in being truthful and objective about what was going on out there.

I soon got bored writing wire stories. It was time for me to move on—1971.

Around then, the *New York Post* was sued for discrimination. For years, it appeared that the *Post* had a quota of three black reporters. They had a practice of hiring blacks and letting them go on the eighty-ninth day because on the ninetieth day, their probationary status ended and they would be protected by contract agreements with the newspaper guild. A lot of black folks would come through the paper and be fired after eighty-nine days. There was an illustrious list of black reporters who didn't make it at the *New York Post*. But when Bill Artis failed the tryout, he sued them.

It seemed everybody in New York jumped on them because the *New York Post* was the ultimate liberal paper in New York. A joke going around said that on the last day of the world, the *New York Post's* headline would say, "World Ends, Blacks and Jews Hurt Most."

The *Post* was hurt that Bill Artis had sued them and that they would be subjected to this kind of criticism. White liberals always are crushed when you suggest that they haven't been totally forthcoming and living up to their principles.

When the AP found out I was talking to the *New York Post*, they decided to punish me by putting me on the night shift, midnight to 8:00 A.M. And the bureau chief was telling other possible employers that I was a black militant. The *New York Post* started hemming and hawing about whether they would hire me. Finally I went to one of the editors and said, "What's going on? The AP people are kicking my butt."

"We're having a lot of political problems," he said. "Your people are out to get us."

When the job came through at the *New York Post*, I moved from white conservative ideology to white liberal ideology—which I think is worse. White liberals don't have any principles that they are going to stick by. They just want to feel good about what they do. But I was actually grateful to work at the *Post* because it was a newspaper. I got a lot of exposure because I wrote feature pieces, and I was lucky enough to have a couple of very good editors who were willing to help me.

One of them had been blacklisted during the McCarthy era. Dorothy Schiff, the publisher, had hired him. She was willing to hire people who had been taking heat, she was good for that.

I think the editor saw a kinship between me—this young black reporter—and him, as an outcast. He worked with me. He showed me things about writing, about technique. He showed me what the stars in the business were doing, how they built a piece. I knew this was a very rare thing that was taking place, because it doesn't often happen to black folks in these organizations.

Black journalists are not really viewed as part of the game. You're an outsider, something to be tolerated. You're not there on your merits. And you don't have mentors. But you have people who are threatened by you. And you have people who feel like it's not going to be good for their careers if you move up.

All kinds of dynamics make them develop a mentor relationship with a young white woman who is cute. She looks like their daughter, or they may think they can sleep with her. There isn't anyone in a white news organization who wants to be a mentor to black men—unless he's gay, and the black men are of a like mind.

Nor are there many women in positions of authority with whom you can have some kind of sexual dynamic. I don't mean you have to be actually involved with them sexually. But relationships where there is some mutual attraction don't exist for us in most news organizations.

Black females run into much of the same thing. But there have been instances where they were able to develop mentor relationships. Janet Cooke, who wrote the phony "Jimmy" story[34] for the *Washington Post*, was the most infamous example. She was cute. She seemed smart. She was not threatening to white men. She came across as a very middle-class person. Everybody seemed to want to protect Janet Cooke. Everybody wanted to believe Janet Cooke.

I never had that luxury. The people who helped me were also outsiders.

I started off at the *New York Post* with a big bang. The *New York Times* sent four people to cover an NAACP convention. I was the only reporter from the *Post*. I did seven stories in four days. The *Times* did three. I was hot! Then they sent me to the Urban League[57] convention. I did the same thing. I was a good reporter, and I was very prolific. But one thing you learn in this business if you are a black reporter is that you never develop a history. It's always the next story you do that matters. And the moment you fuck up, you're hung by your toenails.

In 1972, I was sent to cover the National Black Political Convention in Gary, Indiana, which was pulled together by Gary mayor, Richard Hatcher, and Amiri Baraka, the poet. They were trying to develop some national political clout. Five thousand people were there, wheeling and dealing and caucusing behind the scenes. As the only reporter for the *Post,* I was outmanned again.

I had never covered a political convention, which is much more subtle than a black civil rights convention. I had a very difficult time grasping the story. Frankly, I was overwhelmed.

The moment I got back to headquarters, I got jumped on. I had screwed up. Everything I had done before did not matter.

I decided to concentrate on black politics, from the grassroots up. I wanted to get good at it. I knew the National Democratic Convention in Miami would be filled with good stories. When the time came, Warren Hoge, the city editor, told me "You're not going." He picked another black reporter who hadn't done any similar reporting and had no expertise in the area. It showed how interchangeable we are.

I was told I wasn't going because of my story in Gary. This was my punishment. It was typical of a black experience in any white institutional setting. Any time Hoge was asked about my performance by a potential employer, he brought up Gary. I was a militant, they said. I got so involved in political issues that my work sometimes suffered. Nothing would ever be said about the thirty or forty other good performances. So you pay—you always end up paying.

One day we brought up the business of racial identification in stories to publisher Dorothy Schiff. She had a room like a boudoir, in Louis XIV style, on the top floor of the *Journal American* building. She served us chicken and tuna sandwiches. It was all very genteel. There were four of us black reporters and an editor. We were very uncomfortable, because she had all of our balls in her hands.

We said, "Mrs. Schiff, putting race in stories when it has no particular relevance is very inflammatory, especially when there are racial tensions throughout the country. When a black person is identified in every crime story, it suggests that being black has something to do with crime. This reinforces stereotypes."

She answered, "Well, let's put the person's race on all the stories."

"I don't think that's fair either," I said. "Whites are more involved in white collar crimes, and we don't report a lot of white collar crimes. Are you going to identify someone as Jewish if some Jewish accountant takes off with $150,000?"

She laughed. Then we were dismissed. And that was the end of it.

Late in 1972 I took a fellowship to study urban affairs at the University of Chicago. I really wanted to get away. While at the university, I got a call from Dorothy Gilliam, a black reporter at the *Washington Post*. I dreaded the thought of going back to the *New York Post*. And besides, Watergate was going on. I said, "Why not?"

I had interviews in the same week with the *New York Times* and the *Washington Post*. I found the *Times* very stuffy. It was like being in a bank. The *Post* seemed a little more hip. Zip, zap. And when I saw Ben Bradlee, the executive editor, he came across as a very macho he-man, a no-bullshit type. It took me a while to find out that he was a five-generation Boston Brahmin.

Bradlee always looked for a way to throw you off guard. He said, "How do you feel about coming to work for a paper that's been accused of being racist?" The paper was facing complaints from blacks on the metropolitan staff that blacks weren't being hired, promoted, and given good assignments.

I said, "Well, I've got to eat."

He laughed. And the next day, the *Washington Post* offered me a job. Six months later, so did the *Times*. And they couldn't understand why I wouldn't leave the *Post* to work for them. Ever since, I've been on their shit list for turning them down. This was a rejection that was unforgiven.

I liked working at the *Washington Post*. It was the first classy outfit I had worked for. It was full of itself because of the Watergate coverage. But it was nice to have the clout that I didn't have at the *New York Post*. When you called somebody, they called you back. When you wanted information, people felt they were obliged to give it to you. At the *New York Post*, they'd slam the phone in your ear and the door in your face.

One of the first things I did that got me into trouble happened during the honeymoon period. I was being very prolific in turning out stories. They loved me. And the woman in charge of newsroom recruitment said, "Why can't we get other blacks as good as Joel Dreyfus?"

"I don't think that's a fair standard to set because there are a lot of whites here who are not as good as me," I said. "Hire some blacks as good as they are."

She almost had an apoplectic fit. What I had said spread all over the place. They were very upset. The concept of suggesting that a black person is better than a white person is not something that most whites in America are ready to deal with to this day. At best, you can be "as-good-as."

I was assigned to write for the Style section, which meant mostly feature stories. They were very open to ideas. And I wanted to write mostly stories which had never been done about black people.

The editors said that our readers were tired of reading about blacks. What they were tired of reading about, which I also think a lot of black folks were tired of reading about, was the same old story about welfare. The same old story about illegitimacy. The same old story about people getting their asses kicked and being victims.

I think there was almost a preference among white folks to read about blacks as victims, because it removes a threat, it removes the legitimacy of black people as an essential element of what defines America. So I felt there had been too much written about how down-and-out black folks were, which was not the whole picture. I wanted to show a different kind of perspective in black life, to show other slices of the black experience.

I wrote one piece which many people thought was frivolous. It was about a black Corvette club. Every Sunday, these black folks—all Corvette owners, including government officials and pimps, butchers, and surgeons—got together because they loved this car. You'd see fifty Corvettes lined up on the highways. And I thought the story showed black folks in the fuller American context and got away from the idea that blacks are some kind of pathological issue.

I found that the role of blacks in the media reflected the broader picture of black folks in all white institutions. You got some jobs, but blacks had very limited influence on the entire organization. Blacks were still viewed primarily as outsiders. Even if they had very visible positions, they rarely had intellectual influence on the organization. For instance, the way CBS covered the news had not been greatly altered by the presence of Ed Bradley.[35]

I wrote about a black station manager in Washington, who had no hiring power and no control over the news operation. Even the sales staff reported to a vice president in New York. And I quoted Max Robinson[36] as saying that the more money he made, the less influence he had on what went into the newscast.

In analyzing the *CBS Evening News* broadcast, I pointed out that there was virtually nothing in it that suggested America was multiethnic, or that there was a black struggle for progress. Instead, they did stories about blacks which were either frivolous or distorted. For instance, a story about the Ku Klux Klan tells you virtually nothing about black America.

Although a lot of taboos remained in advertising—a black man couldn't be seen with a white woman in an ad at that time—television commercials were probably the most realistic representation of black people in the American media. You got a cross-section of black people—lumberjacks and professors, athletes and cops. They wanted to sell black people products. And you can't sell people anything by insulting them.

But my Haitian perspective kept saying that the symbolism of desegregation was not enough. I was interested in how power was shared. And the issue of power was at the core of the whole relationship between black journalists and white news organizations. The access that black reporters had or didn't have was related to power. And what kind of power were you going to have? Could a black person expect a normal progression from reporter to editor to manager to publisher? Well, for most of us, the answer was no. And it would be foolish to think that it was even a possibility.

Look at the sports department at most networks, television stations, and newspaper and magazines. There are few black people in those areas, although blacks dominate professional basketball, football, and boxing. But sports are a great white male fantasy area, which is high in pleasure and high in profit.

When *Newsday* first told Les Payne[37] they couldn't send a black reporter to Africa because he couldn't be impartial, they were exercising power. After all, the press sent Jews to the Middle East. Asians were sent to cover Japan and Korea without a second thought. It came down to power. And in this country the issue of black people acquiring power was still frightening for most whites because it undermined the whole thing about superiority and inferiority and qualifications. It scared the shit out of them.

I spent several months on the media series. I interviewed hundreds of people. I wrote 15,000 words. And the *Post* didn't like it. They never challenged whether the story was true. But everybody from Ben Bradlee on down hated it. They felt the picture was too bleak. They wanted to hear that because Max Robinson and a few others had highly visible jobs this meant that everything was wonderful. It was the old why-aren't-you-blacks-happy kind of thing.

There were a number of small mistakes in my series, mostly due to copyediting. I got a long memo saying that if I kept making mistakes like that, my future in journalism would not be bright. I wrote back, "That's interesting because one of your star white reporters just had two front-page corrections in the same week." That was the kind of thing that kept me in trouble.

I felt I was a very conscientious reporter. But mistakes were looked for to be used to knock me down. I never felt that I had the comfort of being in a news organization where I was protected and supported, where people would rally to me and make me better. For the black journalist, it's always a kind of antagonistic relationship— you are the outsider.

I got to the point where I wouldn't discuss racism at the *Washington Post*. Or in any news organization. I realized that racism was totally irrational. You're never going to argue and persuade somebody to change his ways. If somebody were being rational, they wouldn't act racist in the first place. And I learned you couldn't tell somebody they were racist. They'd say, "Right." And then where did you go?

So I addressed issues I felt were important strictly from my perspective or from the journalistic perspective. I suggested that racism produced poor journalism, without really saying that out loud.

When Washington won home rule, the *Post* sent a reporter to Fourteenth and U to interview blacks for their reaction. This was the corner where drug addicts hung out. They published a story saying the addicts didn't care, and the cops told the reporter to be careful or he would get knifed. I was outraged.

I told the desk, "What is this crap? Here's a city that has the largest proportion of middle-class black people of any city in America, except maybe Chicago. And we are interviewing addicts. Why don't you go to the prisons and interview white convicts when Congress passes a bill?"

I never suggested that racism was the problem. I talked about it in journalist terms, and that really upset them. I was showing them that they were guilty of bad journalism, even if they were at fault because they were racist.

And this same racist behavior explained why our foreign reporting was some of the worst in the world. We tied our coverage in many countries to government handouts. Or we accepted whatever our embassies said. We couldn't believe that Latin Americans didn't want to be oppressed. We couldn't believe that little yellow men could kick the shit out of all-American white boys from the Midwest. We couldn't believe that Africans wanted to run their own affairs, that they want to have democratic countries, and that they would have to go through the same experience of slaughtering each other, the same fiefdoms, the same tribalism, that Europeans experienced. Italy was only formed as a country a hundred and fifty years ago. And they had a two thousand year-old civilization.

When Les Payne finally did go to Africa, he became one of the first American journalists to write from the point of view of the majority—the blacks. This was not another one of these, "Will White Africa Survive?" stories. "Will their privileged way of life become extinct?"

I really believed that black folks brought a unique perspective to a national or international story. And there was an audience for it. Not just among blacks but among white people who were tired of the same old establishment view by people who dined and talked only with each other in places of power and privilege in New York and Washington.

The outsider's point of view, which the black journalist could offer the media, was a view many Americans would like to share, because they feel they are on the outside of the parameters of power, too. But there was a great fear among people who ran things about what that perspective could mean, because that perspective would open up channels with readers, which they didn't have.

I once wrote on the op-ed page of the *Post*, a piece critical of American arrogance in foreign policy. I talked about our condescension toward Third World countries. How we couldn't have constructive diplomacy as long as we were so arrogant in our relationships with them.

Nathan Glazer of Harvard University wrote me that I was suffering from Western self-hate. But most letters agreed with me. And most of them came from white readers, including Gary Hart.[38] That gave me a sense that there is a constituency out there for the kind of journalism that black folks want to do and believe should be done, if only they could get past what Bob Maynard[39] called "the gate-keepers." The people who control the access, control the definitions of what is news, and keep everything tied to the status quo.

Because I was outspoken about hiring practices and how the *Post* covered the news, I became a kind of lightning rod for a lot of complaints. Some of the black reporters would meet at my house. We wrote memos to Ben Bradlee urging the paper to be more aggressive in its hiring of blacks, in promoting them, and in guaranteeing equal opportunity throughout the paper. Those points were obviously not welcomed by management. So that time became heated and tense.

After a while, I got tired of the whole thing, tired of being in the middle. I took a leave of absence for six months to work on a book, and came back determined to buckle down and not get into any more hassles. I did my work. I stayed out of office politics. And then for personal reasons, I decided I wanted to move to the West Coast. So when an opening came up in the L.A. bureau, I applied.

I wrote Bradlee a memo saying I was interested in the bureau and would like to be considered. I got a letter back from him saying that while I was viewed as a gifted journalist, they had decided not to offer me the job. Because I had been critical of the *Post*'s policies, I had become a pain-in-the-ass. And nobody wanted a pain-in-the-ass.

I was very upset. I gave a couple of copies of the letter to people and asked them, "How do you think I should respond?"

I finally wrote to Ben Bradlee that I never knew I had to sacrifice my principles to move forward at the *Washington Post*, and that I always felt I was trying to make it a better paper.

But before my letter reached Bradlee, someone made a photocopy of it and passed it around. The next thing I knew, the letter was on the bulletin board of every major media organization around the city. And in New York at the *Times*. It also appeared in the *Village*

Voice, and in an *Esquire* magazine profile of Bradlee. This happened in the middle of the turmoil caused by the printers' strike against the *Post.*

Bradlee was really pissed off. And we had a shouting match.

"I don't guarantee that I can convince you," I said. "But I really did not intend for this to get out."

All our conversations in the past had been private. I had great access to him. I could walk into his office to talk over things. Even higher-ranking people were envious of that. And I always thought we basically got along. We had a sort of mutual respect, if not an actual liking for each other.

Bradlee said he wasn't going to fire me, but I couldn't expect the *Post* to do anything for me in the future. I got the message. This was the end of the road. Two months later, I resigned.

Bradlee and I are friendlier now. And he allows me use him for a recommendation.

It was a very hot time then. Today there are fewer tensions in newsrooms like the *Washington Post.* There isn't the feeling among whites that blacks are putting heavy pressure for concessions. I think it's because black folks got tired, got discouraged. It moves in cycles in any organization, media or otherwise.

But I see more confrontations coming. It was a more simplistic period back then than it will be in the future.

Because now we know what to ask for.

BEN HOLMAN

Ben Holman was always out front—the first black to graduate from the University of Kansas journalism school, the first black to become a CBS correspondent. He had many more designations as "the first."

———

I didn't believe it was happening.

They're punching me. Kicking me.

I'm bleeding all over the place.

I'm big. But, God, they're bigger than me.

It's mad. Confusion everywhere. But I hear one of them.

"You should have known we were going to get you sooner or later."

I thought it had blown over in Chicago. I was convinced they had forgotten about it. It really wasn't such a big deal.

In the summer of 1964, you expected anything to happen at a civil rights rally. The country was tense. But I didn't expect anything to happen to me. I was very identifiable. I was the only black in the whole CBS organization.

They were having a civil rights rally outside the Hotel Theresa, in the center of Harlem. It was a typical outdoor civil rights rally—warm weather, a number of speakers, big crowd, an army of policemen.

In spite of the earlier incident, I didn't feel any alarm. I was plainly visible. I was there for CBS. The unit had CBS painted all over it, the big eye and everything. I was directing the camera crew. I was on top of the truck. I was telling the crew what I wanted them to shoot.

The main speaker finished. I needed to ask him some questions. He was going to his room, on the second floor of the Theresa. I wanted to go up to see if he would talk to me. I yelled to my crew to follow me to the room.

A mob followed the speaker into the elevator in the lobby. I was familiar with the Theresa and knew I could easily walk the stairs. I decided to go up, and then I'd probably get there before he did.

I heard footsteps behind me. I assumed somebody else had the same idea as me. I got almost up to the top of the landing and the footsteps closed on me. It was four of them. They started beating on me fantastically. Really! All four of them beating the hell out of me. I flailed around trying to defend myself, trying to protect my head.

They punched, they kicked. They called me "Uncle Tom." They called me a traitor.

I didn't know them. But I knew who they were. By the way they dressed. They were from the Fruit of Islam, the dreaded guard of the Black Muslims. These were not small people.

They called my name.

"Holman. You should have known."

It was quite a melee. We fell down the stairway. I ended up at the bottom.

I escaped and ran out the door. They disappeared into the crowd. It had happened so fast, I guess in a minute or two. But it started a big commotion. People in the lobby screamed and yelled. Nobody knew what was going on. The cops made no effort to do anything—white, all white young cops, and they were absolutely petrified. They froze. They stood there like tin soldiers.Blood was dripping all over me. I made my way to one of the cops. I looked into his eyes. I have never seen a man so scared before. He did nothing. He was totally immobilized. He was so frightened that he didn't know what to do.

I kept saying, "I'm from CBS! I'm from CBS! They just beat me up!"

He didn't move.

Finally, one of his partners came over and grabbed me and steadied me. I was excited, covered with blood, and I looked a mess!

So he took charge. I finally convinced him who I was by showing him my press pass. He decided to get me out of there. He escorted me around the corner and put me in a police car and took me to Harlem hospital.

The doctors insisted I stay a couple of hours. They took some X-rays. I had a bloody nose, superficial bruises and cuts, but no broken bones. They asked if I wanted to remain overnight, and I said "No." But I didn't get home until close to midnight.

Meanwhile, I had called the CBS office and explained what had happened. They did a phone interview with me to use on the news that night.

One of my childhood friends came over from New Jersey to take me home and stay with me through the night. We didn't know what might happen next. He called my folks. I knew my mother would be upset if she heard what happened on a news program first. She had high blood pressure. I had to warn her.

My mother—a great lady, Joanna Graves. She never said anything to me about my being at CBS, my being the first black. But she told others how proud she was of me.

We were very poor. I was born in Columbia, South Carolina. My father was a barber. He died when I was four. My mother moved to Bloomfield, New Jersey, and became a maid to support me and my sister. She worked for wealthy white families. She married again when I was eleven. My stepfather was illiterate, a garbage collector.

We didn't have much. But she made our home a haven for children. Mother raised six orphans from birth, besides us. She let me make my own decisions and get my own jobs. She always supported me.

I got my first job when I was eleven. I worked as a migrant farm worker from six in the morning to six in the evening, six days a week, picking celery and lettuce. It was back-breaking work, and I was paid sixteen dollars a week. I thought I was rich! Independence was bred into me at an early age.

The first time I showed any real writing talent was in the seventh grade. My cousin, Holly Sims, had a pet dog, Skippy. My folks didn't want a dog. So I more or less adopted Skippy, a tan mutt. I saw him every day. Everyone thought the dog was mine. He followed me everywhere. Once he was hit by a car. I was somewhere else at the time. He just lay there and wouldn't get up. People thought he was dying. When I arrived, Skippy hopped up, he was waiting for me.

I was in the seventh grade, at this mostly white school. The teacher asked us to write a paper, and I wrote about Skippy. She accused me of plagiarism. In Bloomfield, New Jersey, back then, black kids weren't expected to have talent. But I convinced her that I wrote it.

I received good grades in junior high school. But I got no guidance, no encouragement. What could I expect? The son of a maid in Bloomfield?

In senior high all the white boys were preparing to be electrical engineers or doctors. I was bored with math and science. Getting an A in calculus was no big deal. So to the consternation to everyone, I announced that I was going to be a writer. I wasn't going to be crazy enough just to try writing. I played the violin in the orchestra, so I thought I could combine my music and writing to do musical comedy. I wanted to be a creative writer.

When the president of the school board heard what I wanted to do, he had plenty to say. He was one of my mother's employers. He told her that I wasn't being practical.

"Blacks don't do that," he said.

"I'll compromise," I said. "I'll be a journalist."

The president of the school board said, "There aren't any black journalists."

"Then I'll be the first."

Some people laughed. Some just shook their heads. Everyone discouraged me.

I graduated ninth in a class of five hundred. The first eight were girls. That got me admitted to Harvard, Bucknell, and Swarthmore—scholarships to all three. But I didn't have the other money you needed for clothes, travel, and books. So I went to Lincoln, a black school, on a full athletic scholarship. I was a halfback. But after one day of practice, I quit. If I wasn't going to be the greatest, I didn't see the point.

After two years, one of the teachers, Mr. Cox, helped me switch to the University of Kansas.

"If you want to be a journalist, you must go to Kansas," he said.

Kansas was *his* school. Lincoln didn't have a journalism program. When I graduated from Kansas, I was a major embarrassment. I was first in our class in the College of Journalism, and editor of the campus daily.

Everybody had a job waiting for them but me. I had all the credentials except a white face. The only other black in my class went to the *Cleveland Call Post*, a black weekly. I didn't have a problem about working for a black publication, but I wanted to work for a daily. I had started looking a year earlier, knowing that I would have trouble. I applied to nearly a hundred papers. I was turned down by every one of them. They didn't hire blacks in those days. This was 1952.

After commencement, I stuck around for a few months, working as a yard-and-house boy so I could eat. One day the dean called me in. He was a former editor of the *Chicago Daily News*. He said he would try the *Daily News* for me.

Several days later, I was called back to his office. "There's a message here for you." It said to call the *Daily News*.

It took me two more weeks to earn the train ticket. Then I headed for Chicago. When I got there, I stayed the first two weeks in the cheapest hotel I could find, run by the YMCA. The rooms were two or three dollars a day, and about the size of a large closet. I ate one meal of soup each day. That's all I had.

I joined the *Chicago Daily News* in September, as a general assignment reporter. One other black was there when I was hired, Les Brownlee. He switched to another paper soon after. For the next nine years I was the only black on the staff.

Despite my recommendations and college credentials, the editors still questioned whether I could hack it. So they farmed me out to the *Chicago News Bureau* to do police rewrite. I was the first black to work there. It was owned and managed by the four daily papers.

One of the rewrite men said, "Everybody's surprised that you can write."

During the first week on the job, I walked into a precinct police station on the north side, and said, "I'm the reporter from the news bureau."

Everyone was startled. They had a conference.

Then the desk sergeant said, "We've been having a meeting on you. Except for the prisoners, we've never had a Negro in here before."

One night, a patrol car followed me from another station. A head peered from the window. "Hey, kid," he said, "we just checked you out. And you really are a reporter!"

My colleagues had more trouble accepting me than my news sources. Some photographers refused to go out with me. When I was assigned to police headquarters, the night I walked in, every white reporter walked out. All five of them.

The *Daily News* had called ahead to warn them. The reporters called back and said police was a white beat and they would not work with a black. For two weeks, they refused to talk to me, to share information. They pretended that I wasn't there. They were trying to get me recalled. It was sheer hell.

I had no training to deal with this. You just went about your work and didn't let anything impair your ability to cover a story. Finally, Tommy Tucker, a reporter for the *Chicago American*, broke the ice.

He apologized, saying, "This is disgusting." He said everyone was afraid to be the first to break the barrier.

Except for the guy at the *Chicago Tribune*, we all became friends. Eventually, he broke down, too. One day he said, "Hey, kid. Want a Coke?"

Eventually, I covered every beat imaginable—county courts, City Hall, the county building. Then one day in 1961, the city editor called me over. We talked and the subject of the Black Muslims came up.

At the time, Black Muslims caused a lot of apprehension. White people were scared out of their shirts about them because of their secrecy, their strong anti-white rhetoric, and their claim about their growing influence in the black community—half a million members, they said. This frightened white people.

The editor and I agreed it would be a good idea to do a story on the Black Muslims. I told him I knew nothing about them. No specific assignment was made, but it was in my head to do something.

I lived in the heart of the South Side, not far from the Muslims' national headquarters and the home of Elijah Muhammad, their spiritual leader. It seemed easy to attend one of their meetings.

I thought about it and thought about it. Finally, I went back to the editor and said, "Maybe I should go to one of their meetings and get some idea of what it's like."

In those days, their services were closed to whites. Only blacks were permitted inside. And every black was searched first. So this was clearly a story calling for a black reporter.

But I always saw myself as a reporter first. I didn't seek out black stories. At the time, I was covering the Chicago Sanitary District, a utility service. But I thought there were times when it made sense for me to cover certain stories because I was black, and the Black Muslim thing was one of these times.

They met every Sunday. So on my own I went to one of their meetings. The mosque on the South Side had formerly been a big Jewish synagogue. It was the number one mosque in their movement. And on that first day, Elijah Muhammad himself was conducting the service.

Even though I had been with the *Daily News* for about nine years by then, I wasn't terribly well known. My picture had rarely appeared with any of my stories. And except for certain people in the black community who were leaders, or news sources I dealt with, I wasn't generally known. It was obvious that nobody in the mosque would know who I was, and I didn't make any effort to identify myself. I was welcomed very warmly. So as far as they knew, I was just an ordinary person.

My first reaction to their message was negative. It seemed odd hearing black Americans talk about Islam, about Allah instead of God. I was a bit appalled. After all, I grew up in the Baptist church and came from a very religious family.

Then Elijah made some very belligerent statements about white people, calling them devils and so forth, talking about how horrible the white man had been, referring to whites as dogs. But this was psychologically interesting because he worked his audience into a fever pitch. Then he brought them back down. All the Muslim ministers seemed to have a knack for doing that—orchestrating a catharsis.

The audience was made up of ordinary black persons. I didn't see anybody of prominence then or as time wore on. The types that joined were largely poor working-class blacks. And they tended to attract young people who were impressed with the almost exotic air of the mosque, people who tended to get carried away by the headiness of the rhetoric, who tended to look for easy solutions to complex and difficult problems in life. They were very vague—particularly the younger members—about how they planned to get from A-to-B in life. There were some highly educated people in the movement, but very few.

I told my editor that I had gone to one of the services. Although I had found it interesting, I needed to know a lot more about their organization before I could attempt a writing assignment.

He said, "We'll wait for you, Ben."

Since I was the only black on the staff, they had no other option. So I started going to the services on a fairly regular basis. I was curious. I decided fairly early to use a fictitious name—Nathaniel Jones. I had a friend, Betty Livingston, who lived not far from the mosque in Hyde Park, and I asked her to let me use her apartment as an address to give the Muslims. Betty was the only person who knew what I was doing.

This was a strange period. I began to like and enjoy what I was hearing. Malcolm X was a big factor. I had been going for two months when he showed up one day, and he made so much sense to me. I found him a very electrifying speaker. He awakened some of my earlier militancy, like the time I had passed out leaflets against a segregated bowling alley in New Jersey. After I went to work in Chicago, I dropped my militancy.

What struck me, as it did the entire audience, was Malcolm's analysis of the role of black folks in the United States. In the late Fifties and early Sixties, the civil rights movement was just underway. This was prior to the civil rights act of 1964, and there was a lot of segregation. Discrimination was rampant. A couple of blocks from my home, a young black person was denied a drink in a bar. Chicago—1961!

So here was Malcolm, a bold black man, questioning whether blacks were getting a fair deal. And putting it bluntly!

At the end of each meeting, I went home and made notes. I had no contact with anyone outside the mosque. I didn't visit with anyone, I never developed friendships. I was amazed that they didn't get suspicious, because I never participated outside the mosque.

But after three months, I sensed I was becoming a convert. Maybe I was impressionable. I was going to the services regularly. I almost got to the point where I forgot that this had all started out as part of an assignment.

After a while, they asked whether or not I really wanted to belong. They asked this repeatedly. Initially, of course, I wasn't interested because I saw myself as being on assignment. After a while, I said to myself, *Why not?*

They explained that I had to go through an instructional period. I would report every day during the week for instructions. The classes were segregated—men in one group, women in another. The instructions were delivered calmly, and were a lot less bellicose than some of their public statements. The course was mostly about the Muslim religion and about Elijah Muhammad. There was a lot of pep talk, too, about the honor and glory of being a Black Muslim.

Some of it was constructive advice. They lectured about the role of the man in the family and his need to be strong. We were told to dress neatly and conservatively. We heard about the evils of pork, but no one said point-blank, "You cannot eat pork." We were told not to drink or smoke. Fortunately, I wasn't much of a drinker—two beers and I was getting drunk. I wasn't much of a smoker, either. So it wasn't a big sacrifice for me.

After three weeks it was over. We filled out some forms and were told we would be notified by mail whether or not we received our "X." The "X" would replace our last names, which was considered the names given to blacks by the master of the slave plantation.

A few days later Betty called me. She said, "There's a letter from the Black Muslims."

The letter was from the minister explaining that I had received my "X" and congratulating me. I was Nathaniel X.

Now that I was a member, they decided that I was a good prospect for the Fruit of Islam. I was young and big. I didn't smoke or drink as far as they knew, and I looked fit.

They promoted the Fruit of Islam as a service organization. Young men dressed neatly in shirts and ties with close-cut hair. They had training in self-defense. But it became clear very quickly that they were actually guards, trained in martial arts, and very definitely paramilitary.

I dodged the invitation.

Mind you, I was doing all this stuff on my own and not telling the *Daily News*. Occasionally, my editor would ask, "How's your research coming?"

"I'm still trying to get a handle on it."

In the early days that was true. After a while, he stopped asking. I think he assumed that I had lost interest in the assignment. They forgot about the whole thing. So I guess, technically speaking, I wasn't on assignment anymore. But I continued going.

Almost a year had passed, and now I was a member. I had mixed emotions. I didn't know whether I should continue. If I was going to continue, then I would have to surface, to be honest with them and really become a full-blooded member. I didn't know what to do. I was torn.

I made a decision. I stopped going to the meetings. After a while, I got a couple of letters saying they missed me.

I didn't respond. I spent a month of soul-searching about what I should do. It was a very difficult decision. I finally decided I would not join. I didn't want to be a Muslim. I decided on balance that my original Baptist training was too strong. I still believed in God, in Baptist principles. I also had doubts about the viability of their programs. And it occurred to me that they had not attracted a single person of prominence, or one who had a college education that I knew of.

Then I had another decision to make. Did I want to do a news story? That was almost as tough. My initial inclination was to forget about it.

One day I was talking to Betty. She said, "What are you going to do?"

"I'm not going to do anything. I'm going to forget about it."

"You spent all that time," she said. "And you're not going to write a story? Sort of a waste of your time, wasn't it?"

"Yeah, it was."

I started thinking. If I do a story, what kind of a story do I write? I didn't think they would print it if I said the Black Muslims were a pretty good organization, but just not for me.

"Why don't you just tell what happened?" Betty said. "As truthfully and honestly as you can? See if the editors buy it."

"That's a good idea. Maybe I shouldn't be so timid."

So I finally went to see my editor. "Remember that assignment a year ago?" Then I told him what I'd been doing.

His eyes widened.

"You've been doing this for a whole year?"

"Yes."

"Why didn't you tell us about it? I'm amazed. I just assumed you had dropped the idea."

"To be honest with you, I almost became a Black Muslim."

His eyes widened even more.

"Ben," he said, "I'm surprised you didn't have more faith in me."

"Well, I wondered."

"I tell you what," he said. "You sit down and write the story the way you want to write it. We'll print it."

"Okay. It's a deal."

I wrote it pretty quickly. It rolled out of my typewriter, the whole series, all fourteen pieces. I must have written it in about three days.

I began the first article, "My name is Nathaniel X . . ." I described what it was like to be a stranger walking into a typical Sunday meeting and hearing the anti-white rhetoric.

I raised the question whether or not this was a violent movement. My answer was "no." There was a lot of rhetoric, a lot of tough talk. But essentially it was not as violent as it pretended to be.

I pointed out the good things, their admonitions against smoking and drinking, their emphasis on family loyalty and marital faithfulness. I pointed out that as far as I could observe their members conscientiously tried to live up to the principles. I said that their emphasis on business enterprise was a plus, although there was little more than a restaurant being operated by them.

But I concluded that Christianity had such a strong pull historically on American blacks that they would have a difficult time winning over any significant numbers. Their Puritan ethic could already be found in the Christian church.

Yet there was a lot of sympathy for the Muslims, even among thinking blacks. They were sucked into this. It was romantic to hear an articulate black man like Malcolm X giving white America hell. What he said about white exploitation was true—you couldn't argue against him.

But what viable path did they have for blacks to take? They talked business enterprise, but what they were doing was minuscule. They said they wanted some land in the South to create a separate state. I thought that was totally out of whack. Their whole approach as an alternative for black Americans was specious. They really didn't have any programs.

There was a big debate in the city room as to whether or not they should run my picture in the paper with the series. Maybe I was naïve. I said, "Sure, why don't you?"

They were very fearful something might happen. They even wanted to assign a bodyguard to me. I rejected the idea. I didn't think that anything was going to happen. I didn't even change my telephone number. I didn't move. I didn't do anything.

I thought I was fairly popular with them. I was a faithful member. I had the notion that even though I deceived them, they couldn't bring themselves to do anything to harm me.

The *Daily News* realized it had quite a series on its hands. And they did a fantastic promotion job. The whole side of every truck had a big promo as a teaser! They had commercials on the air. They whipped Chicago into a frenzy of expectation. The news syndicate offered it across the nation. And it got a lot of publicity in the Muslim publications. They ran story after story about how I had done this traitorous series of stories.

From the first day the story appeared in Chicago, the Muslim reaction was extremely strong. They started calling immediately, threatening to kill me. They told me they knew where I lived. One phone call shook me up because the caller described the car I owned.

"I would avoid driving if I were you, Ben." the caller said. "It just might blow up on you."

After three weeks the calls faded but not the letters. The *Daily News* had to set up a special section to handle them. I gave them permission to open and screen them. The really nasty ones, and the threatening ones, I didn't see. They didn't want to shake me up.

I got quite a bit of reaction from non-Muslims who were black. They said that I had let myself be used by whites to spy on black folks. They didn't see anything wrong with the Black Muslims. They thought the Muslims were effectively scaring the white man, shaking them up about the plight of black folks. That's why there was widespread sympathy among blacks for the Muslims. One young lady whom I had seen socially stopped speaking to me—and she was a non-Muslim. She said I had done a terrible thing. Gus Savage, who later became a congressman, attacked me in his black weekly newspaper.

It was the only time in my career that I used this approach to a story—a pseudonym. And I didn't feel any guilt. I felt I had done a fair, honest job.

The fact was that the Black Muslims presented themselves as the salvation for black America, not as just another religious movement. They were the solution for the black man. That was their whole platform. Any organization that purported to sell itself on that basis warranted the kind of scrutiny I gave them. They even billed themselves as the fastest-growing black organization, but a little research showed that their claimed membership of five hundred thousand was more like ten thousand.

The fact that they were black, like me, was no reason why I shouldn't have done the story. I would have written the same story if I had been working for a black publication and the publisher had let me.

The week before the series began, Irv Kupcinet, the *Chicago Sun-Times* columnist, was doing his show at WBBM, and had me on. He heard they were looking for a black reporter to hire and he suggested me. In October I joined WBBM, the CBS station. I was the first black on television news in Chicago. The move made sense—more money and prestige. There was a challenge in trying something new, and television looked like the coming thing.

In January of 1963, I got a call to come to New York to audition for the network. The other networks, not long before, had hired their first blacks—Mel Goode at ABC, Bob Teague at NBC. I guess

CBS was catching up. I was made the first. Teague and I were on general assignment. Goode was posted at the U.N.

The CBS executives were extremely cordial. It was a little unusual for a new reporter to meet with the president, but they had me meet Richard Salant.

Salant said, "As far as we are concerned, you're just another reporter on our staff, unless you want it otherwise."

I said, "That's the way I want it."

So I was transferred to New York. Several months passed. Quite frankly, I forgot about the Black Muslims and the threats. I figured nothing would ever happen. The New York mosque had a reputation for some bad actors. But I figured they wouldn't care much about what happened in Chicago.

I was wrong. I was taking the subway one day. I was on the subway platform at the BMT 28th Street station, the station that I used to go to work everyday at the old CBS building.

This brother recognized me. Not many blacks were on television in those days. I couldn't honestly say what he intended to do, but he started down the platform toward me. He may have been approaching me to say something. But I wasn't taking any chances. The subway arrived at that moment, and I ran into the train.

The next encounter was the beating I got at the Hotel Theresa.

In late 1964 I persuaded CBS to let me work on the schism between Malcolm and Elijah Muhammad. I was very much upfront this time. I contacted Malcolm and told him what I wanted to do. He was very cordial. I reminded him of the *Chicago Daily News* situation.

"Oh, yes," he said. "I remember you very well. Come on over. Let's talk."

He was extremely cooperative, and I got all sorts of footage. We talked a lot on camera. We talked a lot off camera.

"I tried to be honest with the first series," I said.

"It wasn't that your series was so unbalanced," Malcolm X said. "Personally, I did not find it unfair. It's just the fact that you were undercover and all that upset us."

He told me that he knew of the beating at the Hotel Theresa. He said it was ordered from above. Then he said, "We did try to bump you off at the subway."

Malcolm was just as impressive when you spoke to him in private as he was speaking from a platform. He talked about his trip overseas, especially about going to Mecca, and his growing realization of the true meaning of Islam. Islam was rooted in universal brotherhood. He talked about the coalitions he wanted to establish with other black organizations. He saw himself as part of the movement to bring about civil rights for black people.

But, he said, Elijah saw him as a threat, a rival seeking to replace him. And worse, Elijah saw him as a traitor. In exposing Elijah, Malcolm had become the enemy. Malcolm said he knew he had been marked for assassination, and that the orders came from Elijah Muhammad himself. He had made a trip to Chicago and barely escaped with his life. He thought they were going to get him sooner or later.

He said, "I'm just not going to be able to stop it." He paused. "I know too much."

Then what he said stunned me.

He thought Elijah was corrupt—morally and financially. He was stealing from the temple, and he had fathered a lot of babies out of wedlock.

Even though I had developed an admiration for Malcolm, I was skeptical. I found it hard to believe. I thought he was telling me this because he was in a political fight with Elijah. Then Malcolm said Elijah's son would confirm everything. I went to Chicago to see him. The son had turned against Elijah. He pretty much confirmed everything Malcolm had told me.

When I got back to New York, Malcolm and I saw quite a bit of each other. It was a warm relationship. We often turned off the cameras and the tape recorder, and just talked.

I decided to film Malcolm at the Audubon Ballroom in Harlem, where he spoke every Sunday. When I got there, Malcolm announced to everyone, "CBS is here." He pointed to me. "This man has been treated unjustly. I happen to know that the beating he suffered was specifically ordered by Elijah Muhammad."

We had it all on film.

I returned to film him the next two Sundays. Each time I sat on the front row beside the camera crew. Everyone could see us. Everyone knew we were there.

On the third Sunday, I told him I had enough footage at the ballroom. I didn't need any more. I said I wouldn't be there the following Sunday.

The next Sunday, February 21, 1965, I did not go to the Audubon.

"For a change, I can sleep late," I said.

I was home asleep when the phone rang. It was CBS. They told me Malcolm X had been shot. They didn't give me any details. I was asked to go to the Audubon immediately.

I can't say that I was totally surprised. But I started crying. He had convinced me it was going to happen. I knew he was going to be killed. It was just a matter of time. I felt smothered in sadness.

I was a little apprehensive on the way to the Audubon. But when I got there, it was all over. Malcolm had been shot several times in the chest. He had been taken away. We took some footage, and I told CBS that I thought I should go to his home.

Before I left, I stood where Malcolm had fallen. It was by a twist of fate that I wasn't there. I could have been sitting up front that Sunday, right in the line of fire. The killers might have turned their guns on me, too. I was still the enemy, as I later found out.

I went to Malcolm's home to see his wife, Betty. I didn't know what to say to her. I've never been terribly good in these kinds of situations. We were both crying. We embraced and went inside.

Then I told her I had a camera crew outside. "Do you want to say anything for the air? It is strictly up to you."

"Yes, I will," she said. "I think I should. What do you think?"

"I really don't know," I said. "It's purely a personal decision."

"I'll try to say something."

"Well, it's not going to be the traditional interview. You tell me what you want to say, and I'll ask the questions."

I knew you should put aside personal feelings and emotions for an interview. But I found it very difficult at this time. I had gotten so attached to her and to him. I wasn't feeling very journalistic. So there wasn't much said on camera. Looking back on it, there were a lot of things I should have asked her. But I was in no mood to be a journalist that day.

Malcolm was killed by two black men, probably acting as agents of the Black Muslims. They acted on orders from the headquarters in Chicago, but not necessarily from Elijah Muhammad. That was the official version. But I suspected that Elijah was aware of what was to happen.

I wouldn't be totally shocked if we learned one day that a government intelligence agency had a hand in his death. Although I have never seen anything pertaining to this, I have been exposed to some highly classified intelligence information as a member of the Justice Department's inner sanctum. Obviously, I could not discuss any of it, but I saw enough to know that the intelligence community in this country was very fearful of black organizations in that period. The CIA and the FBI and others considered almost any black organization suspect. But until I am shown otherwise, I logically must go along with the official explanation for Malcolm's death.

A few months later, I was in Chicago on another assignment, when CBS asked me if I wanted to cover the big Muslim convention scheduled at one of the old armories on Wabash Street. With all that had happened, they were somewhat apprehensive about my safety. But I said I would go.

The place was packed, maybe three thousand people. This was when the Black Muslims began letting the press cover their meetings. When we came in, we were asked to identify ourselves. I started to give my name, but before I could say one word the person in charge said, "Oh, we know who you are. You're that old . . ." I wasn't listening to what he was saying. It hit me. They still hadn't forgotten.

We set up our camera with everyone else. Elijah Muhammad was not there. The meeting was being run by a minister from Boston. I said to myself, *This is television. I am here with a crew. Nothing can happen. There are crews here from all over. There is even a foreign crew here, probably because Muhammad Ali is on the stage.*

I discussed how much more footage we needed with the crew. We were pretty well convinced that we didn't need any more. Then all of a sudden, I saw the floodlights on me. My back was to the audience. I didn't understand it. I turned around and the other cameras were focused on me. They were filming me!

Then I tuned in on what the speaker—the minister from Boston—was saying. He was denouncing me.

"This is the dog," he cried out. "This is the traitor. He is the one who betrayed the beloved Honorable Elijah Muhammad!"

The camera people started to panic. The crew said, "Should we call the cops?"

"Are you kidding? There's nothing the cops can do at this point. I think your best bet is to get away from me!"

They were white. They could get out.

"You get out. I can't move."

The crew left. I was still there, literally down front. Where was I going to go?

Surely, I thought, *this crowd won't take me apart with the world's cameras here, with Muhammad Ali sitting here.*

I looked at Muhammad Ali when this ruckus started, and they were screaming for my scalp. He sat there, didn't say anything. I said to myself, *Surely my ol' buddy is going to get up and save me from being murdered.* He didn't move.

I had spent two weeks with Ali at his training camp. Even though he was a Muslim, we got to be pretty tight, as you do with sources you cover for a long time. I never brought up Chicago and neither did he.

"Hey, Muhammad," I said. "It's your old friend." He looked puzzled.

I said softly, "Oh, God. He's gonna let them kill me."

This Boston minister was really whipping up the crowd.

"He is a traitor! He deserves death!"

The crowd was screaming, three thousand strong, "Kill him! Kill him! Kill him!"

Suddenly, the Fruit of Islam moved toward me. They formed a circle around me. It was almost like the secret service had put a guard on me. The leader came over and whispered to me, "We'll get you out of this."

"Okay," I said. "I'm in your hands."

They led me through the auditorium.

The speaker was still screaming. The crowd kept reaching over trying to get me.

"Let me at him! Let me at him! Let me *personally* kill him!"

The guards warded them off. They got me out. I thanked them.

The leader said, "We weren't going to let anything happen to you, brother. We just wanted to shake you up a little bit."

"That's a hell of a way to shake me up! You scared the shit out of me!"

He said, "Are you okay?"

"Yeah."

"Can we call you a cab? Where are you staying?"

I told him the hotel. And that was it. I was never bothered like that again.

Nearly twenty years later, I learned the name of the Boston minister. It was during Jesse Jackson's campaign for the presidency. NBC had been reviewing the old film taken that day in the auditorium. The minister in the film was the same minister now being accused of threatening the life of Milton Coleman, a black reporter for the *Washington Post*. I looked at the film.

"My God," I said. "That was Louis Farrakhan."[40]

I worked on several more documentaries before I left CBS. They always said they had to do something about the problem of blacks in the United States. But they could never get sponsors. Some problem would come up. I sometimes thought they were paying me to make documentaries that would sit in the can. In one we focused on black teenage unemployment, a serious problem then as it is now. We found a group in Harlem that was making progress in putting blacks to work.

I went with a crew to scout the offices. All they had was a basement hole. Stepping down into it was like going into a dungeon. The crew was white, of course. And they were nervous. By then we only had one black part-time crew person, an occasional black sound man, and one black secretary.

Before we started filming, one of the guys said, "Hey, Ben. How you doing? Or should I say Nathaniel X"?

The crew nearly had a heart attack. They didn't know what to do.

I said, "Oh, you must be a Muslim."

"Yeah."

"Were you one of the guys who beat the hell out of me at the Theresa?"

"I didn't get into that."

"Well, why do you keep giving me a hard time?"

"Brother, you know what you did. We can never forgive you for betraying us. We thought you were a good, card-carrying member. You deceived us."

"Look," I said. "Malcolm told me it was a damn good series."

"You said some good things."

"You're proud of that," I said. "But nobody, black or white, could have gotten that story from the inside any other way. It's a journalistic technique."

"We recognized the publicity," he said.

"Are you going to participate in this interview right now?"

"Why not?"

And he did. The game would go on.

I left CBS in 1965. I hadn't reached a point of resignation that

I've reached now, twenty years later. It was obvious that I wasn't going to get to where I wanted to be at CBS. I was too young—still in my thirties—to throw in the towel. I went to NBC where I was permitted to do some production work, some producing.

That made it difficult when the Johnson Administration approached me about joining the Community Relations Service. Initially I said "no." Then I talked it over with the top brass. I was happy at NBC, but I thought this was a rare opportunity. There weren't many blacks who received a presidential appointment. NBC told me I could assume that I was on a leave of absence.

The Community Relations Service was established by the Civil Rights Act of 1964 to provide alternatives to litigation and to provide mediation in conflicts affecting minorities. In 1969, I became the director with a staff of four hundred. In 1977, I stepped down.

NBC had nothing to offer, reminding me they had already made offers of jobs in their local stations. CBS expressed some interest in me as a street reporter. But after running a government agency for eight years on the level of an assistant attorney general, I thought I had advanced beyond that and deserved a crack at an executive-level position.

I ended up teaching journalism at the University of Maryland.

It is very difficult to succeed as a black professional in this country, regardless of how well you perform, or what your abilities are. Somehow, you just can't go beyond a certain point in many professions. That became clear to me in all my journalistic endeavors.

At CBS I thought the most natural role for me was in the area I best performed—field producer. That's what I made clear to management. I was not a Max Robinson. I wasn't that great on air in terms of delivery. I was not as good a reader. I didn't *want* to be Max Robinson.

I applied for every single producer position that became available. And every time I was turned down. It became very frustrating, when I saw white candidates with far less ability, far less experience, getting those positions. I finally started asking questions.

"What would I have to do to get one of these jobs?"

A benevolent and sympathetic senior producer took me aside. He told me to forget about it.

"They brought you here because they had to have a black face on the air," he said. "And that's all we'll ever do. Forget about being a producer."

I knew in time there would be many black faces on the air. That is what happens in this country. But the question I raised back in 1965 was: When would a black go beyond being the reader—the front person—and rise to the position of having some say over what goes on the air?

It was extremely painful. It took a great toll on me. It even made it difficult for me to function because I had so much bitterness and anger. I tried talking to another official at CBS.

"Ben," he said, "we really don't understand you. There are so many blacks who'd give their right hand just to be where you are. And you're complaining!"

I got so angry that I drew a picture of a black hand, which I intended to slip under his door that night. I changed my mind. It was childish.

I had lunch recently with a guy who was behind me at CBS. He's now a vice president. I think he felt awkward.

"Ben, it's good to see you," he said. "You know, you were always one of my idols. I always looked up to you."

You're the vice president, I said to myself. *I'm sitting here. And you are taking me to lunch!*

That stuff tears at you when it's almost conceded. What has kept me on balance, I guess, is that as I grow older, I say to myself that as a black man attempting to make it in this field, I must resign myself to the fact that there is really just so far you can go, and you must make the best of whatever you can. If you want to keep your sanity, you have to accept this and find some way to submerge your bitterness so that you do not become dysfunctional.

I don't think a lot of white folks even today realize how bitter it is, how painful it is, how much you hurt. And it doesn't get any better as you get older. As you get older, you tend to keep looking back and saying to yourself, *This is what I should have been.* Even today, I can't stop thinking about it.

I think back to that time in 1963. I knew I was on the spot as the first and only black reporter at CBS. News had reached us that a church had been bombed in Birmingham, killing four black schoolgirls. They wanted me on the plane immediately.

Richard Salant was worried. "Dan Rather will be there to meet you. If you feel uncomfortable, give us a call and come right back."

Dan Rather was our Southern bureau chief. He met my plane. Although we had talked on the phone, we had never met face-to-face.

Because of segregation, Dan stayed in a white-only hotel in downtown, and I stayed in the black-owned Gaston Motel. The Birmingham police tailed me everywhere. Once when Dan and I were eating together in a black restaurant, they entered with shotguns and ordered us out because Dan was white, eating with a black man.

We spent the days filming blacks who were organizing to protect themselves against the bombers, the Klan. At night, I invited Dan over to the motel.

One warm night we stayed up to the wee hours in the courtyard, talking about everything. Dan was nice. He was well regarded by management even then. But he didn't have much of a head start on me. We talked about the business, our futures, the usual stuff.

Dan said that one day he wanted to sit where Walter Cronkite sat.

"That's the difference between the two of us," I said. "I know I can never become Walter Cronkite. But one day you can."

John Jordan, of the Norfolk *(VA)* Journal & Guide, *was a correspondent in World War II who covered black troops in Italy.*

———

I was drafted in the spring of 1944, World War II. I drove up to Richmond, Virginia, and went to the induction center.

They put me down for the marines. Can you imagine a black marine during World War II? There hadn't been any black marines since the Revolutionary War. I couldn't imagine what I would be doing. But I drove back to Norfolk, set to enter the marines in thirty days.

I had been working for the *Norfolk Journal & Guide* since 1933. It served the Tidewater area but was read by black folks in every state in the Union and some foreign countries. It was known as "the *New York Times* of black journalism" because of its fine editing.

I talked about going into the marines with my publisher, P. B. Young Sr., and he said that maybe I could get a deferment, because we had been losing a lot of staff to the war. Meanwhile, we had a correspondent, Lem Graves, who had been in Europe six months writing stories on black troops.

Mr. Young said, "I've got another idea. I believe Lem wants to come home. Why don't we try to send you to replace him?"

"I've been drafted. I'm going to the marines. How are you going to fix that?"

Mr. Young said, "Go see your draft board chairman."

I did. And I told him, "Look, I'm a fairly good journalist but I don't know what kind of marine I'll make. I've never fired a gun.

Never shot at anything. I really don't mind serving my country, but I think I might serve it better as a war correspondent. And now I have a chance to go over as one."

The draft board chairman agreed, and said, "We'll find some kind of technicality and get you released from the draft."

Then, to become a war correspondent, you had to be cleared by the FBI. They ran a background investigation. As a reporter, I was well known to the local police department. When the FBI came to check me out, the police told them, "Yeah, ol' Jordan's okay." Two days later, I was cleared and told to go to Washington.

I went to the commissary at Fort Eustis to buy my uniforms. In World War II, you had to wear the same uniform that officers wore. In fact, I was a simulated captain. A sergeant in the Pentagon gave me the oath as a captain in the Army. It meant that I would rate the privileges of a captain on the bases, and if I got captured the Germans were supposed to treat me like an officer.

I applied for assignment to the Mediterranean Theatre of the European command. I wanted to be with the Fifth Army front in Italy, where the black troops were. And as it turned out, I spent practically my entire time there, from the spring of 1944 until the end of April of 1945, a week before the total surrender of German forces.

I thought I had at least thirty days to get my affairs straightened out at home. But after I was sworn in, I was told to come back right away.

"Hell, no," a sergeant told me. "You get back to Washington tomorrow."

They wanted me nearby so I could be notified if transportation came up all of a sudden. I went back to Portsmouth that night and told Erma, my wife. She was as frantic as I was. We stayed up all night trying to get my affairs right.

Next morning I flew to Washington. It was my first time on a plane. I checked in with the Pentagon and was told that I would be leaving on the next available transportation. Well, during World War II, you could hurry up and wait two weeks for the next transportation.

In those days hotels weren't integrated, so I went to Howard University, got a room there, and fell into bed. I hadn't been there but a half an hour—barely gotten my damn shirt off—when the phone rang.

"Come over right away. Your plane to North Africa is ready."

I checked out on the run and caught a cab to the transport command at the army airfield. When I got there, they briefed us on what to do in case the plane went down. It was a four-motor job. Except for that short flight from Norfolk to Washington, I had never been on a plane in my life. Now I was about to fly over the North Atlantic! Since we didn't have jets then, it wasn't going to be some routine four or five-hour hop over to London.

We left late that afternoon. When we stopped at Newfoundland to refuel, we had breakfast. It was 1:00 in the morning. A few hours later, we were in the Azores, and it was time for lunch. Then we flew another five hours to Casablanca. A bus took us to a villa where we spent the night. At 7:00 the next morning, we went to Algiers, where I checked into a GI hotel and waited five days for transportation to Italy.

· I didn't waste time before writing my first stories from Algiers. We had to send them through an army message center. I quickly learned cable-ese, which meant I could reduce a whole column of copy down to three or four paragraphs. But I went over there so damn fast I never had a good briefing on what I could send and what I couldn't.

In the first story, I described the thrill of going over on the airplane, and I mentioned all the stops. Now, the Atlantic route was how we were sending supplies overseas. I didn't know this was top secret, even though by that time the Germans knew our supply route. So there I was, describing it all in the papers for everyone to read.

Then I started writing about the battalions that were arriving. I interviewed the new troops and gave their unit designations. I didn't know all this stuff was supposed to be censored by me. And it was being published without censorship by the army!

Meanwhile, the command in Algiers was bombarded with questions about my copy. Washington asked Algiers, "What the hell have you got there?" So I was called to headquarters and chewed out by the top commander for giving away military secrets.

A war correspondent is still a civilian. Nobody can tell him actually what to do. It's called freedom of the press. Yet I had to remember that the army would be taking care of us. We would depend on the army for supplies, for food, for transportation and, yes, for protection.

When I got to Rome, I could tell immediately that it was going to be the fashion capital of the world after the war. The city wasn't battle-scarred. The people were beautiful. Even with a war on they were dressed in the latest fashion.

Rome was the public information headquarters for the Theatre. Max Johnson and Art Carter from the *Afro-American* newspaper were already there. And Ollie Harrington, representing another black newspaper, the *Pittsburgh Courier*, got there about the time I did. So Ollie and I decided to take a room together at a hotel. We met a maid there who was the niece of Primo Canera, the boxer. Oh, boy. She just loved Joe Louis, even though he knocked Canera out. So she told us we could leave our things any time and they would be safe. Nobody would ever have our room.

If I'd had any sense, I would have spent two weeks in Rome, rested up, and got myself together like Harrington did. But I was anxious to find the 99th, the all-black pursuit squadron that trained at Tuskegee Institute, called the Black Eagles. They were strafing the Germans somewhere north of Pisa.

Not many buses were running. So I hitch-hiked a plane ride up to Naples, trying to catch up with the 99th. I went to the air force operations unit looking for information, and was told that the squadron would be at some little Italian town farther north.

When I arrived at the town, I found an engineering outfit clearing a field. The 99th had not moved up yet. I was where they were *going* to be. I had found out about their advance orders. And the engineers were constructing the air field and doing it under bombardment.

The guys were white, mostly Southerners, and they wanted to know what the hell I was doing there. They weren't stupid enough to be insulting, but you could tell I was in hostile territory in more ways than one. But I didn't let them bother me. Heck, I'm a Southern boy. I've been down with it all my life.

I was told to stay overnight. That night I got my first baptism by fire. The Germans weren't far away, and they started shelling us. We had to dive for cover. They didn't give war correspondents any basic training. Like how to protect yourself. Of course, you found out damn quick. I became a casualty right away because I dived into a hole that had a beer can in it and cut my wrists all up. Then some guy dived in on top of me and almost broke my back. And I hadn't even gotten to the 99th yet!

Before leaving there, I learned how to fall down. I could fall down with a handful of grapes, without crushing a single one. I learned how to hit the ground with a camera. We didn't have the small 35-millimeter cameras. We used the big Speed Graphic[41] with the four-by-four film. I learned how to fall with the lens pulled out without crushing it. You went down on your knees, whirled over on your back, and let the camera rest on your chest. After you broke one and banged your knees a couple of times, you got the hang of it.

I also learned how to sleep under bombardments—ours going out, theirs coming in. I was within German artillery range for six months straight. I woke up one morning and found the window of my room blown out. The shell hit right outside. I'd slept through the whole thing.

The information office in Rome had a record of me leaving Washington but not of me reaching Rome. When they caught up with me, I had to return to Rome.

They said, "We've been looking for you for two weeks!"

I said, "I went to find the 99th. I don't have time to sit around in a hotel in Rome."

When I finally did reach the 99th, the guys didn't look at all like the heroic flyers that we had grown used to from the reports in the black papers. They were just a' belly-aching. One guy was carrying on like hell, complaining about flying three missions a day and getting shot at every time.

"I hope you press guys are satisfied," he said. "We were doing all right at Tuskegee. But you had to make us heroes."

Actually, they were heroes. They were doing their jobs. Before I got to Italy, after the Americans landed in Sicily, the black press headlined that the Black Eagles had downed eight German fighters over the beachhead. After the 99th became part of the 332nd Fighter Group, the group brought down five German planes in a single day over Munich. I learned that in a military outfit, if there isn't belly-aching and griping, you don't have much of an outfit.

From the start, I had trouble with their commander, Colonel B. O. Davis Jr. He was extremely capable and extremely West Point. His father was the first black general, and he knew he was a first, too. He had to dot every "i" and cross every "t". He was obsessed. He couldn't make any mistakes. He had to be as close to the best as possible.

In my first interview, Colonel Davis kept saying, "We don't make mistakes. We're winning the war."

"Of course, I'm looking for victory, too," I said. "But I have to report what I find in a human way. I have to report the truth."

Boy, did I have trouble getting answers!

He was so obsessed with doing well that he told me what to print and what not to print. I wasn't supposed to even hint at anything unfavorable. He didn't want me to mention a single casualty. So we had clash after clash.

I said, "I'm not the kind of reporter to report whatever I'm told. I'm not going to defame you or make you into some kind of villain. I'm here to help and to make our troops look as good as possible. But I can't tell my readers that you don't ever have problems, that you never have casualties."

Although most of my readers were black, I never considered myself a black correspondent or a black guy over there. I just considered myself a correspondent—an *American* correspondent.

The first elements of the 92nd Infantry Division didn't arrive in Italy until July 30th. The army had not been integrated by then, of course, and all the enlisted men were black. The black officers were in the lower grades, such as lieutenants. There were a dozen or so captains, and two or three majors. The higher ranking officers were white. So the 92nd was like a little island of black folks in the Fifth Army front. And the 92nd had never fought anyone before, so it really had no heritage to fall back on.

At that point, the Germans retreated to a prearranged line, known as the Gothic Line, in Northern Italy. They knew exactly where they would make a stand, and they held that line for the duration of the war.

When the 92nd finally got there, its mission was to contain as many German troops as possible. The 92nd held a sector from the north of Pisa inland to the Serchio River. That included some of the most rugged mountain terrain you will ever see. After the Fifth Army made its attack in the fall, it got stymied, and the battlefield became static.

Let's face it. I found out eventually that the overall strategy was not to do much anyway. Just contain as many German troops in Italy as you can. Keep them there so we don't have to fight them in France. It was as simple as that.

I went straight to the headquarters of the 370th Regimental Combat Team, the lead unit of the 92nd, which was in combat before the rest of the division arrived. They were virtually self-contained. They had everything with them except tanks. I stayed with them, filing stories.

After the rest of the division arrived, General Edward Almond, the division commander, called me to his headquarters. He said, "Who the hell is this guy writing about the 370th in *my* division and I don't even know him?"

Major General Almond was a Southerner. I thought to myself, *I get along with Southerners and they get along with me. I understand them and I will get him to understand me.*

When I was shown into his office, he said, "Jordan, you've been writing out of here for weeks and you've never had the courtesy to come to division headquarters to check with operations. I never met you. My chief of staff didn't know anything about you. My public information guys never heard of you. And you're using the army message center and all our facilities."

I had given the message center at Fifth Army headquarters the authority to cut anything from my stories they wished. I didn't want them to send the copy back for me to change. So I had the reputation of sending everything, which included restricted material and stuff that broke censorship rules. I expected them to make the cuts, and I knew a lot more would get through that way. I figured the general suspected me of sending out all this information. Maybe he thought I was working for the enemy.

But without batting an eye, I said, "General, frankly it didn't occur to me that I was to check in with you. The 370th came over ahead of you guys, so I just sort of became attached to them. I found out they are a damn good unit."

"I'm not going to tell you what to print," he said. "I just want you to promise me one thing. In your roaming around, if you find any problems that you don't understand, or if you have questions that you can't get an answer for, then you come to see me."

I thought that was fair. I said, "I'll be glad to do that, but I don't want you to get mad if I ask you some pointed questions."

He said, "That's what I'm here for."

Almond never tried to influence what I wrote. But he often said that his mission was to make the 92nd a really top-flight operation, and I came to believe that he tried to do that.

Whenever I stayed at headquarters, I ate at the General's Mess because they had the best food. About half the officers there were white and half were black. You noticed that one table had white guys and another table had black guys. It was by choice, by custom, or whatever you want to call it.

Well, we—the black officers and me—decided to break up these segregated tables. So on Monday, we showed up first. And at least five of us sat down at every table. It was a beautiful job of integration.

Oh, brother! When the whites came in, they almost fell down. The general didn't know what to do because there was no law against it. And, hell, this was a black outfit! Things went along without incident. The talk was courteous, and about small things like the weather or an operation. Everyone was friendly. But there was a certain stiffness and not the same kind of camaraderie we shared among ourselves.

Tuesday night remained beautifully desegregated. But on Wednesday night, it began to change. More blacks at one table, more whites at another. By Friday, it was segregated again—completely.

It was just that people with things in common enjoyed being with one another. The correspondents' table was always integrated, because we had more in common with each other than we did with the officers. And at night, you were tired. You wanted to let your hair down. So black guys might want to share stories with each other, in a way that they wouldn't feel comfortable with whites present.

I got a good lesson then in what integration should be about. I tell my white friends today, "You don't have to worry about me demanding to come to your club or to your house. I probably would prefer to play poker with my boys. I just resent the hell out of a legal restriction that prevents me from attending anything that is open to the public. That's all it is."

One of my first front-line assignments with the 92nd came when one of the battalions tried to outflank a German outfit. We wanted to capture a thousand-year-old walled city.

Ollie Harrington and I went on the mission together. By this time, I had my own jeep. Our boys were located in the damnedest places, and a car was the only way to get there. I felt guilty about asking a GI to drive me into a combat area. My work really seemed frivolous compared to their duties. And who wants to die trying to get a little news story out? So I did my own driving, which the boys in the motor pool loved me for. And I got to be a helluva good combat driver.

We started out on some of the roughest roads I had ever seen, behind a mountain, through a tunnel, and out behind the Germans. It was a silly place to be, really, as I look back on it. The Germans had very good observation posts. They located the spot where we came in. Soon, we were under terrific fire.

The Germans shelled us with 88s, which started out to be an antiaircraft gun. But when they ran out of field artillery, they just leveled that 88 at us. And it became a horrendous piece, very accurate. They could hit a moving jeep with ease.

We were stuck there for two days. We couldn't get our stories out. I hadn't brought any food so we had to eat field rations. It wasn't the small arms fire that gave us hell. It was those Germans stuck up in the mountains.

Finally, Captain Charles Gandy of Washington, D.C., sent out a twenty-man patrol to locate the artillery guns. He commanded Company G. I decided to go on this patrol—like a nut! A lieutenant was in charge. I made the twenty-first man.

In World War II, the guys didn't like having anyone with them who didn't have some firepower. They want you to be able to do something. I didn't know how to use a Tommy gun or an M-1 rifle. So I put four grenades in my pocket.

I said, "That's the best I can do, guys."

We got to a point where we decided to split up. The lieutenant said, "We'll send the men this way, eleven men, to scout around. Let's meet at this point in two hours. We'll cover more ground this way."

I went with the sergeant on the eleven-man patrol. After a half hour, we spotted the artillery. But we were hopelessly lost. Then the sergeant turned to me and said, "Sir, what do we do now?"

"Sergeant, you have got to be kidding," I said. "I'm a war correspondent."

He refused to hear anything about me being a war correspondent.

"Okay, Sergeant. I'll tell you what we'll do. Let's go back exactly the same way we came in."

Fortunately, we didn't run into any enemy patrols or positions, and we got back to where we were supposed to be. The other patrol found us and we told them where the artillery was located.

On the third night, we were resting behind a stone wall. I was asking guys where they were from, hoping they would be from Virginia or somewhere else where my paper had circulation.

I saw a guy walk by. "Hey, buddy. What's your name?"

"Private Christian."

"What are you doing?"

"I'm on an observation post. I came back to get some food for me and my buddy. We've been up there for two days, and we were out of food."

He had a big box of K-rations, a bag of ammo, and his gun—quite a load. So I said, "I'll take the box of K-rations you have there, and I'll walk with you to the end of that wall but no farther."

When we got to the end of the wall, it seemed quiet, so I decided to go a little bit farther.

"There's a building over there," he said, pointing. "A tower. My buddy's up there."

We started walking. We came to a fork in the road. We made the wrong turn. I was lost again. So here we are. American troops behind us. German troops in front. At night, patrols are out everywhere, probing, jabbing. You can get shot by your own guys. And you better know the password. If you didn't you could get killed right quick. And sometimes they changed the password on you while you were out.

Once the password was "Mae West." I didn't know it had been changed. I was near the 370th's headquarters. "Coming in," I said, "Mae . . ."

All I heard was "Click. Click. Click."

I started talking real fast. I said, "Wait a minute, man. Wait a minute, baby."

When Private Christian and I were lost, I said, "Let's whistle or something. Do something to let our guys know where we are." I knew our men would be so scared to death, so trigger happy, that you could walk right into them and they would kill you immediately.

So here we were walking down the road, whistling. I looked up and saw we were headed toward a bridge. I thought, *This must be the bridge just before you enter the target town, Lucca. And we haven't taken Lucca yet! We're behind enemy lines. Whistling. Walking toward the Germans. And I don't have a gun!*

I said, "Christian, this is Lucca. We haven't captured it yet. I know damn well your observation post isn't here. What's more, the Germans, if they have any lookouts at all, are wondering what the hell we are doing."

We started walking back. All hell broke loose. The Germans opened up with everything. And fire draws fire. So the Americans opened up. And me and Christian were in the middle of it!

We jumped into a ditch and crawled about a quarter of a mile back in the direction we had come. Then we lost the ditch cover and tried to use the trees along the road for protection. When we got back to the fork, we heard movement.

It was a patrol. I didn't know if they were Germans or our people. We hid in the bushes until we could hear them talking. It was our guys. Christian yelled out the password. I didn't know it.

The following February came the most serious attack I covered. We were north, along the sea. We had been trying to do something about the Germans in those mountains for three months. There was a mile of flat land between the sandy shore and the mountains. It was a beautiful beach, like Virginia Beach before the honky-tonk element took over. There were palm trees. And nice weather until you got up in the mountains—then it was freezing.

It started out not as an attack, really. The general wanted some live prisoners to interrogate. We went on a patrol and got the hell shot out of us. Then a brigade got involved. We just kept enlarging the damn thing, trying to get one prisoner. Finally, it became like an invasion. The Germans had some serious fire power on that coast. Pillboxes[42] all over the place. This was one bloody operation—and a needless operation. We lost some good officers.

A special unit of tanks came to back us up. They had integrated crews. We tried to get across a canal with the troops behind the tanks. The Germans knocked out nineteen of our tanks. I went in with L Company. I fell down on the beach and held the camera on my chest to get pictures.

We were trapped.

To get out of that trap, you might step on a mine. I had to crawl in the tank tracks the whole way out. My God! They fought over a week trying to establish a line beyond that canal, and they couldn't do it. It wasn't because anybody was cowardly or "melted away" in combat. We just got the hell shot out of us. We were outgunned, and the Germans were well dug in.

I spent one afternoon bringing wounded guys out—carrying them, dragging them, pulling them. Guys who'd stepped on mines. Feet gone. Legs gone. And I heard shrapnel fly over me every time an explosion went off.

I got the men to my jeep and drove them to the aid station. Then I went back and got some more. Dead bodies lay everywhere. So many dead bodies. I had to keep going. When you found yourself in a forward area, you helped any way you could. Being a correspondent didn't matter anymore.

I was recommended for the Silver Star on three separate occasions during that week—by two chaplains and the general. General Almond said, "I'm instructing my executive officer to contact the right people at the Pentagon after the war so that it will be official."

I'm sure he forgot about me when the war was over.

Before I left, he gave me a plaque commending me for front-line work. And when I got home, I received a commendation from the Defense Department, the same as the rest of the correspondents.

After that canal deal, though, it was obvious that the war would soon be over. The Germans started surrendering. One night a German tried to surrender to one of the guys pulling guard duty near the canal. But our guy had fallen asleep and the German had to wake him up to surrender to him.

A couple of weeks later, we took a little town up in the mountains. We set up company headquarters and moved in. On the second day it was very quiet around that town. I guessed the Germans on the other side of the town had decided not to reveal themselves.

Our guys were walking around town getting acquainted with the girls and buying wine. Some were hanging around the square. Suddenly, a German officer walked up in his fatigue uniform. Nobody paid him any mind. The officer walked a couple of blocks through the town. The GIs were talking to the people. Some were having lunch.

Finally, he went up to the GIs and asked them, in perfect English, "Where is the company headquarters?"

One of the brothers motioned down the street toward a hill.

So the officer walked away. The Italians who were still left in the town got all excited. Their eyes popped. They started shouting in Italian, "German! German!"

The GIs started looking for their guns. They got all excited too and started yelling, "German! German!"

It turned out the German was trying to surrender.

Stories got back to the States charging black soldiers of the 92nd with fading away or melting under fire. The enlisted men of the 92nd won as many awards for bravery as the other outfits in the Fifth Army. I know. I was there. I took the pictures of them getting the medals.

Mark Clark, commander of the Fifth Army, and General Sir Harold Alexander, commanding general of the Allied Forces in the Mediterranean, came to visit us and were looking over maps, pointing out this and that to the correspondents.

Lieutenant General Mark Clark was a lot like General MacArthur, more king than general. He had a photographer with him at all times, taking pictures of everything he did. He must have had a warehouse full of pictures.

When the Americans threw three divisions against the Gothic Line,[43] we didn't break it. The Germans held the high ground and we were on the low. They were set up too well. We took terrific casualties. But the white correspondents didn't write that the white officers in the 91st melted away. They wrote that they failed to take their objectives, or got bogged down, or ran into heavy enemy fire. These were the phrases used for the white soldiers.

I heard rumors that Clark didn't want the 92nd under his command because it was a black outfit. But I never could pin it down. And I never heard him say anything derogatory about the 92nd.

Like all divisions in the Fifth Army, the men of the 92nd were infantry soldiers whose first job was to stay alive. You take a position, you stay alive. You hold it. What else are you going to do?

Let's face it. On the battlefield, you don't have too many guys setting out to be heroes. Mostly you set out to try to stay alive and to get through the next day. I discovered that was how heroes were born. I didn't find too many guys who tried to go out to win a Silver Star—white or black.

Take Jake, a black guy from Mount Olive, Mississippi. He was a real-life hero. It was right after the deal on the canal. I was asked to be on an NBC radio broadcast showing how our boys had courage abounding.

I brought Jake to my room to prepare him for the NBC interview. He had been on the Gothic Line. He found himself in charge of his company after his commanding officer was killed. He was with a machinegun squad at a strategic point. The enemy was pushing our troops back. They were in a real hassle.

Jake held that point for three hours after everybody else was either shot up or had retreated. Then reinforcements arrived to push the Germans back.

General Clark came to the front to award Jake a Silver Star.

We rehearsed for the broadcast. I asked Jake questions to establish his extraordinary bravery.

"Jake," I said, "why did you stay to fire that machinegun after everybody else had fallen back? How could you stay under all that small arms fire, those mortars, all that artillery?"

Jake said, "I didn't know they had gone."

"Where did you think our guys were?"

"I didn't know. I just stayed there. They could have gone any place. You know how the guys will goof off on anything."

"Jake," I said, "You can't say that on the NBC broadcast.

TOM JOHNSON

Tom Johnson covered the civil rights movement in America and the Tet offensive in Vietnam for the New York Times.

———

The worst thing that ever happened to me at the *New York Times* was being offered a promotion.

A. M. Rosenthal, the managing editor, wanted me to take the job of assistant city editor. I had already refused when other editors asked me. I'd spent sixteen years bouncing around the world studying social revolutions, and suddenly they wanted me to sit at a desk and be part of the headquarters staff.

Essentially what they wanted, I knew, was a black for that job.

Abe Rosenthal and I had developed a relationship over the years. He called me in and said, "I wouldn't ask you to do anything you don't want to do. But we need you, the *Times* needs you."

I didn't reply. He continued in a chilling way.

"I know you've turned down the job. Let me say this, I would like for you to take it. But if you don't want to take it, I'll understand."

Now that, to me, was the biggest threat in the world. It didn't sound like he would understand. I knew I had to do some fast thinking. But at least it wasn't like when I first started out in journalism and couldn't find a job anywhere.

I was born in St. Augustine, Florida, from an old family that was part of the migration of former slaves out of South Carolina. When I was eleven, we moved to New York and lived in Queens.

My mother was a seamstress, my father an undertaker. When they broke up, she grabbed the kids. There were three of us. Now and then, my father made a big show of coming to see us and buying us clothes. But my mother mostly supported us; she was a very strong woman.

Before we left Florida we lived on what she made plus—well, it wasn't called welfare in those days. NRA stood for the National Recovery Act—or as the black people around us named it, "Niggers Raggedy Ass." It meant we stood in long lines for hours waiting for flour, apples, potatoes, and such.

Mother, who was very religious, left my brother and sister and me with our grandmother, and she went to Bean City, an area near the Everglades, where thousands of migrant workers came every summer to pick beans. She sent us letters that might contain a dollar and forty-five cents, or maybe something like three dollars and twenty cents. To us, it was a lot.

Of course, you know how color conscious blacks can be. She was naturally dark and then she would get sunburned much darker. That became the family conversation—how black Momma got going down there to pick beans. Her brothers had moved to New York. She joined them and worked for a year as a seamstress and a domestic, and then sent for us.

She had dropped out of school at fifth grade, but she instilled family values. We had to study because, you know, school was going to change things for us. And we were in church every Sunday, every Tuesday and every Thursday, sitting on those hard benches. She held us together.

Sometimes we spoke about our father in a derogatory way, and she would insist, "No, he's your father, you don't talk about him like that."

Sometimes we went to visit him. One day he took us to the barbershop. He was a big man with a big voice. And he loved to talk. He announced to everybody in the barbershop, "This is my son. He's training in New York to become a surgeon. And this is my other son. He's training to be a lawyer."

He had no idea of what we were doing. My brother became a machinist and plumber. He could always do things with his hands, where I was hopeless. My sister died at age seventeen of rheumatic fever.

After high school I joined the army and spent nearly three years in Japan. The army set me on the way, it really did. I had a lot of time on my hands and we had a good post library. I begin to read everything, usually novels—Hemingway, Gorky. I also liked books on philosophy; Unamuno was a favorite.

By the time I got out of the army, I was convinced I was going to have some kind of career in writing. I brushed up on math and English at a private school and then entered Long Island University. I graduated in 1955 and started looking for a job. I couldn't find anything in journalism. So I did a mix of stuff until I finally hooked up with a public relations firm.

In addition to my PR work, I wrote a column for a newspaper called the *New York Edition of the Pittsburgh Courier.* I also wrote three or four news stories a week, sold advertising, just did everything. After more than a year of this I had built up a huge list of bylines and something of a reputation.

Louis Lomax lived not far from me. He was one of the best-known black journalists in the country. Louie called me one night at two in the morning, and said, "Hey, man, I want you to get your résumé over to *Newsday.* They're looking for one."

This was 1962 and of course I knew what he meant when said he said "looking for one." He gave me the name of the editor to see. I made an appointment. When I went to his office, I found a short muscular man sitting with his feet on the desk and a Confederate flag on the wall behind him.

He said, "Tom, we talk about integration around here, but we ain't got a single nigra in this place. We've been reading your stuff, and we want to talk to you about coming over here."

I had to listen carefully when he said "nigra," because I wasn't sure what he was really saying. But we became good friends, and I considered him one of the best editors in the business. He gave me a test, which I passed, and then offered me a hundred and sixty-five dollars a week, considerably more than I was making. And that was the beginning.

Maybe I liked journalism because I was a frustrated teacher. It gave me a real high to think, *I saw this with my own eyes and I'm going to tell the world. Look, World, this is what's going on, this is what it really means.* But mainly I liked journalism because of the practice that went with it, the constant writing, writing, writing. Journalism also was a good place for a self-starter, which I was.

It wasn't long before I was covering race relations. Three civil rights workers had disappeared in Mississippi, last seen in the town of Philadelphia—Schwerner, Chaney, and Goodman. The first and last were two Jewish boys who came down from New York to work on a civil rights project. Chaney was their black friend who lived in Mississippi. The NAACP board of directors for Mississippi, twelve officials, some of them white, was making a tour of the state around that time, in July 1964.

Every place they went the local newspaper would run a headline: TESTERS DUE HERE TOMORROW. "Testers" meant they were testing civil rights laws but, in fact, that was not the case. They were asking for information about the missing kids, and checking on voting registration, examining the general conditions of blacks. They were followed around the state by threatening crowds of whites.

A number of white journalists covered the NAACP tour, guys like David Halberstam of the *Times,* whom I didn't know at that point. I was the only black journalist. The county deputy sheriff, Cecil Price, agreed to meet with the delegation upstairs at the town hall. But he ordered all the journalists to stay in the downstairs lobby.

I sized up the situation and decided to follow the delegation upstairs, acting as a member of the New York branch of the NAACP, as opposed to acting as a reporter for *Newsday.* I was glad I did. I learned that the journalists in the lobby, mainly the photographers and cameramen, were assaulted and beaten by some of the white crowd.

David Halberstam later said to me, "You are a journalist, aren't you? You should have been downstairs with us."

I said, "Fuck you."

I was in enough danger as it was. When we started to leave, Charles Evers, one of the NAACP leaders, walked out first with Deputy Sheriff Cecil Price. Evers and Price had grown up together—on opposite sides of town, of course. The crowd started screaming when they saw the two of them, with the rest of us following behind.

"This is Philadelphia, Mississippi! Niggers, you don't belong here! Get out of here, niggers, and never come back!"

Cecil Price said, "Please move back." When they didn't budge, he yelled, "Get a move on it, goddammit, get a move, we're coming through!"

About twenty or thirty people in the crowd were carrying shotguns and pistols. I said to myself, *You are going to die. You are going to die right here.* I saw the hatred on their faces and knew they wanted to kill us.

Then my fear turned to anger. "Nobody has the right to make me this scared," I said. "And if I'm going to die, I'm going to take somebody with me."

I concentrated on staring at this person and then another, waiting for someone to move toward me. I was going to grab him and try to kill him. And that burning thought got me through the crowd.

The county attorney, who was young and a college graduate, said to us, "We treat niggers here as good as we treat niggers anywhere else."

Cecil Price said, "You've heard from our county attorney. You ready to go now? I'm going to put you in your cars and we can finish your tour."

He was trying to get us out of his county as quickly as possible, knowing full well that he had been involved in the murder of those three civil rights workers some weeks before.

The Public Accommodations Bill was signed the day I left New York for Mississippi. So Charles Evers decided to book us in a white motel, those of us from the north. He didn't want to risk the lives of his own people. We were originally supposed to spend the night at the homes of the local black undertaker, the school teacher, and people like that.

When we arrived at the Sun and Sand Motel, the white women working at the desk started to cry. We were the first blacks to register. The manager came out and hugged the women and said, "Now you just go on and fill it out, everything's gonna be all right."

I had to call my newspaper by 3:00 P.M. to let them know what I would be writing about. Between then and 7:00 I had to find an hour or two to write the story. I was constantly looking for my lead. Philadelphia, Mississippi—what was the significance of the name? Where could I find out when the town was founded? I knew I had to draw a picture of the town. Would that be my lead?

Pretty soon I got good at covering race stories. Not many white reporters wanted to get involved. So I was able to step into the vacuum and make a place for myself. When the riots broke out in the mid-Sixties, I moved from one to the next.

A black reporter on the *New York Times* told me he was quitting the paper to work on a poverty program.

I said, "Since you are leaving, could I give you my résumé to turn in over there?"

He said, "Sure, send it over."

Within several weeks I got a call from A. M. Rosenthal. I went over to the paper and we talked, and we talked, and we argued. I was reasonably comfortable at *Newsday* and had no real interest in leaving, though I knew I would leave for the *Times*. But months went by and nothing happened. Then Rosenthal called again. I was hired.

I did okay at the *Times*. I probably had a reputation for not socializing with white people and turning down their invitations. And not socializing with black people, either, to tell the truth. I could be as extroverted as necessary to do my work. But by inclination I tended to be an introvert.

I was an action reporter, though, and it seemed natural that I would be sent to Vietnam. One day a wire service report said the black death rate had reached upwards of 25 percent in some units. We were talking about that in an editorial meeting, and Abe Rosenthal said he had seen the same report.

So it was decided that I would take a trip to Vietnam to report on the black situation. Rosenthal knew that I was influenced by the Homer Bigart School of In-Depth Reporting. Homer Bigart was a legendary reporter at the *Times* and had been one of the early ones to cover the war. Bigart thought that you should go into a strange place, pull your shirt tail out, and walk around with your mouth open. And you'd learn everything that was going on. What he was saying was that you should leave your note pad and pencil in your pocket and become so unobtrusive that people would continue to do what they were doing before you got there.

That was to be my method of operation. I would cover various war stories for three or four months and then write a long piece on blacks in Vietnam.

My editors said, "Make it very long, make it maybe two thousand words."

In truth, I wrote a series of three pieces running about four thousand words each, and they made the front page. The foreign editor wasn't pleased when I told him what I was going to do. But I saw the story, and he didn't. Once he saw what I'd written he accepted it as it was.

I observed relations between black and white servicemen. But I seldom asked a direct question. I went everywhere, even to Bangkok to watch the soldiers relax. I filed stories on various other things I had seen. But I was getting ready to write the big race piece I'd talked about with my editors, when I went out to the aircraft carrier *Ticonderoga*.

The day I landed on the carrier we started getting reports of something they called the Tet offensive, 1968. Everything had busted loose, and the enemy had taken over parts of Saigon and every other major city. I asked to be flown back to the mainland. The navy understood and they flew me, when the weather permitted, into Danang. The Marine Press Center in Danang became my base for the next few days.

I linked up with a marine unit and we headed to Hue, the city north of Danang which was under attack and occupation by the North Vietnamese. We were strung out on the road moving toward the Perfume River. Two American helicopters flew over and started strafing us. All they saw were people moving, and they couldn't tell whether we were friendly or enemy troops.

A young white guy on the radio cried, "Stop it! Stop it! You are strafing us!"

The helicopters continued to fire. A black corporal ran over and grabbed the radio and said, "*Di di mau*, motherfucker! *Di di mau*, motherfucker!"

That told the helicopters we were Americans, and they stopped firing.

We walked into Hue. The bridge over the Perfume River had been destroyed, so they made a makeshift crossing of logs and ropes. There had been an awful lot of fighting, artillery and street battles, and the dead were still laying out there—men, women and children. We followed the marine column to the U.S. headquarters, called MACV. It was headed by a black colonel who was the senior adviser to the South Vietnamese commander.

They told us they were in bed asleep and the North Vietnamese sappers bombed their doors and broke in. Everyone ran and jumped out the windows and into ditches and got back to headquarters. That's where we lived for the next few days. There were only three telephone lines at headquarters. I tried to phone our Saigon office every night, but it was a matter of negotiating for the line. Sometimes I'd have to pretend to be military in order to get a message to Saigon.

House-to-house street fighting was still going on. The marines were on one block facing the enemy a block away. As an enemy soldier ran from one house to another, somebody would shoot at him.

The civilians from Hue came and stood behind the marines or stood behind the North Vietnamese troops and watched the shooting, as though it was street theater. They said, "Oh, look at that!" And then they stopped to eat their lunch while they watched the war.

I attached myself to the strongest American unit I could find. The shooting sounded like telephone wires whipping in the wind, because first you heard the whistling sound of bullets passing close by, and then the sound of the *pows!* coming from the distance. I saw North Vietnamese soldiers who had chained themselves to their guns and had to be shot or burned to death to stop them.

Dead bodies were strewn all over the place. I asked the survivors how the others died. What had happened, according to many of the citizens, was that when the enemy took over, they went from house to house. They knew where the wives and children of soldiers were. They knew where government workers were. They went in and said, "We're not here to kill innocent people but we do need Mr. So-and-So." Then they took them out and shot them on that basis.

So many bodies were lying in the open that there was talk of disease spreading. Orders came down that the bodies needed to be swept up and buried. But the American commanders bristled at that, and said, "They've got to be cleaned up by the Vietnamese. I will not have any of my men burying dead Vietnamese." The American troops didn't want to do it. The bodies were in such a state of decomposition that you could pull on an arm and it would come off.

The first thing I noticed about the American kids—and they were kids, eighteen or nineteen years old—was their language. I'm talking about both blacks and whites. Whenever a shot was fired, you heard the cry, "Git some! Git some!" And they would jump up and run at the enemy yelling and screaming.

I asked a white colonel, a West Pointer, how was it that his troops had dislodged the enemy from a village. He said, "You've got to understand that those Asian motherfuckers didn't have their shit together."

He had been listening to his black sergeants, of course. Much of the language in Vietnam was black, the language of the ghettos, or what you heard on basketball courts in black high schools.

Blacks and whites did find brotherhood in Vietnam, that was true. "I love you my brother." Because it was so dangerous and a matter of life and death. Behind the lines you saw the races pull apart. But not in battle.

There was an awful lot of plain bravado in their attitudes, the feeling of unformed youth that they could not possibly die. "Man, we got us some gooks today. That's what we did."

But if you listened to them late at night, and didn't try to play the reporter, you found out how scared they were. How they ran the night before throwing hand grenades at every sound they heard. And when daylight came they were so happy to see one another still alive that they hugged and kissed like Girl Scouts— whites and blacks. You had to live with them and let these tales come out naturally.

They developed a sense of humor about each other. A black marine who lent his bed to a white friend said: "That sack has a lot of soul. It's a soul-recharging station. But I don't want you to wake up tomorrow morning thinking you can talk trash and dance the boogaloo, you hear me?"

"All right," a Mexican said, "which one of my brothers is going to buy me a beer?"

He got the beer, but not before blacks and whites laughed, "Give me! Give me! Give me! He still thinks he's on relief."

Black soldiers had no sense of their history. They were telling me, "We're proving ourselves. We're showing them that we can fight." They made up 9.8 percent of the military forces in Vietnam, but close to 20 percent of the combat troops. In 1966 the black-death rate soared to about 25 percent, and the Pentagon ordered a cutback in front-line participation by blacks.

A Harlem-born intelligence officer on General Westmoreland's staff told me: "They feel they're the first Negroes to fight because their history books told them only of white soldiers, and their movies showed that John Wayne and Errol Flynn won all American wars."

I tried to teach them a little of their history. I told them that in the Civil War more than 200,000 black men wore Union uniforms. Blacks were at Little Big Horn with Custer, they helped chase the Sioux into Canada, and they pursued Billy the Kid across the southwest. Some runaway black slaves fought on the side of the Indians. Ten thousand blacks fought in the Spanish-American war, and a group of black cavalrymen rescued Theodore Roosevelt's Rough Riders at the battle of El Caney.

I told them a controversy began over the fighting qualities of black combat soldiers in World War I. The all-Negro 369th Infantry Regiment stayed under fire for 191 days without relief—longer than any other American unit. But the 368th, also all black, was sent to the rear as a result of confusion and disorder after five days at the front. And in World War II there were reports that the all-black 92nd Infantry Division in Italy had "melted" when it met German troops. But a black aide to the secretary of war investigated and reported that some units—but not all—had made "panicky and disorderly" retreats. The controversy subsided during the Korean War as growing numbers of units were racially integrated.

And of course General William Westmoreland, the commander in Vietnam, had nothing but the highest praise for black servicemen. So I told them they had a lot to be proud of.

Certainly, there were blacks in Vietnam who wanted to prove themselves, and they volunteered. Others were on the front lines because they came with a minimum of skills. They didn't get the job as air traffic controller. They got the jobs with rifles and grenade launchers.

A West Point captain told me that he didn't want high school graduates in his company. He wanted dropouts—kids from the farms, from the ghettos, kids who had a certain anger and needed to prove something. He didn't want people who wanted to sit around and discuss the problem. So that kind of thing also contributed to the high death rate of blacks in the war.

After seeing action in Vietnam, and writing my stories on race relations, I knew I didn't want a desk job in New York. But how could I refuse A. M. Rosenthal's offer to make me assistant city editor? The only way I could refuse was by quitting the *Times*—and I wasn't ready for that.

So I accepted. And the job turned out to be worse than I had thought. I spent a lot of my time doing things that were necessary to putting out a paper but uninteresting to me—deciding the number of words that went into a column, the number of words we would devote to an airplane crash.

At 4:00 each afternoon we had a meeting of the editors, and we had to defend the stories that we suggested for the front page. What really got to me is that I would sit in the meetings and watch the white executives, many of them forty to sixty years old, who had spent their lives at the *Times*, act in a pitiful way.

After they suggested a story for the front page, somebody would say, "I'm sick of that."

Then the person who suggested the story would say, "I really didn't mean to suggest that, I really didn't mean it."

It made me ill to see aging men kowtowing and trembling when they made a presentation. I didn't want to become like that. To me, what I did as assistant metropolitan editor was the worst thing in the world. I made assignments, handled a ton of paperwork, and directed traffic. But there was no creativity, certainly none of the creativity that goes into being a reporter or a foreign correspondent.

At the end of the day you made up, or helped your supervisor make up, one page of the paper—and then you went home. The most creative thing you did during the day as a junior editor on the *New York Times* was to buy your lunch.

I was dissatisfied with my work and maybe with myself. I decided to take my kids, who were teenagers, to Mississippi to show them what I'd learned about being black. Charles Evers invited me back for a holiday he was promoting.

I was anxious for my children to see cotton growing. I wanted to teach them why we were brought here, and how difficult it was to grow and pick cotton. I showed them what happened when cotton was picked. After the first going-over, then the gleaners, the poorest of the poor blacks, came along and picked the wispy fibers that remained in the bolls.

"We were not brought here to play baseball or basketball," I told them. "We were not brought here to dance and sing. We were brought here for a purely commercial purpose, and that was to provide the economic base for a new and potentially rich nation. Cotton was so important to it."

And the initial black experience was symbolized in what they were seeing in those cotton fields of Mississippi. I was not sure that I reached them. They listened to me, they always had a way of tolerating the old man. But I don't think they were impressed one way or another.

It occurred to me on that trip that I was just a journalist, a guy with a job, and that if I dropped dead I was worth an insurance policy and shipment back home. That was what my kids would inherit, that was all.

I begin to think about the years when I covered Africa. I was a big guy as a journalist. And I remembered the Africans who came to my house to eat and drink and praise me. They were poor people. But I remembered they were all interested in developing independent sources of income, not just finding a job. They wanted to set up a fishing business or a travel agency. And when any of the successful ones died, their children received a lot more than mine would have.

I asked one of my servants what he would do if I gave him a hundred dollars. He said, "I'll buy a piece of cloth and cut it into four pieces and sell it. Then I'll buy more cloth and sell it."

When I grew up in the South, blacks never had much thought of developing capital. The idea was to find a good job and spend your life working for somebody else. That was a different approach from many other people in the world, who immigrated to America and became entrepreneurs. The Asians, for example, even the Africans.

A journalist found it difficult to move into the commercial area, because as a journalist you were accepted immediately by all kinds of people and taken as an authority on one subject or another. I found it hard to even think of getting away from that. But I realized that Africa had changed my life in terms of what I wanted to do with it.

So I left the *Times* and set up a private business as an international trade specialist.

Do I miss journalism? Oh, sure, journalism was in my blood. But somehow the nostalgia fades when I think back to my promotion as assistant city editor.

KAREN DEWITT

Karen DeWitt, a Washington correspondent for the New York Times, *was on assignment in a small Southern town, when she discovered that she was the only black person for miles around.*

It was the summer of 1978. Jimmy Carter was president. He was talking about the mood of America. So the *New York Times* was getting ready to put together a package of stories on the American mood.

Another reporter had already begun a big story out of Chicago. And our editors said, "We won't do California because we know that California hates Carter." So they told me I could go to any other part of the country—the South, North, New England—anywhere but Chicago and California.

I decided I might as well do some sightseeing on this assignment. So I said, "I'll go to the Ozarks." I had never been to that part of the country. I booked myself to Fayetteville, Arkansas, in the northwestern section of the state. Arkansas, as far as I was concerned, was the South.

I'm a Northern girl. I grew up in Ohio. My image of the South was not just the civil rights things that we saw on television in the Sixties. That imagery certainly stuck in my mind. But when I was younger, I was picking up *Jet* magazine,[44] which my family received, and reading about the lynching of black men. I knew the South had changed. But all that was still in my mind. I had a horrific idea of what the South was like.

Roy Reed, a former *New York Times* reporter, had a farm near Fayetteville. I thought it was a good idea to see him. He could show me the lay of the land.

I flew into the Fayetteville airport. It looked to me like the Dayton, Ohio, airport in the 1950s. It was very small. The field was littered with chicken feathers. Fayetteville was in a big chicken-plucking area.

I noticed there were no blacks around the airport. The airport people said, "Welcome to Arkansas. Is this your first trip?"

"Yes." And I thought, *Gee, this is very nice, they are very pleasant*.

I had made reservations for a rental car to drive to the hotel. You didn't want to show up in these towns without people knowing you were coming. When I got to the hotel, I realized there was not another black person there.

Right away, I phoned Roy Reed. I thought he could tell me the best place to interview non-city people. I liked the country, and I wanted the opinions of country people.

Reed was away. His wife suggested I try a place called West Fork because I could visit the Long Branch Café, where Roy went now and then.

"It's full of local people," she said, "and this is Friday, the best night."

The Long Branch Café—I liked the name.

I had hoped Reed would be around, because I was really very nervous about all this. And I would be walking into a bar by myself, a black female. I thought it would be helpful if another *New York Times* person was there.

It was two in the afternoon. I decided to drive out right away. I didn't like the idea of showing up in the dark at an all-white bar, or at a bar where I assumed there would be not many black people.

This was a small town, like one of those towns out of the 1930s that people drove through on the way to *The Grapes of Wrath*. It was sleepy, there was no one on the streets. Main Street had maybe a dozen houses and a gas station. The gas station was literally a barn with three pumps out front.

As I drove across the city limits, I knew I was integrating the town with my very presence. There were no blacks living there. This was a serious white town.

I drove to the end of the town and saw two very white people. I mean, they looked like rednecks. They looked underfed, inbred, and—I hate to say this—they had rotten teeth, like the backwoods people in the movie *Deliverance*.

I said very politely, "Could you please tell me where the Long Branch Café is?"

They told me to go down the road and make a right. They gave me the name of the woman who ran it, Ethel.

Sure enough, there it was. It looked like Miss Kitty's Long Branch Saloon, except there was no town around it. It just sat there by itself in the dust.

I went to the door. It was locked. The sign said it would open at five o'clock.

I was feeling a little nervous, so I decided I wouldn't wait around. I drove back to Fayetteville, twenty minutes away. I killed time resting and eating. Then about 4:30, I drove back to West Fork. I wanted to be there when Ethel opened up the place.

I didn't want to stroll in there with folks already there. Dum-de-dum-dum. Intruder!

Ethel was opening when I arrived. I said, "Hi! I'm a reporter from the *New York Times*, and I want to do a story on the crisis of confidence in America. I thought this would be a good place."

"Oh, no," she said. "This is not a good day. We got bluegrass on Friday night. People be comin' in and playin' music. It's not a good night."

"Oh, no," I said, "this is a perfect day. There'll be lots of people here."

Her daughter and husband stood in the background. I said to myself, *She hasn't thrown me out yet.* So I merrily settled right in.

"I'm here to do a story on the crisis of confidence in America. Do you think President Carter is doing a good job?"

The daughter talked to me first, then Ethel, and her husband. Gradually, family after family started coming in. Every time somebody arrived, they looked at me, then walked over to speak to their friends. I was the focus of their attention, and they were obviously talking about me.

I imagined they were saying, *"Who's that?"* And being answered: *"I don't know."*

I felt the tension in the air. I was nervous myself. My armpits were wet. But I was a journalist and supposed to be calm. Even as this was happening, I thought, *I'm a sophisticated reporter with a big-time newspaper. I'm not supposed to be feeling scared.*

But I was. I was scared because I didn't know what these people might do.

I started hopping from table to table, interviewing people, trying to cool everybody out. No one asked to see a press card or ID. Gradually, I began to feel pretty comfortable.

I liked to report outside Washington and New York and big cities in general because people will say things and put their name to it. Now the folks in the Long Branch disliked Carter intensely. But I had a feeling that they would be dissatisfied with whoever was in office. I don't mean that they were complainers. They were the epitome of the American independent spirit. Most of them were dirt farmers, gas station attendants, people like that. But they were surprisingly erudite, surprisingly knowledgeable.

I sat down with one guy and asked him, "What are the problems with America?"

"Corporations."

He unfolded a paper napkin and drew a series of boxes. He said, "This corporation here has a product. They don't sell it directly to you and me. They sell it to another company which sells it another company which sells to another company." He worked out the whole corporate structure on his paper napkin.

These people were real revolutionaries, right out of the 1700s. They said things like, "If you ever want to see the military take over, now is the time to do it. I'm tired of being kicked around by these little five-and-dime countries all over the world. There is no reason why America should be like this."

By eight or nine o'clock the place had filled up. There must have been forty people. And they had accepted me. I was their "nigger" basically. But it turned into a delightful evening.

When the bluegrass band started up, I was sitting with a woman who turned out to be a journalist for the local paper. We chatted a little. Then I started humming along with the band.

When I was in college, I sang in hootenannies. Bluegrass. I knew a lot of the songs they were singing—"Banks of the Ohio," "Wildwood Flower," "Don't Come Home Drunk with Lovin' on Your Mind."

So I started singing at the table. Then one of the women I had interviewed said, "Oh, sing 'Amazing Grace.'" I started singing it.

They stopped the band and the folks around us said they wanted me and the journalist white woman to sing a duet together, "Amazing Grace." And we did it. Oh, did we do it! It was wonderful! And the folks loved it. The evening was getting warmer and warmer.

After we finished "Amazing Grace," one of the young girls said, "Can you sing some Diana Ross?"

I said, "No. I don't know any Diana Ross songs."

When the band stopped playing, I started interviewing one of the guys. He told me how poor he had been as a kid, how he didn't have shoes to wear in the wintertime, how his father hunted game so the family could eat meat. He agreed that his kids were better off than he had been. They had shoes. They went to school. But, he said, "I just thought I would be further along."

He was talking about the American dream. He had a real feeling that the dream hadn't been fulfilled for him. That was part of the reason these folks talked revolution. They were disillusioned.

West Fork was a dry town and didn't allow liquor. They were real church-going people. No drinks were served in Ethel's place. So a guy in the band invited me outside for a beer. I joined all the boys from the band on the back of a pickup, to drink Pabst Blue Ribbon and sing country-and-western songs—right there, under the stars, singing redneck lyrics. "I'm red, white and blue. I drink Pabst Blue Ribbon . . ."

The next day, I asked a photographer with the local paper to take pictures of Ethel's place and the Black Oak Baptist Church and the folks whom I had interviewed. He was a young man of about twenty. He asked if I had ever tasted smoked turkey.

I said, "No."

He said, "Y'all come have lunch with my family."

We drove literally through the back woods over the "crick" to his family's house. And as I looked out of the car, I saw something from my childhood.

"Oh, my God, you've got sassafras."

He said, "How'd you know that?"

I told him, and he said, "We'll have sassafras tea for lunch."

And sure enough, we went out and dug up some sassafras at his place, and his mother made some sassafras tea. Before I left, she gave me a bottle of cucumber pickles and pickled watermelon rinds.

That night, I wrote my story. The next morning I went to church with the woman journalist I'd met. Everybody was real nice. But there was a big hoopla going on down the road at a place called Fort Smith. The Ku Klux Klan was having a big to-do.

There was a resurgence of the Klan in the South, so after the service was over, I told the woman journalist, "I know this is big Klan country. I ought to go down there and do a story."

Some of the people overheard me. They said "No! No! You don't want to go down there. Those people are just terrible. It might really be dangerous. You don't want to do that."

For the first time, I think, they had gotten to know somebody black, gotten to know me in a way that they had never done with a black person. That's why they were so protective.

I had the feeling that I had been adopted by these white people.

MAX ROBINSON

Max Robinson set up his first television audition by answering a "white male only" want ad in a Virginia newspaper. He later became an anchor on ABC's World News Tonight.

———

I was looking through the want ads. It was 1959, in Portsmouth, Virginia. I had dropped out of Oberlin College, and was staying with my grandparents. I wanted a job. I wanted to be a news broadcaster.

In those days, the help-wanted ads had two lists. "Help wanted, male." "Help wanted, male (c)." The second one, with the "(c)," meant colored. I saw an opening for a TV announcer under the white ads. I decided to go for it. I figured the worst that would happen was that I wouldn't get the job. But of course the same thing would happen if I sat there doing nothing.

I was raised by people who taught me: "Never assume that you can't do something unless you've tried. Never assume the door is closed unless you've tried to open it. And never assume it can't be opened until you've done everything you can to open it."

That was the fundamental lesson of my youth. I was raised with that kind of incentive.

So I went to the TV station and walked in. There must have been thirty white men standing around waiting to be called for an audition. Every one of them looked at me like, "What the hell are you doing here? He must be crazy!" It wasn't pleasant walking into that kind of atmosphere. You had to muster up as much courage as you could.

Finally, someone said, "You want to do an audition?"

"Yes."

I did the audition. I must confess it was very primitive—reading aloud from *Time* magazine. After a while, a guy came into the room. "We're going to call four names, and the rest of you can go. We wish you well. Thank you for coming."

Robinson was one of the names he called. I was shocked! We did another read, and the owner of the station called me into his office.

"What's your name again?" he said.

"Max Robinson."

"You're fascinating, Max."

"I beg your pardon, sir?"

"You interest me. Good audition. You've clearly had some broadcast experience, haven't you?"

I had done some work on and off at black radio stations, mostly jazz shows, since I was fourteen.

He thought for a moment and said, "I'm trying to figure what I'm going to do with you."

He clearly didn't think he could use me for the main job.

"Could you do a couple of days a week? Would that hold you for a while? We can't pay you a lot of money."

"Sure."

Another guy got the major job, working Monday through Friday. I did weekends. And when I did the news, up went the slide on the screen with the station logo. You'd hear my voice, but I was the invisible man.

I started thinking. *When Walter Cronkite does the news, he's not behind a slide.* And I had all these relatives in the area who wanted to see me. My vanity got the better of me.

One night I was in charge of the newsroom. So I told the guy on the floor, "Take down the slide. We're going on camera."

After the show, my grandparents called the station. They said, "We saw you. You were great!"

I'd hit a homerun, right?

Wrong.

The next day the owner called me. He was really upset.

"You looked fine. And I really hate to do this. But why did you go on camera?"

I said, "Well, what's wrong with that?"

"I'm going to be honest with you. We've been flooded with phone calls. They did not know that voice they were hearing on weekends belonged to a Negro. Max, I've got to be straight with you. You've got a lot of talent, but I'm going to have to let you go. I just don't need that kind of trouble. If you need a recommendation, I'll write you the best I can."

Strangely enough, I felt no bitterness. He was up-front. I kept saying to myself, *You blew it, turkey. You blew it, dummy.*

After a stint in the Air Force as a language specialist, I went to work in Washington as a reporter for WRC-TV, Channel 4. When I walked through the hallways, I spoke politely to everyone. People looked right through me, like I didn't exist. I felt that the cameramen hated me.

I was the only black at the station.

One day a fire broke out in town. I was the only person in the newsroom. The news director looked and saw me, and looked around some more. Then he called a white reporter away from lunch, and sent him to cover the story. Another time he decided to do a documentary in a black neighborhood and was in the process of putting a crew together to go out on the truck.

"Will I be reporting on the scene?" I asked.

"Oh, no. You drive the truck."

"May I ask another question? Why do you need a reporter to drive a truck? You have people here who can drive."

"Well, we can trust you."

Before I ever got on air with a story, I was forced to shave my moustache. I asked why, and they told me it was company policy. But I suspected that it was aimed at my race, because moustaches were more predominant among black men than whites. My sister Jewell told me that I'd just shaved off the only thing that made me look halfway presentable.

When I went to work at WRC, I was told that Washington, a predominantly black city, wasn't ready for a black anchor. Actually, the station wasn't. But the people of Washington, black *and* white, had always been. If you were good and you communicated, people would accept you. I always believed in that, and it has never failed me.

I finally turned in my resignation. I wasn't going to be the "nigger-by-the-door." I will *never* do that.

In 1967, I went to a rival station whose call letters then were WTOP-TV, Channel 9. I sat down with Jim Snyder, the Channel 9 news director, and told him that I wanted to become an anchor. If this couldn't occur immediately, then I would work for it to happen in the near future.

"I will keep this moustache." It had grown back.

Snyder said, "What's with the moustache?'

"Oh, nothing."

In 1969 I started anchoring at Channel 9. There were surprisingly few bigoted responses. In fact, then and throughout my career, you would be shocked at how little hate mail I've gotten, and how very heavy my share of the white audience has been. I wasn't limited in terms of demographics. We got more black viewers than the rival stations. Apparently, I appealed to a very broad spectrum.

In the 1970s the local stations in big cities were hiring blacks faster than the networks, because the FCC made them follow federal affirmative action requirements. Communities had much more influence than the networks over what local stations did. And local stations learned that they could turn around their ratings much faster than the networks by appealing to black viewers.

My greatest fear when I started anchoring was of being late, of not being there when it was time to go on. One evening, just before it was time to go on, I noted that the show was being juggled by the producer. And we didn't seem to have the lead story ready.

I asked where the reporter was.

The producer said, "We can't find him."

"What! You can't find him?"

I discovered that the guy was making idle chatter with a secretary. He came in fifteen minutes after the show started. And it was the lead story! I was livid at first. It mystified me how anybody could do that.

After I went off the air, Snyder, the news director, called me into his office. Jim knew me well. He knew I would start protesting.

"Now wait a minute," he said. "I don't care what you say. Wait a minute, Max. You gotta look at . . ."

I hadn't said a word.

Jim suspended the guy for a week without pay.

The person happened to be a black reporter, but I would have fired him. That was an unpardonable sin.

One morning in March 1977, I got a call from Jim. By then the evening news show I was anchoring with Gordon Peterson was solidly in first place.

Jim seemed anxious.

"Max, something's going down," he said. "Some people have taken over the B'nai B'rith building. We think it's the Hanafi Muslims. Do you know those guys?"

"Yes. But, Jim, those guys don't do things like that."

"Well, that's the rumor we got."

"I'll be right in."

A few years before, I had shopped at a jewelry store in Georgetown. At the time, it was the only business down there owned by blacks. That was when I first met Abdul Aziz. I was impressed by the shop, and I bought gifts from him.

Aziz belonged to the Hanafi Muslim group, which had its headquarters in a mansion that Kareem Abdul-Jabbar had purchased for them. Aziz invited me to meet Jabbar.

"I'd be happy to."

Then he said, "Would you be interested in joining us?"

"No. That's not my cup of tea. But I'd be happy to join you on a social occasion."

I could sense there was some courting going on.

The Hanafi group was small, an orthodox part of the Sunni Muslims. They were led by a black guy, Ernest McGhee, a former jazz musician who had some college and who now called himself Hamaas Khaalis.

Hamaas basically preached peace and racial harmony. It was said he had been in the Nation of Islam—a Black Muslim. Hamaas broke away after some Black Muslims were convicted of killing Malcolm X. But that changed on this day, in 1973, when his family was massacred at the mansion. They found five of his children and grandchildren dead. His wife and his daughter, who was married to Aziz, were seriously wounded. The killers had drowned the ten-day-old grandson in front of his mother's eyes.

I went to their headquarters. The surviving members of the family were devastated. They asked me to help them set up a news conference and to give them a few suggestions—and I did. I took myself off the story. I didn't feel I should cover it. I didn't like any hint of conflict. I had always played it very straight in terms of how I operated as a journalist.

I saw Aziz at the hospital and offered him a ride. As we drove away he said, "Max, why are you doing this? People are treating us like the plague. You know this car could be hit at any time?"

"Aziz," I said. "Please don't talk that stuff. I'm not into macho man. I don't walk down dark alleys, either."

"But why?"

"You're a person. And I think a good person. You need some help. And I would want someone to do the same for me."

He nodded.

"I ask only one thing," I said. "If they decide to hit this car, just tell them I'm the cab driver."

But I was really concerned for Hamaas, because he didn't show the grief that most of us would show. He seemed too calm.

Two years later, five Black Muslims were tried and convicted for the massacre. It was said that Hamaas had been writing to Black

Muslim ministers around the country, calling their leader "a lying deserter" for deviating from the orthodox religion.

Before I went to the station, I called Aziz. He didn't answer. I left a message for him to call me at the station. Then it hit me. *Oh, my God!* I thought. *They probably are involved.*

Hamaas stayed bitter. And that bitterness drove him to revenge. That was what was happening when Snyder called me that March morning.

As soon as I got to the station, Aziz called. They had done it.

I said, "I must talk to you immediately."

He said, "Come over here. I'll talk to you."

By this time, we knew that a hundred and thirty-four hostages had been taken at three locations. Nineteen people had been injured. Someone had been killed at the District Building. We learned that it was a young black reporter, Maurice Williams, who covered the mayor's office for the Howard University radio station.

I went to Jim Snyder's office. "I'm going to talk to Aziz now," I said. "Get the camera crew."

Gordon Peterson came in, and we apprised him of the situation. "I'm going now."

"No," Jim said, "you can't do that. You can't put your life on the line."

"Jim, this is a story *I* have to cover."

"I order you not to go," Jim screamed.

"My story, friend. Fire me after I finish."

I went to the headquarters and waited a long time to get in. They must have had ten locks on the door. A few policemen were around, but they were not so evident. I kept thinking, *I know these people. What's happened to them?*

They let me in. I saw a couple of guns and a lot of machetes. Finally, Aziz came in.

"What in the world have you done?" I said.

He told me what had happened, and said that they had drawn up a list of demands.

"My God, by your logic, you could have taken me hostage!" I said.

"We talked about that and rejected it," he said.

Hamaas was now calling the headquarters and asking for me. He said this was a holy war. He was ready to die for his faith. And he started reading off these demands.

I stopped him and asked, "Would you like to talk to me at the station?"

"I will do that."

So I gave him a time to talk.

I rushed back to the station and told Jim, "We've got to go on the air immediately."

"Glad to see you're still alive," he said.

Gordon Peterson was opening up the news show, and I was on the phone to Hamaas. I was the first person he talked to, the first to hear the demands, and to learn why he had made this move.

Hamaas demanded the killers of his babies. He wanted the people who killed Malcolm X, too. And he wanted a movie made in Libya, called *Mohammad, Messenger of God*,[45] withdrawn from distribution. He said it was a fairy tale.

Later that evening, I was called to the control room. I picked up the phone, and the person on the other end said, "You are a rat. You betrayed our cause. You're dead. And your family is dead."

When I got back on the air, I didn't mention anything. I finished out the show. Then I called my brother Randall and told him to pick up my wife and child and take them to my house. A police guard was there to protect the house. And then I was assigned a police guard around the clock. They took me to stay at the Sheraton Park Hotel.

When I got up the next morning, I went to the station and headed straight to the typewriter and wrote a four-minute piece. Then I did a stand-up in front of the headquarters as if I were talking to Hamaas.

It was clearly an editorial piece. I explained how the Hanafis had been treated without any compassion during their earlier ordeal, and now they were doing the same thing to innocent people.

I found out later that Hamaas had heard it and was very moved.

The siege ended thirty-nine hours after it started. Three Middle East ambassadors got Hamaas to release the hostages and surrender his men.

Later Aziz told me, "We always knew that you understood us better than most people. Incidentally, the threat on your life?"

"Yes?"

"We had nothing to do with that."

How he knew about that, I don't know. But he certainly had pretty good intelligence.

Some people said that I was hired by ABC because Roone Arledge[46] saw my Hanafi work. Or he discovered me sipping a soda at Schwab's in L.A. The public myth was that I was picked. I was discovered. Which was not true at all. And I found that dangerous for young people to believe. It suggested that all they had to do was what they tended to do—sit and wait.

It didn't happen that way. A year before the Hanafi incident, my brother Randall, who was the head of TransAfrica, a lobby for Africa and the Caribbean, said, "I need to talk to you."

That sounded strange. He had never said that before: "I need to talk to you." We usually just talked.

"What's the problem?" I asked.

"There's no problem, but we need to sit down and talk, so arrange a time when we can carve out a couple of free hours," he said. "A lot of people feel very strongly, as I feel, that you should be the first black evening network news anchor."

"Well, that's a nice compliment," I said.

"I'm serious."

"It's a big piece of work," I said. "I don't think I'm prepared to take it on."

"You're crazy. You always underrate yourself."

I had a habit of doing that in my short life.

"Nobody's more prepared, and it needs to be done," my brother said.

I pointed out that I was a local anchor and a black anchor. One would be a problem for anyone—and two was very difficult.

"Time for you to pay more dues," Randall said.

We had another session, and I argued that I was doing well in Washington. I liked what I was doing. Sometimes I was a little bored, but that's one of the drawbacks of life.

Randall said, "If your mind is working, you won't be bored."

I'm not sure what propelled me to act. Vanity might have been a part of it. That drives us all, I suppose, certainly in this business. But there must have been something else. A feeling that I needed a challenge, and I knew this would be one.

Finally I said, "Okay. It's a big piece of work."

I looked down the road and saw that I would be doing more than just making an adjustment from local anchor to network. I could also see all of the pressures that would be brought to bear on a black person in a seat of authority in America. This would not be acceptable to many people who were in positions to make decisions. I also knew the support system wasn't there. And I was frightened, very frightened.

First, I needed an agent. I'd been using Vinnie Cohen, a very fine black lawyer and dear friend, to do my contracts at Channel 9. As a matter of courtesy, I let him know that I appreciated the work he'd done, but, clearly, he could not be the agent going to New York and knocking on doors. Then that became a problem, too, because agents picked and chose who they wanted to represent.

Gordon Barnes, who was doing weather at the station, knew about the decision I'd made. "You have an agent?" he asked.

"No."

"There's a guy you really ought to talk to. You're a hot commodity. If you want to stay here, he can get you more bucks, too."

So he gave me the agent's name. I picked up the phone and called.

On the other end, "Hey, it's good to hear from you. I see your work. I love your work. You do a great job."

"Thank you."

"So what do you want to do?"

"My goal is to be a network evening anchor."

"Well, Max, let's be realistic. I don't see that in twenty years. It's no disrespect to you. I'm talking about the marketplace. I'm talking about reality."

"I appreciate what you're saying. It's been nice talking to you."

"No, wait a minute, look: New York market. L.A. market. Big bucks. We ought to get together."

"No," I said. "There's no reason for us to get together. There's something that I want to do, and clearly you don't see it. You can't help me."

"I'm sorry," he said, "but that's the way I feel. I wouldn't be dishonest with you."

"I appreciate that."

And I hung up.

I realized that I had a real dilemma just getting to first base, just getting somebody to believe in me. So I cast about, talked to people, and the name Alfred Geller came up. He didn't have any black clients, but that didn't bother me. I figured that might be a plus. He might find it a challenge. So I called him.

"I'm really flattered that you called me," he said. "I've seen your work."

"I need your help."

I told him what I was interested in. I didn't hear a "no."

"May I come down and meet with you?"

"Sure. Come have dinner at my house."

So we talked, and he said, "Where do you think you will end up when you do this?"

I said, "ABC."

"Why do you say that?"

"Because they're the ones in need. Obviously, I'm not taking Cronkite's place. And NBC is well situated. ABC's in terrible trouble."

"Good point."

"We need to talk to all of them. But let's focus our energies on ABC."

At the time, Bill Sheehan was president of ABC News. As we dealt with Sheehan, Roone Arledge, the president of sports, arrived to take over the news. So we didn't know what Sheehan's position would be.

"Sit down, Mr. Robinson and let's figure out how we get you to ABC," Sheehan said.

I was astounded. This was rare. They usually put you off.

The last time we talked, he said, "Look, I'll tell you what we're thinking about. We may not be talking about evening news anchor, but we are thinking about that for down the road. It may happen in a year or two. But first we want you to do the news brief, weekend anchor, and some reporting. How does that appeal to you?"

"Fine," I said.

"We'll be back to you in two weeks."

Two week passed. We heard nothing. We didn't want to look like we were hungry, like we were knocking at the door. So we let a month go by. Finally, my agent called them.

He didn't get Sheehan. He got somebody else who said, "I think you're talking to the wrong person."

Alfred said, "What are you talking about?"

"I don't think Mr. Sheehan has any authority."

I thought, *Oh, holy hell*. We'd spent all this time negotiating with a dead man. We had to start the whole process all over.

When Roone Arledge replaced Sheehan, he brought David Burke as his assistant. Burke wasn't in the business. He had worked in politics for Senator Kennedy. But he was a good man—very savvy, very bright.

So Burke was the man we were dealing with. We found that Roone had ordered tapes of my broadcasts and had them stacked up almost to the ceiling in his office. Apparently, he was a bit nervous about this decision, possibly on several levels. Burke told me later that he'd never gotten so tired of seeing one individual in his life!

ABC was third in a three-way race. The chemistry between Harry Reasoner and Barbara Walters had not worked. So Roone was casting about. Dan Rather. Tom Brokaw. Robert McNeil. But he couldn't find a major anchor to go against Cronkite.

It was a nervous time for me. Alfred and I weren't sure what would happen. But we knew we were close to something.

Then, when I was in Richmond, my hometown, Alfred called. "You're in!"

"I'm in?"

"Yes."

"Wait a minute, Alfred. What does that mean?"

"You hit the jackpot."

It was incredible. Not only was I the first black evening anchor, but I was also the first local anchor ever to go directly to a network. This had never happened before in the history of the business.

Roone had to figure out some way to make an impact on the ratings without coming up with a major person. So he hit upon a multiple anchor concept. Initially, it was four anchors: Peter Jennings in London, Frank Reynolds in Washington, Max Robinson in Los Angeles, and Tom Jarriel in New York or Chicago. He said he was doing this to give more immediacy to the news reports.

One day David Burke said, "What are you doing this weekend?"

"Going to L.A. to look for a house," I said.

"Why don't you put a hold on that?"

"Why?"

"We don't want to let too much out, but I don't think you ought to go to L.A."

"Come on, David. You can't have me out here not knowing exactly what I'm going to do. I've got to make plans. I have a family."

"All right. But keep it to yourself. Don't tell anybody. Don't even tell your wife."

"Okay."

He tossed me a couple of pages of notes. There were three anchor locations, not four. No names. Chicago. London. Washington. I thought, *Holy hell. I just lost a job.*

"David, there's an immediate question I've got to ask you," I said. "Am I one of these three anchors?"

"Of course you are."

"Am I in Chicago?"

"Probably."

David wasn't trying to be coy, he was sincere. It was my first introduction to Roone Arledge, a man who made decisions very rapidly but vexed over them before he came to the final announcement. You thought that he was going here, and suddenly you found him over there.

After I joined the team, he called me to the Washington bureau to announce his decision to the correspondents. I was seated between him and David. At one point, Roone leaned over to me and said, "I want you to know something, and I want you to believe this. I never thought of your race when I hired you."

It was almost as if he expected me to say, "Thank you."

I said, "Okay."

I went on the air July 10, 1978. When we started *World News Tonight*, jokes were made about us being floating anchors—a difficult concept to grasp for anybody. What's a *floating* anchor?

There was a good deal of competition among us in the early days. We were all vying for our share of the show. And I think that was a mistake—setting us against each other. After that was resolved and Frank Reynolds became the lead anchor, things got better. And we really had cordial relations.

Chicago was a very *serious* white market. They gritted their teeth when I came to town. Here was a black man coming to a town that didn't have any major black local anchors—and he was the *network* anchor. So I ran into a lot of professional jealousy.

One of the local anchors said, "I don't know how a black man can identify with the wheat fields of Kansas." That was the strangest statement I had ever heard from anybody. A television critic warned me, "When you come to Chicago, you better be humble, or Chicago will humiliate you."

Where am I going? I wondered. *What am I getting into?*

A critic wrote in the *Chicago Sun-Times* that I was an "airhead." He said I couldn't edit, couldn't write—the network had to prop me up. Usually, I never dignified such charges with an answer. But this was one time I really wanted to say something. Roone cautioned me: "Just ignore it."

I understood that some people resented a black person being in that position and starting to do well. But when people said Max Robinson wasn't prepared, I knew there was a grain of truth in that. I'm not talking about my intelligence or my capabilities as a journalist. But I had never been at a network.

Frankly, I had to learn a hell of a lot during the time I was on the job. I played catch-up. There were lessons you had to learn in order to be prepared to assume that major anchor chair. There was no question that if I had had two or five years doing national reporting, it would have been helpful. And I was surrounded by correspondents at ABC who felt that they should be the anchor person. I arrived at the network with no support structure.

Who were my allies? I had no allies.

It was true of many black people, if not all of us in the business, be it electronic or print, that we found ourselves in roles without having had an old boy network to help prepare us for it. Yet, in the early days, there was a bond that linked David Burke and Roone Arledge and Max Robinson, because of the backbiting people did toward all of us.

Of course I knew Roone wouldn't have taken the chance with me unless ABC was in trouble. But as it turned out, Roone's hunch bore out. They never had a problem with ratings. It worked. Nobody argued the point. And although Frank Reynolds, Peter Jennings, and Max Robinson were three members of a team, each of us was very valuable as individuals. Each had his own constituency.

Clearly, I brought a substantial minority audience. But if you looked at my mail, you found a cross-section of America. I came across on the tube with a warmth that both black *and* whites could feel.

I had just arrived in Jamaica for a vacation, when I got a phone call from one of the producers. "Sorry to disturb you," he said, "but I knew you wouldn't mind."

"What's wrong?"

"Nothing's wrong. Guess where we were last week?"

"Where?"

"Number One, friend. First place. Never before in the history of ABC News, right? And we want you to know that you should take a large share of that credit. That's why I had to call you."

On occasion, when I replaced Frank Reynolds in Washington, the ratings went up. And that was strange. Management was aware of it, but they wouldn't talk much to me about it. Even when I replaced Peter Jennings in Washington, after Frank was too ill to go on, the ratings went up.

For a long time, I wanted to beat myself over the head for what happened to me during the election coverage in 1978. I'd been at ABC for six months. I had some senatorial candidates to deal with, and obviously I had never done that before. I felt that I wasn't prepared enough, so I tried to digest material that I didn't need, which complicated my life.

Attempting to deal with all this, I drained my energy. I was too calm, and Roone was screaming in my ear, "Pump it up. Pump it up." I didn't know what he was talking about—"More energy. More energy." I retreated into myself.

I think that really hurt me in Roone's eyes, which was critical. The terrible thing about this business was that your mistakes were more memorable than the good things you had done. Instead of just writing it off as a bad night, I worried about it. It weighed on me. It haunted me up until the 1982 elections, when I really came on strong.

Once, when my agent and I were meeting with Arledge, Roone looked at me and said, "Max, let's be honest. We have some problems. When we move you about the country, you need to have a TelePrompTer."

"I need to have what?"

Roone had this look of did-I-say-something-wrong?

I turned to my agent. I could see that he had already heard some of this stuff, too. They were saying that Robinson was glued to the TelePrompTer. If they took it away from me, I would collapse.

"Roone," I said, "remember the piece I did in Philadelphia?"

"The July Fourth piece?"

"I didn't have any PrompTer."

"Those were stand-ups?"

"We had to do them right before air time."

"Max, I'm sorry."

"I understand."

But what galled me was that some people outside the company heard the rumors and then began to repeat and repeat it.

I could do a minute and thirty-second stand-up without a TelePrompTer, if it was about one story. But I couldn't do five stories. I didn't know anybody who could. Some correspondents recorded what they had to say and played it back through an earpiece, repeating what they heard themselves say. I never used that technique. I found it disconcerting. It made your face look like a zombie because you were concentrating on hearing what you were saying in order to repeat it, rather than thinking about what you should say.

You saw people on the air who didn't seem to be aware of what they were saying. They smiled through death and destruction. But viewers noticed one thing about me: I was aware of what I was talking about. They told me, "I appreciate watching you because when somebody dies, you're not smiling."

When it was time to cover President Reagan's inauguration and the release of the fifty-two American hostages in Iran,[47] one of the executive producers called and told me to stand by. I waited by the

phone. And I was totally ignored. I'm not a mind reader, and spec-
ulation can be dangerous. But I guess I thought—well, let me put
it this way. It was a slap in the face. If he had called and said, "Look,
we're not going to include you in this coverage," I wouldn't have
liked it, but it wouldn't have been half as insulting as to leave me
hanging on and to be ignored.

Within twenty-four hours after the inauguration, I sent a
telegram to Roone informing him I could no longer tolerate such
treatment. It fell just short of offering my resignation.

Roone phoned and said that he would be talking to me. He said
they were very happy with my work, but there were some things he
wanted to run past me. I said that I looked forward to meeting with
him. And then I heard nothing.

It's almost better to have somebody tell you that you're a dog,
we don't like you, or we don't like niggers. Then you would know.
But I heard nothing. And there was no way I could approach the
subject. Communications between us were bad. The frustration
level was high.

The snub I felt weighed heavily on my mind when I went to
Smith College in Northampton, Massachusetts, three weeks after
the inauguration. Before the speech, I had dinner with a group of
students. I was disturbed by the tone of what I picked up from some
of the black students. They were upset about the insults they had to
put up with. Like going to a cocktail party where whites served
drinks with Zulu Lulu swizzle sticks.

In my speech, I mostly talked about racism in America, about the
need to start communicating with each other honestly, to come to
the table as equals. What I had to say about the network was a small
part of the speech. But that was what got picked up and carried by
the wire services across the country.

I said that I had met with a stone wall when I questioned things
that were damaging, demeaning, insulting, and dangerous to black
people in this country. I said it was not peculiar to ABC. It was
peculiar to white America. And I talked about watching the coverage of two very patriotic events from the sidelines, even though I

was a national desk anchor responsible for a good deal of the ratings at ABC.

When I got back to Chicago, Roone called. He wanted me in New York the next day. He was upset.

I flew in and that night I had dinner with two black colleagues, Ed Bradley and Earl Caldwell.[48]

"Did I do something wrong?" I asked them.

"Earl Caldwell said, "No. What you said is true. But you clearly bought trouble in saying it.""

I was very concerned. I got little sleep. I thought I had let some people down, especially young people.

I walked into Roone's headquarters the next morning. Not at the news office where I always had met him before. This was the first time I'd ever seen this other office. There was a black secretary outside his door. She looked at me, and it really shook me up. It was like, *I feel so sorry for this brother, this poor dead man.*

She must have been puzzled when I cheerily said, "Good morning. How are you?"

I was psyched up because I kept telling myself, *You are right! And even if you're not, you're going to look and sound that way.*

When I walked in, I said, "Roone, good to see you." He was caught off-guard.

"Max. You want coffee? A Coke or something?"

"I'll take a Coke."

I stayed four hours.

I told him this was the first time I'd had a real conversation with him, and that it was sad it had to be under those circumstances.

"Max, you're playing politics with this race thing," he said. "Using it to your advantage."

"If anybody can let me know the advantages I have because of race, please tell me. I can't figure it out. You've got to be out of your mind!"

"Calm down, Max," he said.

I told him about a top-level executive who deliberately tried to sabotage my work at the Democratic National Convention the year before. I mentioned what he'd said to me when I joined up, about how he didn't recognize my race.

He struggled to tell me that he hired me because I was good.

"Of course you did," I said. "But to suggest to me that you have to disregard my race means there's something wrong with my race. I don't want you to disregard that I'm black. That means that being black is a drawback, and you're taking a burden off me. It's not a burden to me, Roone."

"My God, I never thought about it like that."

"That's one of the problems I was trying to address in the speech I made to the students. There are so many things that happen in this country that we don't think about which injure and damage people. My people have been hurt, not so much by the Klansmen, not so much by the open bigot—in fact, they have been rather helpful— than by the thoughtlessness of so much of white America, because we can't talk to people like you. Because you know you're right."

Another ABC executive walked in. Someone had phoned him.

He said, "You think you've got all of black America behind you on this?"

"I'd be very surprised if the majority of black people in this country weren't behind me. You'd be very hard pressed to find any black person who says that racism is not a significant factor in American life."

"A black leader," he said, "called us and said that you should be fired."

I said, "Why did you tell me that?"

"I just thought you ought to know."

"You don't even know who you're talking about. Most black people don't know who he is."

"Who do they know then?"

"For good or ill, Jesse Jackson."

"You've got to be kidding! Who really gives him the time of day?"

"I didn't say who *you* respected, because black people don't care who you respect."

When the meeting ended, Roone said, "You know, you've taught me a lot of things. You opened my eyes."

Then I issued a statement, which said in part that I did not intend to leave the impression in my Smith speech that decisions at ABC News were based on racial considerations. I also said that I regretted any impact those remarks may have had on my colleagues and on management. I said I was talking about a problem that exists in every part of our society, and was not singling out ABC News for criticism.

If we had had a healthy internal dialogue within the network, I wouldn't have made that speech. I won't say that I was correct in doing it. Certainly, it wasn't politically smart. And unfortunately, I got a reputation because of it as being some kind of militant, which was not true.

Many well-intentioned white Americans, I believe, want to make progress on race relations. But they must suffer the pain of recognizing the problem. And people in my industry, especially, feel that it is wrong for a journalist to talk about the issue. If a journalist isn't going to do it, who is?

The following year I was invited to host the DuPont Awards[49] at Columbia University, along with Dan Rather, Tom Brokaw, Barbara Walters, and Charlayne Hunter-Gault.[50] I could feel everybody waiting to hear what I would say. I knew that there were those who thought I would come out and talk about racism in America in a very heavy way. And I still felt that was a reasonable thing to do. But I didn't want people to think that I was limited to one subject.

I got up and said, "I have been given three minutes to talk about the state of broadcast journalism—which is not enough time." I talked about the tyranny of the clock. How we were ruled by it. I dealt with a subject that we all wrestled with every day. Unlike print journalists, we didn't have editorial meetings. We didn't have time to sit down and have philosophical discussions.

I think we failed because we had such legitimate reasons for not addressing the problem. We had so many excuses. Everything was so immediate. We had to deal with the breaking story. We were not putting important issues aside because we were evil people. We just made decisions without thinking about it.

I added that the presence of black people, Hispanics, Asian Americans and other minorities in our business was important, not simply because you had to hire a person of color, but because all of us should bring our perspectives to bear on these problems. If we were brought to newsrooms and expected to think like white people, then we had lost all the fundamental reasons why we should have been valuable to this country.

The people at ABC were happy that I didn't come out blasting the audience as racists.

Frank Reynolds's condition grew worse. He had terminal cancer and had to go off the air. I had sent him three plants and called his wife from time to time. She wrote me twice. There was no bad blood between us. And when he passed, Peter Jennings, Ted Koppel and all of the others were called on the air to talk about Frank. I think it looked odd that Max Robinson, one of the co-anchors, was not invited to say anything. And I felt insulted.

This was the kind of treatment that they might have thought insignificant, but which really bothered me all along during my relationship at ABC. Common courtesy was involved—things that they just seemed not to think about. And I was very hurt by it.

Shortly after Frank died, I thought ABC would go to a single anchor. Then Roone called me to New York. He said we needed to talk. I suspected why. I knew I was going to be bounced. No one told me, but if you're in this business for any amount of time, you have a way of reading the handwriting on the wall. If you need to be told, then you're in trouble.

There's a joke in this business. When you understand things are not going very well and that your stock is not too high, then don't hang around the water fountain. Make yourself scarce. Don't let them find you.

So I went to New York and talked first to Alfred, my agent, and told him what I thought was happening.

"Don't prejudge it," he said.

"Alfred, let's not be foolish."

"They wouldn't bounce you," he said. "That's crazy."

"Sometimes craziness prevails."

"How do you think you'll react?"

"When they announce it to me, I will say, 'Roone, you're not known to make any bad mistakes. What I don't understand is why you would install one-third of the team rather than two-thirds of the team, given the fact that we each have our own following. That doesn't make sense to me.'"

When I met with them, they announced the decision: Peter Jennings would go on as the sole anchor.

I said, "This is not appreciated by me."

Everybody nodded.

I said, "It's as mystifying as it is unacceptable." I laid out the ratings that I'd brought to the show.

"If you are reducing the show from the three-anchor concept, why wouldn't you reduce it to the two who are remaining? What's wrong with that? Clearly, there is an audience which has found me very acceptable as a major player at ABC News."

I hadn't heard anything from David Burke. Now he looked very sad.

"You make a very good case, Max, and we can't argue with it," he said. "But we have made another decision."

When I returned to Washington, on my way out of working for ABC, I was given a reception by the Capital Press Club, which represented mostly black journalists.

"I am a little concerned about being singled out as a person who speaks about racism," I told the black journalists. "Because I didn't seek that position, and I don't want that position. What concerns me the most, however, is that you are silent when those of us who feel we must speak out do so."

"Your silence is dangerous and damaging," I said. "It is a hurtful noise."

Jimmy Hicks, a correspondent for the National Newspaper Publishers Association, covered the Emmett Till trial, sitting at the "Jim Crow table" in a Mississippi courtroom. Hicks was a decorated army captain in World War II.

———

I went to this town, it was September 1955, and introduced myself to Sheriff Strider. He was an All-American from Ole Miss. I was covering the Emmett Till case. The lynching of Emmett Till.

"I am James C. Hicks from New York. I'm a reporter for the National Newspaper Publishers Association."

Sheriff Strider looked over my head like I didn't exist.

"Sheriff, I understand that you control press conferences. I would appreciate it if you'd let me know when you have a press conference. I'm living in Mound Bayou, but I can get over here in a hurry if you'll have somebody in your office call. Just let me know when you're going to have a press conference."

He said, "What makes you think I'm gonna let niggers come to my press conference?"

"I would hope you would," I said. "I certainly would appreciate it."

"All right. Give me the number."

He never really called a press conference. But I was there every day, in this little town of Sumner, Mississippi, which had to be the most segregated town in the most racist state in America.

I was actually a roving correspondent for NNPA, based in New York. At first they had me in the Washington bureau with

Louie Lautier, who was the first black White House correspondent. I was Louie's assistant. I covered the State Department as the first black.

Then they decided to expand the news service and send me to New York. I had no office. My office was my inside coat pocket, a telephone booth, and the Theresa Hotel bar.

Gradually, I stayed on the road for one month, two months, three months at a time. They gave me as much money as they could, and I'd go packing. Miami. Then San Antonio. Or Los Angeles. I remember driving one thousand, three hundred and twelve miles once without stopping.

In the South, you didn't want to stop. We faced Jim Crow travel then, so you wanted to drive. And traveling by car in the South, your first problem was staying out of jail.

The first time I got arrested was in Dalton, Georgia. This was before the Till case. On my way through the South, I stopped in Atlanta, and some of the guys at the *Atlanta Daily World* told me that the best thing to do was to always gas-up in a large city.

They told me not to go out on the side of the road to take a leak. If you're black, that was indecent exposure down there. You hold on until you can get to a place.

When I got near Dalton, Georgia, I was completely out of gas. Not only that, I had to go. Believe me, I had to *go*. So I pulled into this roadside gas station in the hinterlands.

I told the guy, "Fill it up."

I said, "Where's your rest room?"

He looked at me and said in a very soft, mild voice, "We don't have a rest room for niggers."

"Wait a minute, wait a minute," I said. "I don't want any more gas. Don't put any more gas in my car."

The gauge showed $1.80 worth.

He said, "You gonna give me that $1.80 that I already put in there?"

"Sure."

I threw two dollars on the concrete mount that held the gas pump. I threw it up there, and I jumped in my car. I was so mad I wasn't thinking properly. Then I started speeding off. I looked in my rearview mirror, and saw the guy was back there yelling at me.

"Come back here, nigger, come back! I'll get you!"

I gunned that little ol' Ford. And as I went up the road a mile or so, I started thinking. All he has to do is pick up the phone and say, "Stop the dude on the road in his little blue Ford."

So I became quite concerned about speeding. But I didn't want to go too slow either. Apparently he did call ahead, because a state trooper stopped me. It wasn't in a town. It was at a wide spot in the road. He called a guy in a warehouse and turned me over to him. The guy was rubbing grease off his hands. Evidently he was a mechanic.

The mechanic said, "You come on over here."

I found myself sitting in a room in this warehouse.

"What have I done?" I asked.

"When you came through Dalton, boy, there was a school bus, and you didn't stop."

"I haven't seen a school bus all day."

I had New York tags, which I later learned was a mistake.

"Don't you have children in New York?"

"Sure, we have children in New York."

"Don't you folks stop for a school bus?"

I said, "They don't go to school in August, you know."

He said, "Well, boy, you're going to *jail* in August."

"Am I going to court?"

"Any time you sit down with an officer of the law, you are in court. And I am an officer of the law."

Nobody asked me for money or mentioned a fine.

I stayed in the warehouse overnight. Next morning, when I told them I had $100, they let me out. Bernard Young, the secretary for the news service, always had us carry as much cash as the service could afford.

The second time I got arrested was in Alabama. I was trying to get from the airport to the site of a story, and I refused to sit in the back of the bus carrying me in. I sat in the white section.

Carl Murphy, publisher of the *Afro-American* newspapers, was a great editor. He prided himself in being on top of an event. Instead of relaying the assignment through Young, Carl Murphy picked up the phone and said, "Mr. Hicks, I want you to go here."

He said, "Mr. Hicks, do you know about Emmett Till?"

"Yes, I know."

"I want you down there tomorrow."

"Mr. Carl, I'll try."

The only thing I knew was that they had lynched a young man, a boy really, whose mother was in Chicago. Till was fourteen years old. His mother had put him on a train down to Mississippi for summer vacation, to visit his granduncle, Mose Wright.

The charge was that he had grabbed the hand of a white woman when he paid her for some candy. In that part of Mississippi, at that time, you did not touch the white people. If you had some change coming, they'd put the money on the counter, and you'd pick it up.

The lynching happened in another place called Money, but the trial was in Sumner. I had been told to go to Mound Bayou, because that was an all-black town. I could get myself a room at the motel. The first thing I did was call Murphy. You established where you were.

The trial was held in the little city hall. The courtroom was segregated. The blacks had to sit in the back. They filled up three rows from the back. But if more whites came, they had to give up their seats.

I started putting together the facts. Money was really just a small hamlet. And Till's granduncle, Moses Wright, was a sharecropper. One day, Emmett, his cousin Curtis Jones, and some other kids went to Bryant's Grocery and Meat Market to buy some candy. There was a white woman storekeeper, Carol Bryant. When they left, Till was supposed to have rolled his eyes and whistled at her.

Two days later, Till was kidnapped from the granduncle's cabin at gunpoint. A few days later, they found his body floating in the

Tallahatchie. His eye was torn out. His teeth were knocked out. One side of his head was crushed in. He had been shot in the head. And there was a cotton-gin fan tied around his neck with barbed wire, to weigh him down.

The woman's husband, Roy Bryant, and his half-brother, a guy named J. W. Milam, were charged with committing the murder. But they denied everything.

The white reporters sat at a press table near the jury. Reporters or not, we blacks had to sit on the other side. So Sheriff Strider set up a bridge table for us on the other side of the courtroom. He made it plain to all of us that we were not going to mingle with the white people. Of course, the jury was all white.

We sat at this little Jim Crow table every day. Simeon Booker was there from Washington, the Johnson Publishing bureau chief. Also this beautiful girl from *Ebony*, Clotylde Murdock. Jackson, this crazy photographer from *Jet*. Another writer, Moses Newsome. And Ernie Withers. He was a good photographer, from Memphis. He was so good at getting along with those Southern whites that he was just amazing.

We sat there every day. And a white deputy sat a few feet away watching us, with a .45-caliber pistol dangling from his holster.

Every morning, the sheriff walked over to our table and said, "How you niggers doing this morning? Are you niggers all right?"

Ernie would say, "We're in good shape. You looking out for us just fine."

Oh, man, I was so mad. We sat there smoldering. Booker, he was gnashing his teeth.

"All right, boy."

And Strider would pat Ernie on the shoulder.

At recess, we left the courtroom and stretched out on the sidewalk. The blacks stood on one side, the whites on the other.

One day I spotted Murray Kempton of the *New York Post*, an old friend. His wife was an old friend, too. Then I saw her. Murray brought her down to look at the court proceedings.

She said, "Murray, there's Jim Hicks."

And boom, she walked right over to me.

"Jim, it's so nice to see you," she said.

Then she kissed me.

Murray said, "My God, come back here!"

Murray, he was a right guy. They were staying in another town. But Murray came to Mound Bayou every night to my room. I couldn't go to his. We'd knock off a bottle of bourbon and talk about how bad it was down there for blacks.

One day I came out of the courtroom during a recess and all of a sudden who but Charlie Diggs[51] runs up to me.

"Jimmy, Jimmy, I'm so glad to see you. Jimmy, look, can you get me in the courtroom?"

Diggs was a U.S. Congressman. He came down more or less as an observer of the trial.

I said, "Yes. I mean, the sheriff is a . . . I mean, I go in there every day. We got a Jim Crow table where we sit. Sure."

"I sent the judge a telegram from Detroit and told him that I was coming," Diggs said. "I got a telegram back from him saying I could observe the trial. But this sheriff won't even let me come in the courtroom. Here's my card. I want you to go in there when court opens and tell the judge I'm out here."

"Okay."

As soon as court opened and people started filing back in, I went right up to the judge. It seemed like every courthouse in Dixie had a big door in the center, with a wing on one side and a wing on the other side. You walked straight through, and the judge was sitting in front, in the middle.

I walked up to the judge, Curtis Swango. When I got to the middle of the courtroom and didn't turn right to go to the Jim Crow table, one of the deputies stopped me.

"Where you going, nigger?"

"I'm going to see the judge."

"You can't go up there."

"Sir, look, there is a Negro congressman outside. I have his card. He told me to take it to the judge because he has communicated with the judge, and the judge has agreed to let him be an observer at the trial."

He said, "You stand right there." It seemed as though they had deputized every able-bodied white person in the country, every chow-hound in the army. God only knows. They walked around with .45s slung on them. Everybody was a deputy, except the blacks.

The deputy left and returned with another deputy. This one was a real police officer, on the sheriff's staff.

He walked up to me and said, "Boy, what are you talking about?"

"Sir, I'll explain it to you."

I told him the story. And he went to find another deputy.

We were standing in the middle of the courtroom. He said, "This nigger here says there's a nigger outside who says he's a nigger congressman."

The third guy looked astounded. He said in amazement, "A *nigger* congressman?"

And the second guy pointed to me and said, "That's what this nigger said."

I can't believe this, I said to myself. *I can't believe this. Hicks, you gotta be cool. You gotta be cool.*

And he added, "I don't know anything about it."

About this time Sheriff Strider came in.

"Sheriff," I said, "can I see you a minute?"

"Yeah, boy. What is it?"

I told him the story. That makes four. And I showed him the card. He said, "I'll take it to the judge."

He showed the judge Diggs's card. The judge told him to bring Diggs right in. Actually, it turned out the judge was a fairly decent fellow, as they go down there.

Strider came over to our table and said, "You got a nigger congressman down here who's coming to observe the trial. I'm gonna bring him over here and sit him right down with y'all."

And I'll be *damned* if he didn't make Diggs sit there at the Jim Crow press table with us.

When I was working on the story, I picked up some information about the fan that had been used to weigh down Emmett Till. A white reporter with one of the local papers said the fan they found on the boy's neck came from the cotton gin on J. W. Milam's farm.

I started thinking. Having been an army man, I thought there must be rifling on the fan that would match the cotton gin, just like rifling on a bullet coming out a barrel. I told Ruby Hurley about this. She was a field secretary for the NAACP. I told her I wanted to go to the farm.

She said, "Jimmy, get yourself a pair of overalls. Find out exactly where the place is. But be careful. If they catch you, you're in big trouble."

I spent the day reconnoitering the place. It was a big cotton farm. His house was right in the middle. I don't even know how he got to his own house, because I drove around fifteen or twenty times, and I couldn't find a road that led to the house. But I finally established that it was the Milam farm and saw the barn.

One night, I made my way there. It was after dark, after supper. I picked out a place to park. Damn near a mile or so from the house. I went to the barn. I had a flashlight with me. I felt the flashlight could serve as a weapon too. It was one of those three battery things, pretty long.

I was scared.

Then I thought, *What if I find this damn thing, and I don't know where the hell the fan is?*

Now, I'm not proud of this. I didn't know what a cotton gin looked like. I did not know the South. I hadn't traveled in the South before I became a roving correspondent. I grew up in Akron, Ohio. I went to school at Akron University and then to Howard. I didn't know *anything* about cotton.

The barn door was open.

One of the things I was afraid of was dogs. Fortunately, no dogs. I went into the barn and looked around. I saw this huge thing. Then I saw a motor.

I said, "This has got to be it."

I looked for the cam shaft, the place where the fan belt fits. And there it was. I had found it.

I got close. I wanted to feel if there was any rifling on it, like when the propeller turns around on an axle. I bent down and put my light on the cam shaft.

Suddenly a light was shining on *me*. I straightened up. I felt this terrible pain race through my head.

Oh my God! Somebody hit me over the head.

"Goddamn," I blurted out. "Jesus, oh, Jesus."

It had happened in one second. But nobody was there.

When I shone my light, it went beyond the cam shaft and hit a broken mirror. The reflection flashed back on me. When I straightened up, my head hit part of the machinery.

I got back to the motel and wrote the story. I said it was nonsense that there was no evidence. I said I had it on good authority that the fan found around the neck of the boy came off the cotton gin at Milam's farm. I had been there and felt the cam shaft. Now the problem was: How did I get the story out?

Thirty-two black papers subscribed to NNPA at the time, such as the *Washington Afro, Atlanta Daily World, Norfolk Journal & Guide, Cleveland Call Post, Pittsburgh Courier*, the *Chicago Defender*. I mailed a copy of my story to each one. So I walked around with my little portable Royal typewriter, with reams of tissue and carbon paper, and stamps.

Ol' Ralph Matthews[52] taught me that if you rub the stamps on the oil of your forehead, they wouldn't stick when you put them in your pocket. I would pound out five copies at a time and mail them off. Or I would send the original on Western Union to Bernard Young, and he would make copies and mail them.

In those days, Western Union was kind of a friend to the reporter across the nation, because you would go in there and write your stories on their beat-up typewriters. You turned it in, and the man sat down and typed it on the wireless. I sent my stories press-wireless collect.

When it came time to file my story, I said, "The White Citizens Council[53] is very popular down here. It was started to fight the Supreme Court decision on school desegregation. A kind of thinking man's Ku Klux Klan."

So I said to this fellow at Western Union, "Everybody talks about this White Citizens Council around here. Does everybody belong to the White Citizens Council?"

He said, "I don't know whether *everybody* belongs to it. But *I* belong to it."

I thought, *Hicks, you gotta be careful. You just can't let anyone in the South see what you are writing. You don't know what to expect.*

But I took a chance. And the Western Union guy sent it just the way I wrote it.

I was stunned.

Two days after I filed the story, I drove from Mound Bayou over to Sumner. I parked where everyone did who covered the trial. When I got out of the car, a wrinkled old man walked up to me as if he had been waiting for me. He had a gun in his hand pointed at me.

"Nigger, you're under arrest."

I thought, *My God, what the hell now?*

"I have a report that you passed a school bus on your way into town."

The school bus again.

I said, "Sir, could you tell me . . . ?"

"No! I won't tell you nothing."

He looked like a dirt farmer if ever you saw one.

"Sir, I haven't even seen anybody on the highway."

"You can tell that to the sheriff. Start walking."

This man was in broad open daylight holding a gun on me. I looked at the gun. It was a .38. His hand started shaking. He had palsy.

I thought, *Yes, it's time to start walking, all right.*

I walked to where he motioned, away from the courthouse, toward the bayou and the warehouses. Some of them had windows. I looked in the glass and saw his hand shaking behind me.

Then, as we turned into a building, I looked back. There were three white reporters following behind. I owed Murray Kempton[54] for this one.

The old man with the gun said, "Sit down."

There was nothing in the room but a table.

Murray Kempton walked in. "What's going on?"

One of the reporters from the local paper came in with Sheriff Strider.

He said, "Sheriff, you are getting ready to give this town the biggest black eye it ever has had."

Somebody else said, "Yeah, Sheriff."

So the sheriff said, "What's going on here? What's wrong?"

The old man said, "This is the one that was driving the car. He broke the law."

The local reporter said, "Sheriff, could we see you in another room for a minute?"

The old man sat there, his hand trembling on the gun.

The reporters and the sheriff came back. With them was a new person.

The new guy sat down at the table and said, "This court is open."

Court again.

"Boy, you are one of them New York reporters that's been writing all them lies in the paper about us decent folks down here. Well, boy, I'm gonna give you a break. When you get back up to New York, you write a story saying that a white man in Mississippi gave you a break. I know you're guilty. But I'm dismissing all the charges against you."

He hadn't even told me what the charges were.

"I want you to go now, boy. Go write that a white man in Mississippi gave you a break."

I said, "Thank you very much, sir."

There was no sense in arguing.

Outside, Murray said the local reporter had told him the sheriff had me arrested because he was going to give me the whipping of my life.

"Jimmy, you're lucky. I'm glad you got out."

"Murray," I said, "I never was so glad to see somebody in my life than when I saw you following me."

I figured then that the White Citizens guy at Western Union had been showing the sheriff every bit of my copy.

When the story about the cotton gin on Milam's farm got to Washington, Betty Phillips was on the desk at the *Afro-American* papers. She contacted the National Council of Negro Women. And they took the story straight to J. Edgar Hoover.

Then I got word from an FBI guy who was on the case down there—a white guy. He said he had a message from his chief that I had some evidence that should be turned over to him. I was in Mississippi. This guy was a native-born Mississippian. And the son of a bitch lived down there!

I said to myself, *I'm not telling him a thing.* Besides, it had already been in print.

When Congressman Diggs left, a tense moment came up at the trial. Milam's wife was scheduled to testify. All the blacks in Mound Bayou told me not to go that day. "If that woman testifies that this black kid put his hands on her, they're going to break up the courtroom and probably kill somebody."

I talked it over with Murray, and told him, "I'm covering."

Booker said he was covering. Clotylde said she was, too. All the black reporters and photographers. But we had to formulate a plan in case anything happened. The first thing we would do was to get Clo out. When something started, I would go for the .45 dangling from the deputy's holster.

I told Jackson to get Clo to the window and hold her as far out as he could, then let her drop. It wasn't too high.

When Milam's wife testified, nothing happened. No emotion. Nothing.

The really startling testimony came later when Emmett Till's granduncle, Mose Wright, testified. Medgar Evers was really worried. He was an NAACP field secretary.

The day Uncle Mose testified, Medgar said, he would have to get out of town. Black people did not stand up in public and accuse white people in those days. Not in Mississippi. And he had already pointed his finger at J. W. Milam.

Medgar said, "I can't take him out of town, because they're gonna be watching me. And if he stays here, they're gonna lynch him."

I said, "What are we going to do?"

"I've got a plan if you're game for it," Medgar said. "You want to help?"

"All right. What do I do?"

"We've got to get Mose to Memphis. But everybody knows my car. I'm going to head south. Then I'll go east. Then I'll head north. I want to meet you and Mose in a pecan grove. I'll give you the directions. Then I'll transfer him to my car."

So I was to drive Uncle Mose to the pecan grove and wait.

The day came. The prosecutor asked Mose what happened when Milam and Bryant came to his house. He told the court how they demanded the boy and took him away. Then he was asked if he could identify the men who took the boy away.

The prosecutor said, "Look around, Uncle. Do you see any of the men who came to your house that night?"

Everybody hung on that moment.

The old man got up.

This is it! I thought.

A black person standing up to testify against white people in Mississippi!

"Thar he!"

He didn't say, "There he is."

"Thar he."

He pointed at Milam.

A ripple rumble went through the courtroom.

I whispered, "Oh my God."

I could feel my heart pounding.

I didn't walk out with Uncle Mose. I met him at a little black restaurant down by the bayou. He got into my car. I took off.

Goddamn, I thought, *I've got the hottest thing in Mississippi in my car.*

Uncle Mose knew exactly the place where Medgar was talking about. The pecan grove. It seemed like an eternity getting there. And I didn't see a car or anything else in the dark. All of a sudden, I saw a blinking light.

I said, "Damn, is that you, Medgar?"

He was there.

It was an air-tight case. Another witness saw Emmett Till in Milam's pickup. Somebody else saw the truck outside the barn and heard somebody shouting, then saw Milam with a pistol.

It took the jury one hour and seven minutes to come up with a verdict.

Not Guilty. September 23, 1955.

Look magazine ran a story later saying the killers said they killed Emmett Till because he didn't repent or beg for mercy. Milam and Bryant received $4,000 for this story.

Uncle Mose got to Chicago. Safe.

I can hear him now.

Thar he!

Bill Raspberry came through the back door of the Washington Post *as a teletype operator and worked his way into a job as a reporter. He became a nationally-syndicated columnist.*

———

I'd come to Washington initially because I had been drafted into the army out of Indianapolis. I had worked four years as a reporter, editor, photographer, and social critic for the *Indianapolis Recorder*, a black weekly. I had learned enough to know that I wanted to make journalism a career.

I was stationed in Washington for two years with the army, attached to its exhibit unit, which included artists, photographers, and a small group of publicists. I was one of the publicists who did radio and TV spots, and press releases.

I was reading the *Washington Post*, and I decided I'd really like to be a reporter on the paper. But my inquiries convinced me that although I'd worked four years for the *Recorder*, I had zero experience as far as the *Post* was concerned. I started looking for a way to get in the newsroom. I was confident that if I could make it into the *Post*'s newsroom, I could arrange to get myself discovered and become a reporter.

I called a friend and he said the *Post* was looking for teletype operators. I figured that would be a way to get inside. This was 1962, the year that the *Post* and the *L.A. Times* were starting their news service. I managed to get a look at a teletype machine, which was my first look, really, at any teletype machine. I saw that that the keyboard was the same as a typewriter keyboard. So I went to the personnel department at the *Post* and told them I was a teletype operator.

I was hired. By the time they found that I *wasn't* a teletype operator, I *was* a teletype operator.

Then I found a sponsor or, rather, a sponsor and I found each other. John Paul was an assistant managing editor. He had some free time, and he took an interest in me. He quickly learned that I didn't want to make a career as a teletype operator. I wanted to be a reporter. He smoothed things out so that it could happen. I was hired on the *Post* in August, and before the year was out, they told me to report to the city desk, prepared to do obits.

Six of us came on at the same time as reporters. The other five were white. I started looking for ways to separate myself from the rest so I could get a career going. I wanted a way to make myself indispensable to the editor in charge.

I was without any special skills or unusual knowledge. I thought I was a pretty good reporter and writer. But I had nothing that I could bank on as an expertise.

Then it occurred to me: *Gee, who am I? I'm black. I've got a lot of experience at being that. What can I do with it?*

The *Washington Post* covered the national civil rights movement, and had a couple of reporters on that beat. But there was a lot of civil rights activity going on in and around Washington, which was handled by the general assignment desk. Whoever was free that day was assigned to the story—to that demonstration or to that picket line.

I began asking for as many of those assignments as I could get. On my days off, I went to meetings of CORE[55] and SNCC[56] and the NAACP and the Urban League[57]—all the black organizations that were making news. I accumulated the home telephone numbers of the organizations' leaders.

Pretty soon, if Ben Gilbert, the city editor, wanted to know what was going on with any of the black groups, he'd ask me. I made it my specialty. I was never formally assigned to that beat. But it became mine.

In the 1960s Black Muslims gained fame, and the Black Power Movement developed into something nationally known. The blacks often barred white reporters from attending their meetings. So under those circumstances a black reporter had to ponder whether he was there as a reporter for his newspaper or as a public relations agent for the black groups he covered. It wasn't easy to sort that out.

At my first Muslim meeting I sat there trying to look inconspicuous. Malcolm X announced: "There are spies for the white man in this audience, and we know who they are."

That did make me feel like a spy for the white man, which is how Malcolm intended I should feel. And yet I knew that I had to go back to the *Washington Post* and write a story about what happened at the meeting. I couldn't go back and tell my editor, "Look, I'm not going to be a spy."

You had to make some serious decisions when you came into the business. But you got no help in sorting things out. You couldn't talk to a white city editor about this. And there was no black elder statesman who had been through some earlier wars and who could say, "Hey, brother, this is how it is." We had to develop a sense of professionalism and learn to sort out what was real and what wasn't by ourselves.

For a while I found myself wanting to write things a certain way and to ignore other things. Sometimes I got tossed out of black militant meetings. It dawned on me that if you played the public relations game, your editors would have no confidence in you—and you were dead as a journalist. But if you chose to play the PR game, you didn't even serve the cause of the black people you covered, except for maybe a day or two. Then you were no longer of any use to them.

I had to develop a rational way of dealing with this dilemma. I realized that black people had suffered not so much from not having public relations agents, but from having too little truth told about us. More than anything, we were victims of distortions by the white media.

I realized there was a value to having a black reporter whose background and ethnicity created a certain level of sensitivity and sympathy. It was necessary that such a person tell the truth, as he could determine it, about what was going on in black America. When I reached that understanding, I began to sort things out. And it sensitized me to the point that I talked as much as I could to younger blacks as they came into the business, especially during the riot years. I was sensitive to the mixed emotions they were undergoing and about problems they couldn't talk about to their white editors. They were a little embarrassed even to talk to each other about these things. They had a strong feeling of "Have I sold out?"

You began to ask yourself whether you were in the position of a slave being present when a runaway was brought back and whipped. Or when somebody planned an uprising or a slave revolt and you were there. Were you the slave who would go back and tell the master?

You certainly didn't want to be in that position. Neither did you want to be in the position of pretending to work for a white employer when, in fact, you were working for the black movement.

In general, white editors were not sensitive to what black reporters were going through. White reporters had no need to sort out that kind of thing. So it didn't occur to white editors that I had any problems. And I never felt there was anybody I could talk to about these things. I always had to work them out on my own. And I was very uncomfortable for a time.

A reporter had started a local column of commentary on District of Columbia affairs. But he got tired of the column and wanted to cover the Hill. So Ben Gilbert, the city editor, approached me and asked if I'd be interested in taking it over. I was to write four columns a week on local affairs.

My first response was "no." I said, "I have three or four column ideas and I can sustain the thing for maybe a week or two. But after that, what do I do for ideas?"

The *Post* talked me into it. They said they liked the way I wrote. And all of us on the staff would generate ideas. I don't think I got an idea from any of them after that. But after I exhausted my original half dozen ideas, it didn't take long before people who read the column came up with their own ideas. In those days, we ran the writer's picture with the column.

When black Washingtonians, who always thought of the *Post* as a horrible institution to which they had no access, saw this black picture in the paper, they said, "Maybe we've got a door to this powerful organization." So for anything that concerned them, that bothered them, that excited them, I became their entrée to the *Post*. As a result, my problem became one of having to sort and sift through ideas to find which four I was going to use in a given week.

Some black Washingtonians were angry about something they had seen in the paper. Or they were dismayed because something didn't get covered. They knew I didn't have any influence over these things, but they still called me just to ventilate.

My column was syndicated throughout the United States in 1976. It drew about a hundred and fifty clients. Under the arrangement, there was not much I could do about whether a particular column got printed. I was paid for writing it. But if the *Post* or any of other newspaper didn't want to run a particular piece, it was beyond my power to do anything about it.

Yet I never had a problem writing a column that disagreed, even completely, with the *Post*'s stated editorial position. They took the attitude that my stuff appeared under my byline, and they didn't have to take responsibility for it.

I don't think I ever had a column killed for opposing their editorial line. I had a couple of columns killed for questions of taste. I wrote a column once in which I took Jerry Ford to task for being on the lecture circuit while his wife was going through a period of alcoholism. She was in the hospital, and he had refused to cancel an engagement to come home to be with her. This was after he was no longer president. The editors told me they thought my column was unfair to Ford, and they killed it. Ultimately, I thought their decision was correct.

Once I came very close to a gaffe. This was during the Nixon administration. One morning I got three calls from people I didn't know—wives of African ambassadors. Nixon had had a dinner the night before at the White House for African ambassadors and their spouses. The occasion seemed to have gone reasonably well.

But one of the wines the White House served created a controversy. It was a Schloss Johannisberger. The wives said that this couldn't be accidental. The president had invited black African diplomats and their wives to dinner at the White House, and then served them a South African wine. In their view, it had to be a calculated insult.

I made further calls and found there had been a general buzzing within the African diplomatic community about the incident. They were quietly outraged, but being diplomats, they didn't want to make a public protest. And I got somebody to give me a copy of the menu to confirm their charge.

I typed the lead of my column to suggest that this was beyond sensitivity and had approached the realm of a deliberate insult. Then I got a flash. I called a friend of mine who runs a liquor store, and said, "Schloss Johannisberger. Where does it come from?"

He said, "Gee, I don't know, but I'll look it up." He came back to the phone a few minutes later and said, "Oh, yeah, I found it. That's a German wine."

The story, of course, evaporated. I guess every reporter in the business can tell you about the story that evaporated because he made one phone call too many. But if I had published that story and then discovered that the premise was wrong, I could have apologized for getting the wine's country of origin wrong—but how could I have apologized for the assault on Nixon?

You can't undo such things. And you can't simply say that you regret the error, because your reputation is tied too much to what you write. That happened more in a column, I think, than in a news story. If it was in a news story, you could apologize for the mistake and that was the end of it. But if you built a column on something that turned out to be nonfactual, you had really put yourself out on a limb.

The first memorable phone call I got from writing columns came from Hubert Humphrey, the vice president. He said he liked something I had written about a youth training program. I was terribly impressed that this busy man, who held the second-highest office in the land, was actually on the phone when I picked up the receiver.

President Reagan also took to phoning me. I'd come very close to calling him a racist for his behavior in the Bob Jones University matter.[58] I thought he had bought into something that had no legal justification, not even any philosophical justification. The university wanted a tax exemption as a Christian institution and wanted to be able to discriminate at the same time. Reagan wished to do these bad people a favor.

President Reagan called and said, "I saw your piece and I'd just like to say a few words on my behalf." He proceeded to give an account, which turned out not to be completely accurate, about how this controversy had come about. But I was impressed, I must admit, by the fact that he wanted to speak to one journalist.

It also showed a psychological shrewdness. Because the fact was, no matter how profoundly I disagreed with Reagan, if I wrote a column that hit him hard and then he phoned me, I couldn't savage him for at least two weeks. I just couldn't. That was the president of the United States! If he called, I had an automatic deference. I had to respect that office.

The toughest columns that I had to write dealt with Israel and the Middle East. I once wrote a series of columns essentially saying that while it made sense for the U.S. to support the policy of providing security for Israel within internationally recognized borders, it also made sense to note the fact that Palestinians were homeless, and that America's Israeli policy was flawed if it didn't take into account the legitimate aspirations of Palestinians as well.

My position differed from that of Israel. So I was branded as anti-Semitic. Letters were sent to the editor about this, and telephone calls were made to me, which included obscenities. There were calls from the Jewish community, and I was excoriated at one synagogue.

The rabbi said in his newsletter that I had praised Yassir Arafat[59] for killing Jews. This was a deliberate and, I thought, quite vicious distortion of the column I had written. I wrote another column accusing him of distortion. The men's group at the synagogue invited me to talk to them about it. We parted, maybe not quite seeing eye to eye, but at least respecting one another.

If you wrote anything other than the official party line with regard to Israel and the Middle East, you expected to come to work and face a morning's worth of outraged telephone calls. Then came scores of outraged letters. It followed almost like clockwork. The idea was that this would prevent you from writing about the subject ever again. And I think, not just me, but almost everybody who did this kind of writing, went through the same thing.

We'd like to say it had no effect on our journalistic effort. But in fact it did. You wanted to walk away from it because you didn't want this stuff coming at you. Nobody liked to be browbeaten that way.

How did we keep doing it? Most people in this business write about these things when circumstances get so bad that one feels one has to write about them. I believed that I didn't have any choice. It was important to readers of the column. It was important to the policy formulations of the U.S. It was important on every level I could imagine. And it never occurred to me that I had a choice about saying things that I felt strongly about.

I didn't escape criticism in the black community, either. Shortly after I started writing the column, the *Afro-American*, the leading black newspaper in town at the time, took after me. Chuck Stone, I think, was the editor. Chuck used to go after me quite a bit in those days.

A group of black kids had gone out to Glen Echo amusement park. It was the Easter break from school. The management had oversold tickets, and suddenly they closed the park to further entries. The bus drivers panicked and left.

The kids came back through town on foot, breaking windows, throwing things, assaulting people. This was before the riot season in the mid-Sixties had started. So it seemed very major. Looking back now, it seems insignificant, although a lot of people were scared silly because they weren't used to seeing black kids over in that part of town.

I condemned the management of the park for starting the commotion. I also condemned the kids for their behavior, and black Washingtonians for not being angry at what the kids had done. I called it disgraceful and inexcusable. And the *Afro-American* gave me hell for criticizing blacks.

I certainly wasn't going to apologize for anything I wrote. I was determined to stand tough. But still, you tossed and turned at night wondering, *Did I blow it? Have I done the number? Which side are you on?*

It was a dilemma not uncommon to that period. We were only a handful of black journalists in the business, working for white newspapers. And we didn't talk at lot about it even among ourselves.

The results of a columnist's work, the impact, the influence, were mostly imperceptible. You'd like to think that if you addressed the controversies of the day, analyzed them and wrote about them in the way that made sense to people, then you could move people in the direction you thought was correct. But the movement was infinitesimal. You couldn't photograph the results and call home to mom and say, "Look, I was able to move the world yesterday."

As it turned out, my columns that had the most obvious and most measurable results tended to be the less significant columns— things that were important only to individuals. For instance, I wrote columns that resulted in getting somebody out of jail who shouldn't have been there.

But my work did not affect the criminal justice system in any significant way. It didn't make the system fairer to poor blacks than it was before. When you effected philosophical change, change that permeated the system, it tended to be glacial change. You might get some key members of Congress to view things a little differ- ently, and this might seem more significant, but it was much less measurable.

A young man named Eddie Harrison had been convicted of a murder that he said was an accident. Harrison was a kid from the ghetto, a street hustler. He said he'd gone to a big-time racketeer to hock a gun. The racketeer saw the gun, panicked, and slammed the door in Harrison's face, and the gun went off.

Actually, whether it happened that way or not was irrelevant, because I discovered that everybody who came into contact with Harrison in the prison, from the warden to the guards, to his fellow inmates and the parole court—everybody who saw him and spent five minutes with him—was impressed that this was a man who could make a contribution to life. He had undergone a remarkable transformation while in prison.

At the time I came across Harrison, he was already out of prison. He was on parole from a life sentence. He was working. In fact, he was doing some work at the antipoverty agency in Washington. Partly through my efforts—a series of columns—he managed to obtain a presidential pardon from Nixon. And it had a very positive effect on his life. Harrison ran a youth program out of Baltimore.

Then there was the case of George Smith. He was out on parole for some crime, and got picked up by police for another crime that he couldn't have committed. He had started a family. He was making a delivery for somebody at the time he was picked up. So it was physically impossible for him to have done the thing that he was accused of.

He tried to tell the judge that at his arraignment. All they had to do was make a phone call to his boss. It would prove that this crime couldn't possibly have been done by him. But nobody would make the phone call.

Here he was, knowing that if he got convicted, he not only would have to do the time for this crime, but he'd also have to go back to do the time remaining on his unserved sentence. And he was sitting in a courtroom with a judge who wouldn't listen. Finally, he got so frustrated that he threw the microphone and turned away.

The judge accused George Smith of throwing the microphone at *him* and charged him with assault and destroying government property. And there it was—his life down the drain.

I wrote a couple of columns about him, explaining the situation, explaining the nature of his frustration, and explaining how he had managed to get his life together after having already done some time. His record was clean up to then. I said that if the problem was the destruction of government property—i.e., the microphone—they should send me the bill, and I would pay the damn thing myself!

The judge read the columns and decided that there was no point in prosecuting those charges. And Smith went home.

A police chief in Prince George's County in Maryland made a promise that D.C. crime wasn't going to flow across Southern Avenue into his county. At the time, in the late Sixties, the police force in Prince George's was overwhelmingly white. I don't know whether the chief articulated his attitude to his men at roll call. But clearly he believed that it was okay to do what was necessary to send the signal to D.C. criminals that they'd better confine their criminality to D.C.

The police not only intimidated and harassed, even brutalized young blacks, they also did the same thing to young whites with long hair, which was anathema in those days. So black motorists would be stopped for minor traffic violations and wind up being beaten and hospitalized, their cars impounded, their lives disrupted. And the incident would wind up in a major confrontation that was so pointless.

I wrote a series of columns exposing these things after talking to both the victims and the officers involved. Everybody in Southeast Washington knew about the PG cops. And yet, the fact that they knew didn't mean that Washington knew. My columns came as a revelation to the white readers of the *Washington Post*. And some of those white readers had influence on the way things happened in the county.

Still, the day didn't arrive when the PG cops said Bill Raspberry has caught us, and therefore we're going to reform. The change was much more gradual. But it happened in ways that were perceivable, and it did leave me with a feeling that some good had been accomplished by my work.

My columns were about people who had never had access to something like the *Washington Post*, who never had had any organization of that size take seriously their complaints. They were always wrong. And in any confrontation with the authorities, nobody ever took their word for anything. When they went to court, it was them against a duly sworn police officer who was white. And the judge looked at the two of them and his decision was obvious. In every confrontation, they were unable to find anybody who would give credit to their statements, to believe them, to see them as creditable people.

It was interesting to watch how their attitudes changed when they felt that at least here was somebody who would listen. "He may ask hard questions, and he may try to shoot down the things I'm saying, but at least there is the impression that somebody is finally paying attention to what we're complaining about."

You are always struck with the question of what your proper role should be. It was not like covering the news from day to day. There was a sense in the Sixties that something revolutionary was going on, and you didn't want to be an antirevolutionary. At first I wasn't comfortable with my ability to judge these things. I didn't think I'd seen enough or experienced enough. It took me a while to develop confidence.

I started feeling comfortable, I think, when the feedback from— not from white people but from the black community—came back in positive ways saying, "That looks good, you're right." Even when they disagreed, they credited me with being honest. So it was mostly positive feedback from blacks that made my life bearable.

Yet I thought it was a mistake for me to set out to deliver a black perspective. I believed that if I delivered Bill Raspberry's perspective, it would inevitably be black. It might not be *the* black perspective, although some readers took my views as *the* views of the black people of America. I discovered that sometimes they were, and sometimes they weren't.

All of my life I have been an integrationist. Growing up in Mississippi made me that way. I came up in a small town called Okolona, which was seven miles from Tupelo. I saw what segregation did to us. But later I didn't always agree with the conventional black wisdom about how to achieve integration.

The black conventional wisdom held that school busing was the best means to achieve integration. Black leadership was hot for busing. But it occurred to me some years after the *Brown* decision that we were spending a lot of time trying to get our black kids into school rooms with white kids. And not nearly enough time overseeing what happened to our black kids in the schools where they already were. I watched what happened to our children, and saw that their conditions were not improved greatly by merely having them in classrooms with white kids.

Let's assume that the reason the schools were segregated was because white people didn't love our kids. If we forced our kids on white people, were they going to begin to love them? And did loving our kids have anything to do with what happened to them academically? If not, that was not likely to improve conditions for them.

Some of our children could, in spite of not being loved, handle an integrated situation, if they had the kind of support systems they needed at home and elsewhere. I was forever in admiration of such groups as the Little Rock Nine,[60] for instance, who integrated Arkansas schools in the face of a mob. Those kids paid some heavy, heavy dues. I can't see how they could have concentrated on academics. But they saw themselves not really as students going for an education but as people changing a society.

It seemed to me that the reason our children were getting an inferior education before busing was not that there were too many black kids in the classroom with them. There were other reasons. And if the fact that their classmates were black was not the problem, then getting them white classmates wasn't the solution, either.

We went through a period when we looked for easy solutions to difficult problems.

The NAACP's reaction to me was understandably negative. Busing was a major aspect of their program. What surprised and pleased me was that the great unaffiliated said, "I'm so glad you said that because it's exactly what I've always felt."

Then I started talking to people who had been parties to some of the lawsuits that resulted in busing. I was even more surprised by what I heard. What concerned them most was the fact that white kids in predominantly white schools had facilities and equipment that their kids didn't enjoy.

They said, "Our kids don't have a water cooler. Their kids have air-conditioned classrooms. We want our school drastically improved. We don't want our kids bused over to their schools because the white school will take away their social life. My daughter wants to be homecoming queen, she wants to be cheerleader, she wants to be all these things, and she's not going to be that in the white school."

But when they took their complaints—which were legitimate, quite specific complaints—about the disparities and the treatment of their children to the black organizations, it wound up as a busing case in the courts.

That wasn't necessarily what the parents wanted. They went along with it because they were told that was how it had to be done. And they couldn't easily argue for segregation. They were just looking for what would be best for their children, their children's best educational chance, and their children's happiness. It was the same thing all parents look for, regardless of race or color.

I don't recall one incident being more painful than another growing up in Mississippi. I suppose the most painful memory was just the general feeling of being cheated. You knew this wasn't right. But I don't want to give the impression that I grew up brooding about this. I was more specifically aware of segregation in Indianapolis, where I moved after I left Mississippi, than I was in Mississippi.

The reason was that in Indianapolis, in the mid-Fifties, I was never sure whether I could eat in a certain restaurant or not. I didn't find out until I went. I presented myself and then was told "no." And that was very unsettling.

In Mississippi, there was no place for me to present myself. Segregation was so thorough. There was a black school, and there was a white school. We had our school, and we had a principal. The white kids had their school and their principal. Their principal was our superintendent. We got textbooks after the white kids had been through them for a year or two. We even got used basketballs from the white school. And I looked at our little school and thought that the white school was the size of what I imagined UCLA to be.

I wondered what it would be like to go to the white school, because I just knew that wonderful things were happening for these white kids. I thought I could hold my own with them, but I wasn't quite sure.

As it happened, a few years ago I was invited back to Okolona to make a commencement address at what had been the white school. The school system was completely integrated. There was a single high school for everyone.

They honored ten Okolonians who had done well—five blacks and five whites. Only one athlete was among the five blacks invited back, a professional basketball player. The blacks also included the superintendent of the schools of Lansing, Michigan—and me, a newspaper columnist.

But all five of the whites honored were athletes. I thought that was nice, that it sort of said something.

When I spoke, I spoke as a black man, as an American, as an individual—as all of these things, just as I do when I write my column. Questions as to whether one is a journalist first, or a black first, or any of these things first, amuse me. You're everything simultaneously.

There is no time when I become a black man rather than a father. I'm both. I'm also an American, and I react to things as an American.

I discovered early on that while one can identify with and perhaps have some special sensitivities to the Third World and to Africa, you only need to spend a week in Africa to know that you are an American. It is so overwhelmingly clear that your assumptions, your values, your ideals, that all these things are thoroughly shaped by the fact that you have grown up in America, even an America that needs serious perfecting.

I'm not more a journalist than I am a black. I'm not more a black than I am a journalist. I'm not more a husband than I am a father. I'm not more of a human being looking at a nuclear threat than I am a person who's worried about his income taxes. And I find that what works for me is to not even try to make the effort to separate them out.

It's Bill Raspberry talking. And Bill Raspberry is all of these things, and they are not detachable. They are one.

HENRY M. "HANK" BROWN

ABC cameraman Hank Brown was the first journalist on the air with film of the attempted assassination of President Ronald Reagan.

———

I was a cameraman for an ABC crew that had often covered President Reagan. We noticed that the crowds were getting larger wherever he went. He was drawing closer to the people. So we thought we needed to stake out a position at the Capital Hilton in Washington earlier than usual, because we would have to film with a big crowd in the way.

To create fewer problems, we usually didn't tell the crowds who we were actually waiting for. We tried to throw them off the scent. In this case we said, "Bo Derek." Everyone started looking around for Bo, giggling.

"You're not really waiting for Bo Derek," they said.

"Sure," I said, "she's going to come walking down those steps there and we'll interview her."

So we had them looking for Bo Derek.

I had been shooting out of the Washington bureau of ABC since 1978. But this was only my second week as an official hire for the network, and my assignment was to cover President Reagan's arrival and departure from the Hilton on March 30, 1981. He was scheduled to speak to a session of the AFL-CIO's[61] building and construction trades department. Upwards of thirty-five hundred union representatives would be in the hotel's International Ballroom, Reagan's biggest audience since his inauguration.

The day before the Hilton assignment, Max Robinson asked me to serve as his cameraman on a mining accident story in West

Virginia. At 7:00 that morning we were at National Airport unloading twenty-one cases of gear. A red cap had the dolly and was putting the gear on the conveyor belt to send it to the airplane.

Then suddenly the West Virginia trip was canceled. It was decided by headquarters that we should do it at another time. So we got all the gear back and went off to do the assignment we were originally supposed to do—cover President Reagan.

On the way to the Hilton, we stopped at the Treasury Department to film a story on a new penny being minted with less copper in it. It was raining off and on by the time we got to the hotel. The street was puddled with water. But it was a balmy day with temperatures in the mid-70s.

When we arrived at the hotel, we found cameramen from NBC and CBS and other networks in the lobby. Secret service agents began arriving, then the police. They went to the lower-level VIP entrance on T Street, which had a concrete canopy and a steel double door. The entrance opened onto a sidewalk about twelve feet wide, which ran along a curving retainer wall.

I asked the secret service agents if this was where they were going to set up the press line. One agent shrugged noncommittally, but a policeman said, "Yeah, that's it." They roped off the area about twenty-five feet from the doors, along the curving walkway.

I ran to get my camera and told my partner, Harry Weldon, the soundman, that we would set up on the walkway—get a good position before any of the other cameramen came outside. I was using the Ikegami HL79, a minicam that weighed about thirty-five pounds.

When I returned to the lobby, I told the other cameramen where they were setting up the press line. So everybody else followed me outside. Then spectators who wanted to see the president followed the cameras.

People said, "You're waiting for the president, aren't you?"

"Yes," I said. "But this is a press line. We have to work here."

By then there were thirty to forty spectators with us, and I thought, *I'm not going to be able to work*. I tried to get the police's attention, then the secret service's attention. A policeman looked at a secret service agent, waiting for instructions, and the agent said, "Move all the people."

The policeman moved the people out of the street and onto the sidewalk, which made everything even tighter. One kid wanted to take a picture right under me! "His head will hit my camera," I said. So a policeman moved the kid. But people were crowded all around me. One lady, wearing a white and blue polka dot dress, was standing between our cables. We were trying to get her to move.

"There's a real problem here," I said to one of the secret service agents. "It's getting too crowded. They really can't be here. We have to work."

The crowd said, "We have a right to be here just as well as you do."

"That's true in one sense but maybe not true in another," I said. "This is really a press line. And a press line is basically for the White House press."

Dozens of reporters and cameramen had arrived on the scene. Some of the reporters figured they might get a comment from Reagan on the situation in Poland.[62] Some of them wanted to record what he would say to the union. Others were there on the "body watch," in the event the unthinkable might happen.

Shortly before 2:00 the president arrived. I got a shot of him getting out of the armor-plated black limo, which the secret service called "Stagecoach." "Rawhide" was the president's code name. I got a picture of him going inside. Then I rushed to shoot the cut-aways. When I went inside, I spotted one of the White House advance men I knew.

"We've got a problem," I said. "There are too many people out-side. We've got a press line set up, and the spectators are intermixed with the press people. The police and the secret service have got us all bunched together. It's not only hampering me from taking pic-tures, it's also got to be a security problem for you guys."

Then I said, "If anything was to happen, those people would get hurt. We are here in case something happens, that's part of our job. But these people shouldn't be there."

"I want you to say exactly what you said to me to the head secret service agent as soon as I can get to him," he said. "We'll see if we can get this corrected."

He couldn't find the head agent in charge. I went inside the ballroom to talk to Sam Donaldson, our White House correspondent. I asked Sam if he wanted any particular shots of anybody. He told me to hang in there for a while because the president might say something. Or Sam might ask him something on the way out.

"I'll have to stay outside," I said.

"Okay. I'll run outside and hold the position for you," Sam said.

So I took the cutaways, which were pictures of the president speaking, pictures of people applauding.

The president prepared to leave. I rushed outside, Harry and me, so we could get a shot of him coming out the door. They escorted the president through a carpeted corridor, about a hundred yards to the VIP exit.

When we got outside I saw about ninety people in that one area where we were before.

"Oh, my God!" I said. "How am I going to get through all this?" I started going, "'Scuse me. 'Scuse me. National press! National press!"

I was trying desperately to push through the crowd. I thought I might have to climb over the wall and squeeze in from there. But then I saw Sam Donaldson, and Sam saw me.

"Come here!" Sam yelled. "Come here!"

I squeezed in front of Sam. Then he squeezed out, and I squeezed in.

"Harry," I yelled. "Over here!"

Harry squeezed in, and we had our position. It was still tight. People were shoving and pushing, saying they wanted to get a photo of the president, saying they had a right to take a picture of him, too.

Five minutes had passed since I got into position.

I saw the agents moving. He was getting ready to come out.

I started filming immediately because I wanted a shot of him walking out the door. I was rolling in case somebody like Sam yelled him a question, or in case something did happen.

As the president came out, I zoomed into him. He flashed a smile and moved toward the car. He raised his right hand to wave at the people across the driveway.

I was on his left, to the right of the door. I widened out with the camera.

Shots rang out. Pop! Pop! Pop! Pop! Pop! Five shots from a .22-caliber pistol. In less than two seconds, they said.

I saw bodies going down in front of me. People were screaming and hollering. Agents ran toward me, carrying pistols. Police everywhere!

I'm going down. I'm down on my knees.

Jim Brady, the presidential press secretary, was right in front of me, three feet away. I saw him go down. Blood came up in front of the lens. Somebody had fired a gun, and I followed it to Brady's head.

I was still filming down on my knees. A police officer jumped over me and my camera. I turned in that direction. There was a young man in a tan raincoat. He stood two people away from me toward the president. Between him and me were a cameraman and Walter Rodgers, the AP radioman. The young man was John Hinckley Jr., the would-be assassin.

The police officer who jumped over me came down on Hinckley and engulfed him.

I stood up and kept filming.

The agents kept coming, pulling out Uzi submachine guns, trying to get the weapons off safety. One of them jammed. The agent had actually jammed the weapon trying to get it into operation.

My mind was working incredibly fast. And everything I saw was unbelievable.

The president had been shot.

An agent, Timothy McCarthy, was hit in the stomach. Thomas Delahanty, a D.C. policeman, was shot in the shoulder and neck. A bullet had penetrated Jim Brady's brain.

I moved back, thinking, *Oh, God. I'm scared. I'm going to be caught in the middle of a crossfire.*

I didn't know it was just Hinckley. It could have been other people attempting the assassination, too. I thought it was more than one person. I saw guns coming at us left and right.

I backed up and continued to film. Finally they got control of Hinckley and were trying to get control of the crowd.

"This has got to get on the air!" I said.

I yelled to my soundman, "Harry! Harry!"

He had forgotten that he had the radio.

"Radio in! Radio in!"

He was stunned, but he radioed very quickly. I was still filming.

"Tell ABC shots have been fired," I said. "Shots have been fired at the president! We don't know if he's been hit. People are down. People are hurt. That's all we can say right now. We'll get back to them."

Sirens came from left and right. People struggled to get out of the way. I said, "We need a courier here instantly." I remembered that Larry, the courier, was across the street on his motorbike.

Everything was chaos. I had to get it to him!

I shoved the tape to our lighting guy, Oscar Haynes. "Get this over to Larry."

He gave Larry the tape. Larry was kind of stunned. I yelled at him, "Get your little fat ass out of here now before I kick your butt!"

Larry got on the bike and took off.

"Wow!" I said, "I got the tape out! I got the tape out!"

The ABC bureau was about eight blocks away. Just after 2:30, our anchorman, Frank Reynolds, went on the air with the tape. He said into the monitor, "You and I are going to look at this for the first time."

I had the first film on the air.

The other cameramen had gotten so upset that they went inside the hotel to sit down and calm themselves. I saw that two more ABC crews had arrived. That put me more at ease. I started shooting a second tape, pinpointing my shots. I figured they might need people in the crowd for witnesses.

Then Sam came up to me.

"Where's the cassette?" he said. "Got to get it back! Got to get it back!"

I said, "Sam, it's gone."

"It's gone?"

Sam was stunned.

"You mean it's gone?"

"Back at the bureau."

"Fine. Terrific!"

And he ran off to keep reporting.

Then suddenly there seemed to be hundreds of photographers on the scene. They were pointing at me, pointing hundreds of mikes at me. I was trying to film, and they wanted me to talk to them.

Sam came back and said, "It's okay. Just go ahead and talk. Tell them what you saw."

I told my story. I said that I had complained about there being a security risk. Then I stopped talking.

"I have to keep working," I said.

A detective from the homicide squad asked me to come inside the hotel. They wanted me. They wanted my camera. They wanted the tape. They wanted it now!

I told them I couldn't give it to them right now, even though I had shipped the first tape long ago. The guy didn't know what to do. So he left, and the FBI came.

This FBI agent said, "You're coming with us now."

I handed my camera to my partner who was across the ropes.

"I don't have a camera. I don't have a tape."

"That's all right," the agent said. "We got you!"

They took me downstairs to a little VIP area, where they were questioning other witnesses.

"I'm sorry," the agent said. "But I'm taking you into custody."

They asked me my name, address, phone number and what I saw. Then an agent drove me to a building on First Street in Southwest Washington that I didn't know existed. He drove into a garage and escorted me upstairs.

He said to the others as we walked in, "This is not the guy. He's a witness. He's okay."

He told me to sit down, to relax, take a break.

"Can I get you some coffee? Anything to drink?"

He calmed me down.

"How old are you?"

"Thirty-two."

"Do you have a family?"

I told him.

"What did you do yesterday?"

I told him.

He was trying to build up my memory from beginning to end.

"What did you eat for breakfast this morning?"

"My usual. Egg and cheese omelet."

Then I told him everything from the hassle over getting our gear back from the airplane at National to the shooting. I told him the whole story.

He said, "You actually warned somebody about there being a security problem?"

"Yes."

He read back my statement. Then he gave me a ride to the ABC bureau. I told him I didn't want to be dropped off in front because there might be reporters trying to intercept me.

"I can understand that. Where then?"

I showed him the back entrance.

The ABC bureau was trying to find out where I was. They had lost me during this time.

When I came in, one of the assistant news directors said, "Hank, they want you now."

"No, they don't. I need to get myself a drink!"

"No, Hank. They want you now."

So I went upstairs to the assignment desk.

On the way, the public relations director grabbed me. "We've got hundreds, thousands, of calls. People want to interview you!"

"First, let me talk to the people on the desk."

I walked in, and the desk editor for assignments said, "Hank, it's fantastic. Everything you shot is beautiful. We're knocking everybody dead. We got phone calls from everybody in New York congratulating you."

"Can I go home?"

"I don't think they want you to go home. Frank Reynolds and Ted Koppel want to talk to you. For the air."

"Do I really have to?"

"We can't force you."

They put a little makeup on me to try to stop me from perspiring. And I went on the air. Ted and Frank interviewed me. Then Joe Templeton interviewed me live nationwide.

"You're a very brave man," he said. "We're very proud of you, that you were able to stand up there and take those pictures, so that the American people would know what happened."

People who looked at the tape told me how incredibly close I was to the shooting. "You could have been killed," one of the directors said.

"What are you talking about?"

He slowed the tape down. You could see Jim Brady get hit. Suddenly, blood appeared across the lens. I started trembling. I had to take a breather. I was tired. I lay down on a sofa. Then I decided I had to have something to eat and drink. I went over to the Greenery, hoping no one would recognize me. They did.

Somebody said, "Hank, that's really great."

I had a bite and a drink, then struggled back to the bureau. I had to do *Nightline*.

Over the next couple of days I worked the White House beat, but it became impossible. Everybody was trying to interview me! So

I got moved to the Hill. But the calls kept coming in, requests for interviews by phone from West Germany, London, Paris. A reporter in Australia wanted to fly here to do an interview!

I was drained. And I got sick. I went to the hospital for kidney surgery a week after the shooting. I think it was caused in part by stress.

My brother James in Philadelphia called me the day after the assassination attempt. Like many black people, he hoped when he first heard the news that the assailant wasn't a black person. Then when he found out it was a black man who took the pictures, he said the family was really proud of me.

People have asked how I had the guts to keep filming. Everything was running through my mind at the time. I wanted to show what black people could do, that we could make the right calls, get the job done.

I thought of my grandmother, how blessed I was by the way she raised my six brothers and me. My father was killed when I was seven by a hit-and-run driver when he crossed the street. My mother died when I was fourteen. But my grandmother kept us off the streets, made sure we went to school, and encouraged us to go to college.

I was representing her that day. And my family. And the streets of Philadelphia. And young blacks everywhere who wanted a chance in journalism. And black people in general.

I think I did them justice. I was sure telling myself in those moments that I had to.

Having come home from Vietnam was another factor. I was drafted into the Army in 1967 because I was a part-time college student. I was stationed in the Saigon area as a weapons specialist.

When I was in Vietnam, I was nervous all the time. You heard a round, and you reacted instantly. Hit the dirt. Looked for cover. When I returned home I told myself, *Don't be nervous anymore. If you hear firecrackers or cars backfire, ignore it.* It was kind of like self-therapy. So when I heard Hinckley fire the shots, I continued to work rather than hit the deck like everyone else.

Another thing that kept me on my feet was because I was new in the position as a full-fledged cameraman. I had to fight to get that position. I knew they wouldn't have blamed me at the bureau if I had put the camera down and run. Some in my business would have expected a black to run away. I wanted them to know that I could stand fast like anyone else.

For a couple of years I had watched people get signed up with the title of "cameraman" ahead of me. I wondered why. I was qualified and already doing the job. I brought up the matter. Finally my bosses did an evaluation on me. They couldn't say I wasn't qualified. A lot of producers liked my work. They said I knew the business, that they couldn't have gotten the show done without Hank Brown.

Then they came up with this "attitude problem" I was supposed to have. They said, "You don't smile enough." They said I was organizing a coalition of black employees and conducting meetings with them. Actually, I was working when the meetings were being held, but I got blamed for them because I was demanding the job title for the work I was doing.

When I first came to ABC there were no black photographers. Joyce Allen, a black woman, was doing sound at the time. She wanted to be behind the camera.

I told her, "The only way you're going to get the job is to raise your voice and demand to shoot. You were here five years before I came. You're not shooting because you take whatever people throw at you. This business is rough, it's full of backstabbing and throat cutting. If it takes you going after me to get the job, then you have to go after me!"

Eventually she got the job. I was told that I was next in line. But I saw others pass me all the same, so I got a lawyer who told ABC I was going to sue.

Before one of my supervisors left ABC, he put in a recommendation that I get the next opening. But he warned me that the people around me were totally racist, that they just had a problem with me being black, basically.

When a soundman got the next position, I asked them to prove he was better than me. I said, "I've been walking around here with a grin on my face from end-to-end, smiles all around, so you can't say I don't smile or that I have an attitude."

They said the other guy was a tad better than me on the camera. I said, "Prove it."

They compared our tapes and said, "We can't show it to you. You're both real good."

So they offered to let us share the single position. I wanted it outright and they agreed that if I followed through with a lawsuit, I would get it. But a black guy who was the personnel director in Washington suggested that I wait for the next opening, which he would guarantee so that it wouldn't appear to my colleagues that I was taking the camera away from the white guy.

I didn't want the image of creating problems, of being some kind of bad guy, so I agreed. I figured my decision might make it easier for them to promote more blacks in good faith than to react to the demands of a quota system imposed by a judge. But basically I had gone through the kind of plea bargaining that blacks experience in this business, because you don't get what you deserve when you are black.

Anyway, it turned out okay. The network soon had five of us blacks shooting worldwide.

Sometimes I remind myself of what a news director told me when I worked at the station back in Philly. He was leaving the city at the time he called me in.

"I have to tell you that I'm a bigot in my heart," he said. "But you have to understand something about the news business. You're a damn good cameraman, and you have damn good news judgment. That made me overlook my bigotry. I admired your professionalism, your go-gettedness out in the field. I'm proud of you. Keep in mind that no matter how racist a person may be in this business, if he is truly a good newsman and wants his station or bureau to be the best, he will overlook his bigotry.

Because it is hard to find good people with good news judgment."

A lot of my associates thought I should have won an Emmy for coverage of the Reagan assassination attempt. At the ceremonies in New York the award went to another ABC news crew who had photographed the assassination of Anwar al-Sadat.[63] But they filmed it at a considerable distance away.

Three days later a second Emmy in the same category was awarded to the NBC cameraman. I felt bad. We were wondering at ABC what was going on. I got on the air first. I kept rolling. In the NBC footage you could see Hinckley's gun in the corner of the frame. But you could see everything in mine. ABC filed a protest, but it was too late.

The Washington chapter of the National Academy of Television Arts and Sciences did give me a special Emmy for standing fast. It said, "In the finest tradition of our industry, even when his life was in danger, he brought home the pictures."

President Regan recovered, as did McCarthy and Delahanty. Every time the president saw me, he smiled and waved "hello." I didn't want to talk to Jim Brady when I first saw him. It seemed too painful. He was hurt so bad.

I saw Brady again and again but never went over to speak to him. Then at the Christmas party at the White House in 1982, I got up the courage to walk over to him.

He looked up at me and smiled.

"How are you doing?" he said.

"I'm all right."

"I'm glad to see you again," he said. "I'm glad to see you are okay."

LEON DASH

Leon Dash served in Africa in the Peace Corps and later returned as a Washington Post *correspondent. He won wide praise for his coverage of the guerrilla war in Angola.*

———

A simple phone call. That's all it was. Right out of the blue. One day you are plowing through tax records in comfortable and safe Montgomery County, Maryland. Two weeks later you are in the African bush, hiding alongside guerrillas. It was May 1973. Ahead of me lay a twenty-one-hundred-mile trek into the middle of a bloody civil war.

I was a Montgomery County reporter for the *Washington Post* when the call came. I'd been investigating housing and industrial property assessments on real estate taxes, hoping to prove that the county was overassessing individual homeowners and letting industrial property slide. It was boring stuff, but I hoped to turn up something meaningful.

That day I was at my desk in the downtown office rather than out in Rockville. The caller identified herself as Connie Hilliard, a graduate student in Afro-American Studies at Harvard University. I learned that she was the girlfriend of Jorge Sangumba, foreign minister of the National Union for the Total Independence of Angola.

She said, "Leon Dash?"

I said, "Yeah."

"I understand you are the person to call."

"It depends on what you are calling about."

"Would you be willing to go into Africa with the liberation movement?"

"You've called the right person," I said. "I'd love that."

I came to the *Post* in 1965 as a copyboy but left in 1968 for a two-year stint with the Peace Corps as a high school teacher in Kenya. I became fluent in Swahili because the parents of my students didn't speak English. I guess I always dreamed of going to Africa.

I grew up in the Church of the Master at 122nd Street and Morningside Drive in Harlem. Its pastor was the Reverend James Robinson, founder of Operation Crossroads Africa.[64] He got me interested in Africa. As a junior high school student, I did volunteer work for Crossroads, stuffing envelopes, typing, and running errands. But my parents were civil servants and couldn't afford to send me on one of the Crossroads-sponsored summer trips.

When Connie Hilliard said Angola, it seemed as though fate was at play because my greatuncle was born in Angola, the son of a Guyanese missionary. She didn't know how anxious I was to get back to Africa. Connie said she would send me a special delivery letter explaining everything.

I said, "Fine."

In the letter, she told me she was recruiting American reporters, particularly black ones, to cover UNITA[65] first hand. She had approached several black reporters, all of whom said they were too busy. But they all said, "We know one crazy fellow who would be willing to go. Leon Dash." That's why she called me. As I read the letter, I thought, "How am I going to convince the *Post*?"

Knowing the politics of the *Post*, I figured I had to do an end-run around Harry Rosenfeld, who was the metropolitan editor. I decided the best thing was to go to Phil Foisie, who was the assistant managing editor for foreign news. The next morning, I went to the office earlier than normal to give myself a half-hour lead time with Foisie before the other editors started coming in.

I had become somewhat famous at the *Post* for doing all kinds of end-runs. The year before, I had led a group of metropolitan reporters in filing an EEOC[66] complaint against the *Post*. We wanted an affirmative action program with goals and timetables. But I think some of the brass thought we were Mau-Mau-ing[67] the *Post* for personal gain, and that I would settle for a raise if I became an assistant city editor.

So one night, after I had a disappointing interview with Jimmy Hoffa[68] because his lawyer kept butting in, I telephoned Ben Bradlee, the executive editor, and asked if I could come to his home for a one-on-one, no-holds-barred rap session.

Bradlee said, "Sure, come on over."

I had a couple of drinks, then grabbed a cab, and went to his house. When he came to the door, I said, "No gloves." He understood what I meant.

He said, "What are you drinking?"

I said, "Scotch."

He got a fifth of scotch, a fifth of bourbon, a bucket of ice and two glasses. And we went into his den.

It was a nasty session, lasting several hours. I let him know that I didn't want to be isolated, I didn't want a bullshit position, and that we were attacking the *Post* as a class, demanding promotion and fair play for blacks in all departments from the seventh floor on down to the janitorial level.

He sort of blanched. He had to be thinking, *Here's this guy, a guest in my home, I'm his supervisor. And he's calling me names, drinking my whiskey, and upsetting my wife. And he's also trying to sue the* Post, *which hires more blacks than most papers, for racial discrimination.*

Bradlee had a hurt expression on his face when I left. I knew he hadn't been through anything so ugly before with a black. But he began to understand that we weren't talking for ourselves. Afterward, negotiations became very serious and really productive.

I showed Phil Foisie the letter from Connie Hilliard, and explained that I would sneak into Angola with UNITA guerrillas, one of the three groups of liberation fighters opposing the Portuguese. Angola was still a Portuguese colony. Foisie was excited about the prospect. We went immediately to Howard Simons, the managing editor. In a fifteen-minute conversation, the decision was made that I would go. When I came out of Howard's office, Kevin Klose, the Maryland editor, looked at me curiously because Foisie and Simons were animated. I laid it out to Kevin.

"Rosenfeld is going to be furious," he said.

"Why?" I was playing innocent.

"He'll think you should have come to him first."

I said, "Oh? I didn't realize that."

At any rate, Rosenfeld was presented with the fait accompli. I was ready to go. To prepare myself, I interviewed a number of specialists on southern Africa at the State Department. I didn't tell them I was going to sneak into Angola. I said I wanted to write a general story from Washington about liberation movements all over the world. I was worried that they might leak my plans to the Portuguese government.

I was going into a dangerous situation. A war was raging, an anticolonial war. I took notes on all the groups so they wouldn't know which one I was particularly interested in. And they all said that UNITA barely existed beyond being a press conference organization—which made me a little nervous.

I established my rendezvous points in London and Lusaka with Connie Hilliard and booked my flights. A UNITA representative met me in London, and then I flew to Lusaka. As I went through immigration, I could see through the glass doors a group of five bearded men in the waiting area. I knew who they were. One of them was a fellow I had gone to Lincoln University with. We weren't really friends, I just knew his face. His name was Jorge Sangumba.

He said, "Leon?"

I said, "Jorge?"

We shook hands and they spirited me off in a Land Rover to disappear into Lusaka for the night. The next day, we traveled north to the home of a black American woman who taught at Kwame Nkruma Teachers College. After several days, we traveled west and picked up a Zambian Airways flight further west. Then it was off in a Land Rover again until we reached the border. We met a band of twenty-five guerrillas and off we went on foot into the Angolan interior.

I traveled with them across eight hundred miles by foot for three and a half months, from June into September. Our objective was the railroad line. Reaching it would prove that the UNITA guerillas could move deeply into Angola.

I was surprised to see a British freelance journalist with the guerrillas. He and I just didn't get along. We resented each other because we both thought we had an exclusive. And the guerrillas kept trying to put us together, because they reasoned that journalists should stay together. It was a total disaster because, beyond the rivalry, I could sense that he was prejudiced. Yet he came to respect me, and I think he grew a great deal before the journey ended.

The leader of UNITA was Jonas Savimbi, a socialist, who broke away from the National Front for the Liberation of Angola, led by the anti-Communist, Holden Roberto. Savimbi was getting help from the U.S., China, Romania, and South Africa.

Savimbi was very curious about black and white relations in the States. He asked a lot of questions. His early education in Angola was through American missionaries, and that had a tremendous impact on him. He said some of the seeds of the Angolan rebellion had been sown by black American sailors who preferred to mingle with black Angolans when they came into port.

They asked him, "How come you haven't thrown the Portuguese out of your country? This is Africa. They don't belong here."

Savimbi got annoyed when I interviewed him. He had never experienced such intensive interviewing.

"Most journalists spend a half-hour with me," he said. "I have already given you two."

I said, "I'm not finished."

After several days and twenty hours of interviewing, he was exhausted. "Why do you ask so many questions?"

I said, "I can't speak for other journalists, but I want to know everything."

The closest we got to the Portuguese was the railroad. We hid in the bush overlooking the train track, and I photographed one of the trains with an armored car in front. There was never any real danger from the Portuguese. They had a reputation for being clumsy, moving in convoys that you could hear for days before they reached you. We worried more about the other guerrillas attacking us because they moved with stealth.

I returned to the *Post* and wrote a four-part series on life among the UNITA guerrillas, which appeared during the Christmas holidays. That was my last contact with Angola until the following April, when the *Post* received a telex message from the Armed Forces Revolutionary Council, which had just overthrown the dictatorship in Lisbon. The message said they had read my series, thought it was a fair comment, and invited me to enter Angola legally and report on the Portuguese side.

Howard Simons said, "Sure. Go." As before, the *Post* picked up the tab, and I flew to Lisbon where I was given a visa.

In Luanda, the Angolan capital, the military government provided me with a press contact, a naval officer, and told me I had carte blanche to travel to any part of the country. I told the African Angolans I met that because there had been a coup in Lisbon the whole situation had changed. But they didn't believe it. They feared that it was merely a ploy to get them to expose themselves as belonging to one movement or the other.

On this trip I wanted to see how intense the feeling and support was for the three movements in the different areas of the country. And I wanted to see for myself the colonial system, which was still intact. I also wanted to establish a record of Portuguese atrocities against the civilian population since the fighting broke out in 1961.

I believed that there would be civil war after the Portuguese left because of the strong personalities of the three leaders of the movements, and the tribal differences they exploited. The FNLA[69] was very conservative, more so than UNITA, and got help from the U.S., China, South Africa, Zaire, and mercenaries. Agostinho Neto followed a Marxist-Leninist line as head of the Popular Movement for the Liberation of Angola. They were helped by the Cubans and the Russians.

In Luanda I made extensive contact with officials of the FNLA and the MPLA, because I wanted to balance my reporting of the year before. Government officials were always cautious and careful, even stilted in our talks. But they were cooperative because they knew I had been invited to come by the powers in Lisbon. So if I needed any special help, I got it. A helicopter? Pop. The next day I was on a helicopter.

I couldn't get any of the Portuguese farmers or plantation owners to say directly that they had participated in or seen any massacres. But as I traveled from place to place with the Portuguese army, I met a lieutenant who began telling me how much he hated the war. Naturally, I wore the same kind of uniform as he did, so that I wouldn't stick out and become a target. The lieutenant described the settlers as criminals who, historically, had been sent off to the colonies. He had been middle-class, a schoolteacher. Then he was drafted. Now he was in this "hole," protecting criminals.

He complained that there were no women, the wine was terrible, there was nothing but heat, and every time he left the base the guerrillas shot at him. He offered me a rifle. I refused. I said I had my camera and would be too busy taking pictures if we were attacked. He thought that was crazy, but said okay. Then he told me how he had heard that soldiers and vigilantes had entered villages and slaughtered everyone—men, women and children.

In central Angola, my interpreter, a lieutenant named Jose Guerre, was equally antiwar, a sort of Portuguese hippie who had been drafted into the army. He loved to wear beads, like a peacenik. We were able to share a good deal because of his opposition. He was the guy who translated my series for the army. He was also a secret MPLA supporter. He gave me MPLA literature, and introduced me to other Portuguese commandos in his barracks. I would find one supporting the MPLA, another supporting UNITA. It was all mixed up.

But one of the commandos was upset that the war was ending, because he had come to enjoy killing. At first, he had tried to avoid the draft and fled to France. When his mother got sick, he returned home and was arrested for draft dodging. As punishment, he was put into the commandos, because of their high mortality rate. He was willing to tell me anything because he thought I would hook him up with gangsters in the U.S. after the war. He believed—from movies, no doubt—that all Americans were gangsters. And since he now had no compulsion about killing, he thought he would be a good bodyguard for American gangsters.

The commando described mowing people down as they ran from the villages or camps. They shot women in the back because they fed the guerrillas. They shot the children, too. Then they torched the villages. Jose, my translator, interpreted his words matter-of-factly.

"Are you translating correctly?" I asked.

"Yes. That is what he said."

Jose wasn't shocked by anything. When he and I went into the bush, to the villages, to talk with civilians, it took much cajoling to convince them that nothing they would say would be held against them. They were still very frightened.

Around this time the new government in Lisbon offered the guerilla leaders amnesty, promising elections, and invited them to return to the capital to discuss the future. I figured that I could get this journalistic coup. I would get to Savimbi and be the first to interview a guerilla leader who came out of the bush.

Jose introduced me to a priest who had acted as an intermediary between Savimbi and the Portuguese military forces. Through him I got a letter to Savimbi, but Savimbi declined, saying politically and physically it wouldn't work. I wanted him to talk about the amnesty offer and the coup in Lisbon. I thought he was being foolish because I was giving him a forum, at least in the *Post,* and I would have walked to his camp. Eleven days? It was no big thing.

This second trip gave me a chance to explore Portuguese racism. Until the fighting broke out in 1961, the government divided the population into a caste system. At the top were some half-million white settlers and administrators. Then came about ninety thousand *mestiços*, who had automatic citizenship because they had some white blood. They were further divided by the lightness of their skin and the straightness of their hair. The closer to white they looked, the more privileges, the more access to high-paying jobs they had.

The African population, nearly five and one-half million, was divided into *assimilado* and *indigena*. The "assimilated" were those who shed their African language and culture for Portuguese and were given citizenship. The "natives," about ninety percent of the black population, remained "uncivilized."

I referred to myself as black. But the Portuguese corrected me. In their context, I was *mestiço*—mixed, because my skin is brown, my hair too straight. They assumed that since I represented the *Post*, I was educated. So they talked to me as if I were white. It felt strange because this was the first time anything like that ever happened to me. In my gut I felt offended. But intellectually I understood what was happening.

At a camp where the Portuguese trained Africans to fight the guerrillas, I encountered a Portuguese major who was trying to teach the Africans how to improve their raising of livestock. I thought it was strange that Africans needed Europeans to teach them livestock after so many thousands of years.

In Kenya I had learned a lot about cattle-raising from the masters. So I asked the major some questions about it. The more specific I became, the more difficult it was for him to answer, until finally he could answer nothing. He became very annoyed and screamed at me in Portuguese.

Jose, separating himself from the major's words, said, "The major said he is trying to teach these uncivilized blacks. That has always been the case. And he does not understand why you have to know so much about cattle."

Before I left Luanda, I visited friends and relatives of Jose. I was the only black in the room, but they didn't consider me black.

"What have you seen in Angola that is good?" they asked.

I thought and thought. "The system I have seen here is not good."

One of the men became angry. He stood up and said, "How can you say that?"

"The system you operate here is inhuman," I said.

"But we're bringing civilization."

"I don't think it is civilized to tax the Angolans and give them back nothing in services, such as education or health."

"Why are you so concerned about the blacks?" he asked.

"Because I consider myself black."

"That's foolish. You are *mestiço*. You have white blood. You are civilized because you are educated."

"In the United States, we all consider ourselves black."

He didn't know how to handle that.

He said, "The United States is a racist country. You have the Ku Klux Klan. They have lynched and slaughtered blacks."

"Yes, that's true," I said.

He hadn't been able to attack me when he called the U.S. racist, and I had pointed out his own racism. The Portuguese believed that since they had mixed with Northern Arabs, they got along better with nonwhite people than did other European groups. And it was all a myth. This man saw me as *mestiço*. And I was sitting in his living room denying that I had anything to do with him and that I identified with the Africans. It was a shattering experience for him.

I left Angola after six weeks. On the way back through Lisbon I didn't bother to interview any officials because I knew they wanted to talk about what kind of independence the movements would accept. I knew that none of the movements would accept anything less than total independence.

My new series, in three parts, was published in August.

Exactly three years later, I was writing a series on drug abuse in Washington when the new foreign editor asked me if I would go back to Angola. The UNITA guerrillas had contacted our African correspondent, but he didn't want to go in. By this time, the Portuguese had left, and in the ensuing civil war that I predicted in the 1974 series, the MPLA and the Cubans had defeated the FNLA and UNITA. The FNLA had retreated into Zaire, but UNITA was continuing a guerilla struggle in southern Angola.

What could I learn that was different from the 1973 trip? I wasn't interested in wandering around the bush again. The foreign editor said this time UNITA was offering Cuban and MPLA prisoners for interviews.

I said, "They've got Cuban prisoners?"

"Definitely."

"That's good stuff," I said. "Good copy."

I had done something out of the ordinary before. To do it twice would make it all extraordinary. And I liked adventure. I was off.

I planned to spend no more than three months with UNITA. I ended up staying seven-and-a-half months. We covered, on foot, twenty-one hundred miles.

The Zambian government was no longer helping UNITA, because of UNITA's South African connection. Most of black Africa had become anti-UNITA by then. UNITA was becoming a pariah. So the guerrillas really had to sneak me through. To avoid Zambian army patrols on our way to the border, we traveled at night and hid in the bush by day.

When we traveled through the swamps, we took off our pants, socks, and shoes. You had to. Your pants became too heavy with the water. And if someone attacked you, you wouldn't be able to run. The smells were terrible from the muck and the swamp grass.

The swamp grass cut you. After three hours of walking, my legs were a mass of blood. But once we got out of the swamp and dried off, the blood coagulated, and you could put your pants back on.

We crossed the border on October 4. Then we could march during the day. But it rained all the time, and I had to learn to sleep in the rain unprotected. It took me two weeks to learn how to do that. As we headed towards Savimbi's camp, I stopped three times from bouts of fever. The diarrhea, I had expected.

Even though this was the rainy season, there wasn't much cultivation in this expanse. Only one person there for every four or five square miles. So we subsisted mainly on wild mushrooms, honey, and bee larvae. I drew the line on caterpillars—they were so hairy. Even though the guerrillas fried them, they didn't bother to take the hair off.

Finally, we resorted to eating the rancid hippopotamus meat they had stored. We boiled it and added a little salt. Then you had to chew, chew, chew. I filled up on it. You had to do it if you expected to walk another thirty miles the next day. And we did this every day.

The first day we walked eight or ten miles, no more. The guerrillas built you up. They watched me very closely, looked at my face, at my pace, for signs of pain. They didn't want to repeat the tragedy that happened in 1973. The UNITA representative in Switzerland was late in crossing the border for the UNITA congress. They moved him too fast. He lost too much body salt. He wasn't able to walk. He was recuperating in one of the camps when the Portuguese soldiers attacked. They walked up to him and fired five rounds into his side.

On the trek in 1973, I asked myself, *What the hell are you doing here? Because you gotta walk outta here. There's no going to the nearest town and taking a plane out.*

But this time was different. I knew what I was getting into. And I was enjoying it. In 1973 I had run out of body salt on the marches, and my leg muscles knotted up so badly that I wasn't able to walk for several hours. This time I had plenty of salt tablets. And I had ten notebooks and a camera in plastic bags. I didn't even have to carry a knapsack. One of the guerrillas always insisted on doing it.

It took me five weeks to reach Savimbi's main camp, because we had to avoid contact with a major offensive which the Cubans and the MPLA had mounted against UNITA. In one camp the word came that MPLA soldiers were arriving. Within fifteen minutes, three hundred people—men, women, and children—moved off in every direction in groups no larger than ten, without a sound. I don't know when the MPLA got there, but I felt safe after watching the guerrillas move the way they did.

When I arrived at Savimbi's camp, the guerrillas whom I'd met in 1973 were very excited. "Leon. Leon," they called out. I wouldn't respond to Mr. Dash. And the people who hadn't met me were very warm. Translations of my articles had been read to them in the camps. My name had preceded me.

Savimbi was very reserved, very distant. He believed that I shouldn't have come into Angola in 1974 on the Portuguese side. That practically made me a traitor. And in both series of articles, I had critical things to say about all the movements, especially about them fighting each other. Like the others, he claimed the fighting among them was ideological.

It was not. It was tribal—ethnic. The FNLA was Bakongo. The MPLA was Kimbundu. UNITA was Ovimbundu. These tribes were all afraid of being dominated by each other. The guerilla leadership may have had varying degrees of ideology, but they recruited on the basis of that fear.

But for one to say that to Savimbi was a no-no, and since I had traveled with UNITA, I was supposed to be a UNITA supporter. He was flabbergasted by the message I sent in '74. He didn't understand that I was neutral. He wanted to control me. And all guerilla groups were the same way. But Savimbi did not tell the others that he was angry with me. And I didn't feel in any danger because he had invited me back in.

When we sat down to talk, he said, "I suppose you have millions of questions again."

"You're right. I have even more than before."

That broke the ice.

Then I made it clear to him that to function as a reporter I had to be neutral. I told him I *may* like him personally, but that would have nothing to do with what I would write. And never will.

One of his commanders raised the issue too. "Leon, which side are you on?"

"I'm not on your side," I said. "I am neutral. America had nothing to do with starting this war. I'm here to report the war."

"You know, Leon, I like you. But I don't like you as a journalist."

Of course I was anxious to see the Cuban prisoners. I was told that all eight of them had been executed. God, I was angry. I was never so angry in all my life.

I yelled out, "You had me come all the way here, and you don't have any Cuban prisoners?"

One day Savimbi pulled out his maps. "We're up here," he said, pointing well above the rail line.

I said, "Oh, really? That's where I want to go."

"Well, it's going to take you a long time."

"I don't care. I've got all kinds of time. Show me."

He said, "I'm not going up there."

"I want to go."

He said okay, and off I went, with about a hundred bodyguards, who passed me from one group of fifty to another. The way ahead was really dangerous because a lot of MPLA and Cuban troops were moving around. And they were under orders not to come back if I got killed.

Being passed from group to group provided me with a gold mine of information. No group ever understood what they were supposed not to tell me. These were young and naïve warriors. They didn't know that they weren't supposed to tell me the South Africans were helping them. And I didn't think I was taking advantage of them by asking.

I asked questions, and they gave honest answers. If I asked the UNITA leadership where South African equipment came from, I heard, "We cannot reveal that." When I asked a warrior where he got the uniform he was wearing, he answered, "From my South African friends."

Many of the guerrillas carried World War II rifles, provided by the CIA, which I knew would be useless in a firefight. So did the guerrilla leaders. We learned after the MPLA takeover that the U.S.

didn't give UNITA much support because we didn't expect them to win. But the guerrilla leaders told the recruits that if they wanted effective weapons, they should kill a Cuban or an MPLA officer. That would mean a quality AK-47.

I was amazed at the large area UNITA occupied, but I remained conservative on their claims. What guerrillas control is not the same as what they occupy, because they do not confront major offensives head on. And I found that they were less disciplined because they expanded so rapidly after it became clear the Portuguese were serious about getting out.

As I walked through one destroyed village or town after another, I said, "How could I be anything but neutral?" The UNITA guerrillas, the FNLA, the MPLA, the Cubans, the South Africans—all were destroying the towns so that the others would not have them. It seemed a classic case of the legacy of the Portuguese conquest in the sixteenth century.

With the exception of their mutual suspicion, which the Portuguese fostered to divide and conquer them, the tribes had few differences among them. Their languages and cultures were essentially African savannah. With friends in all three movements, I said, "How could I favor one side?"

In the camps, the peasants found it strange that I, a black man, could not speak their language. Their perspective of that part of the world was the only world they knew. One young guerrilla asked me how long it would take for him to walk from Angola to America. I told him there was an ocean in between. He was surprised to hear that. And he was *mestiço*. That showed me that even a privileged person had been kept ignorant by the Portuguese educational system.

Life passed routinely in the camps. I didn't join in their dancing, but I watched them play soccer. There were marriage ceremonies, and babies were born. I learned how fiercely the women guerrillas fought. If attacked, their children were placed behind them, so the women would not retreat like the men. They could not run, carry their children, and fight at the same time.

In the first of Savimbi's camps, I met Anita. I'd known her

brother, a guerrilla commander. She was the only girl I was ever interested in. She was very attractive and very intellectually sharp. In the old colonial system, she would have been an *assimilado*, a pure black who finished the university and became "civilized."

Now Anita carried a gun. She was a guerrilla.

Nothing was more painful to me than when insects burrowed into my feet. Like chiggers, they laid eggs, which had to be dug out very carefully. The sores were crippling, and I couldn't walk for three or four days. One time Anita heated a pin over the fire and carefully dug them out. It took her eight hours over two days.

I wanted to bring Anita to the States and marry her. We talked and talked. She had mixed emotions. It was a very tough life she was leading, but she had become very dedicated. She refused my proposal.

Finally we reached Mongo, in the center of Angola, at the foot of twin mountains. The guerrillas wanted to kill all the government troops there and destroy the town.

The attack took place at dawn. I remained on the eastern twin of the two mountains, half a mile away. About twenty-five guerrillas opened fire with automatic weapons and mortars. The hundred soldiers broke out of their homes and fired at the flashes in the bush. Quietly, a hundred and twenty-five guerrillas slipped behind the soldiers from the south and opened up on their backs. Half of the defenders turned to meet them.

It was a trap.

The twenty-five broke off the fighting and ran to join another hundred guerrillas in a line of grass on the town's eastern side. The soldiers were caught in the classic L-shaped ambush. It was horrible. They were chopped to pieces. It was the first time I had ever seen anything like it. In a few minutes, forty-two soldiers were dead and seven of their wives were killed when a mortar hit a house they were hiding in. The guerrillas claimed only three wounded.

I came down from the mountain and walked a bridge across a small river. I was strolling into town when suddenly we saw movement. A guerrilla was carrying a wounded comrade out. The commanding officer had failed to provide a force to ambush any reinforcements that might come down the road into town. And the reinforcements were there. If they had wanted to, the government troops could have chased us out of the town. We wouldn't have gotten across the river in time, and we would have been mowed down.

I came out of Angola on May 22, 1977. And in August the *Post* published my seven-part series.

I have a very fond memory of Anita. I can still see her beautiful smile. And personally, I liked Savimbi. He was an attractive, Machiavellian character. I found him brilliant and charismatic—but a total opportunist. I wouldn't trust him, would never have trusted him.

He was angry with me because I said all those things about him after the second series of interviews. But all those things were true. I think that gave him a better understanding of who Leon Dash was.

A reporter.

BARBARA REYNOLDS

Barbara Reynolds was a reporter for the Chicago Tribune *who covered the civil rights movement and became a friend of Jesse Jackson.*

———

In 1972 I lived on the South Shore in Chicago three blocks from the home of Jesse Jackson. One day I ran over to the house and burst into his kitchen.

"Reverend, they have asked me to write a book about you. Isn't that wonderful?"

He was silent.

"Reverend! Isn't that wonderful?"

He looked at me coldly.

"Barbara," he said, "don't write that book."

Nothing else.

I left dejected, confused, and very heartbroken.

I first met Reverend Jesse Jackson in 1968, when I was writing for *Ebony* magazine. I saw him at his Saturday morning meeting for the Operation Breadbasket[70] campaign. I was just a face in the crowd. I said, "I have never seen such a man." I was awed by his presence, by his use of words, by his effect on people.

I grew up in Columbus, Ohio, and I had no real understanding of what the civil rights movement of the 1960s was about. Our parents sheltered us. We didn't know about black history. We didn't know that blacks couldn't eat in restaurants. We didn't understand the rigid segregation in the South.

When I saw blacks being beaten by the police in demonstrations, I said, "Mother, why are they doing that?"

She said, "Oh, you don't have to worry about that." She tried to put my mind off of it.

But when I went back to school—Ohio State University—the next day, everybody on campus was talking about what was going on. Some of us said that if the police were going to beat blacks like that, then we'd have to go down to help them. We heard about a movement in Brownsville, Tennessee, to register blacks to vote.

I went to Brownsville with white students and church people. I went into the cotton fields to beg and cajole the sharecroppers to vote. I never understood until years later that if they had voted, they would have been put off their land. It was 1964.

In Brownsville, we had thugs to worry about—*and* the police. One night we went to a roadside inn to relax. Someone pulled the jukebox plug, and they chased us out. Then we were chased up and down these dusty roads, driving with our lights out. Another night we were coming back from a meeting to appeal to blacks to vote. People stood in the middle of the road.

"Oh, you better pull over," I said. "Maybe somebody is hurt."

"No, this is a roadblock," the driver said. "They are after us."

He gunned the motor. We flew around the roadblock. It was up the dusty roads again with our lights off.

After that we had a rally to dramatize the need to vote. The police came to break it up. We were supposed to lock arms, but as soon as I saw the dogs and the police, I ran and got into the car and hid! When I looked out, I could see what it really took to face down dogs and people with clubs and guns. I thought it would have been easier if I'd had a gun to shoot than to stand there and be clubbed and bitten. And that is why I gained a tremendous respect for the civil rights people.

When I returned to Columbus, I wrote about my experiences for the local daily and the campus newspaper. They were my first published articles, and they were not written dispassionately. I believed you couldn't be objective about the movement, that it was something that you had to live in order to write about.

When I got back, I called a white classmate, and received the shock of my life. We had shared a bed together in the in the home of a black family in Brownsville. She had told me, "Come to see me when you get back." So I called to say I was coming over.

"My sorority doesn't like Negroes," she said. "And I don't think you should come over."

After Martin Luther King was assassinated, I felt bad, of course. I felt very bad that I had missed working with him. I worked in the movement, but not with him. And *that* made me feel I hadn't contributed very much. So when Jesse Jackson told me he was the new King, I wanted to believe it. And I did believe it.

I didn't quite put him on a pedestal next to God like some people did. At that point in my life, he just seemed remarkable—young, strong, intelligent, wise, caring. I felt safe around him. I used to fly with him when I was covering him. I was afraid of airplanes at the time. And I'd sit next to him, and I wouldn't be afraid. He was remarkable. That's what I first saw in him. He was the first great person I'd ever known close up.

Coming from Columbus, I didn't have an identity of my own—a black experience. Jesse gave me one. It was to serve the leader. If you served the leader, then you served black people. Journalism for black reporters was service to the movement.

Jesse also seemed to know more about what reporters should do than we knew. He indoctrinated us. And I assumed he was correct. He defined the role of black journalists as those who protected black leaders. By serving the leader, you advanced the movement. Journalism wasn't about being objective. He always told us that white reporters weren't objective. For example, they weren't objective about the state of Israel, he said.

Then he scared me to death! He said that character assassination preceded physical assassination. That made all of us afraid to write anything negative about him. Since he identified with Dr. King so much, we felt that we didn't want to be a party to anything that might happen to him.

I became one of Jesse's leading cheerleaders. After I joined the *Chicago Today*, I wrote maybe fifty favorable stories about him. I was never critical, I served him well. That's why Nelson-Hall, the publishers, approached me to do the book.

Sometimes a black writer, like Lu Palmer or Vernon Jarrett, asked me to quit being such a cheerleader. I said, "Look, I'm doing what I'm supposed to do."

I became an adjunct to Jesse's staff. I advised him on what to say to the press. Reporters like me were involved in defining the movement, acting in the movement, critiquing the movement. You switched back and forth from being a person in the movement and being a writer.

When I first told Jesse about the offer I had to write a book about him, he didn't explain why he would not cooperate. Later, I asked for an explanation. He said he wanted to tell his own story. I was shocked because I was one of his best friends. I used to go in the back door of his home without knocking. I'd play with the kids. I was his wife's confidante. I was part of the family.

I had uneasy thoughts about some things that I thought should be in the book. I told myself, *He'll clear those up, and they won't be a problem.*

But he only gave me interviews on subjects that he wanted to talk about for the newspaper. I did the interviews anyway, but our relationship grew strained. It was almost like breaking from your own relatives.

I faced the dilemma of being a black reporter who wanted to write a full portrait of a great black leader. What do I put in? What do I leave out? I often wondered if what I went through was experienced by white reporters who wrote about a white person they greatly admired, such as John F. Kennedy.

I wondered if black people really wanted to know the other side of their leaders. I wondered if black reporters *should* tell the other side, expose it to the world. Are we black people first? Or reporters first?

Jesse had always told me that he was standing on the balcony of the motel in Memphis with Dr. King when he was killed. He said that he cradled Dr. King, the dying leader, in his arms.

I heard stories that Jesse lied about what really happened on the balcony. The rumors said that he smeared King's blood on his shirt and took a plane for Chicago, more concerned about emerging as the new leader than with staying with the others in Memphis, or going to Atlanta to help bury King.

"He'll probably tell me about that," I said. "It's no big thing."

It got very shaky between us is when he wouldn't tell me anything. All he had to say was, "Barbara, they lied." And Barbara would have written that. I believed everything the man said! I never would have challenged anything. But when he wouldn't say anything, I was left with nothing to do but research the question.

So I talked to many of the people who were at the King assassination. Andy Young,[71] what happened? Ralph Abernathy,[72] what happened? Hosea Williams,[73] what happened? Bernard Lee,[74] what happened? I reconstructed what I heard. I didn't editorialize. I didn't even give my impressions. I wrote it as it happened, starting the day before the assassination.

They had been in Memphis to help the striking garbage men. At one point, Jesse wanted to do things his way and everybody else wanted it another way. Dr. King had told him, "If you don't want to do what we're requiring you to do, why don't you get out of the movement."

I'm not sure King meant it, but the exchange demonstrated that they were not on the good terms that Jesse later claimed they were, or that Jesse was his closest aide, as Jesse's followers later introduced him.

I also learned that Jesse was not on the balcony when King was killed, that he was not the last to be with him in his dying moments, and that he must have put his hands in the blood after the body was removed.

Hosea Williams told me, "I don't know why he would lie like that."

When King's people met the next morning to make funeral plans, they were stunned to learn that Jesse was appearing on network television. He had told them he was going to Atlanta to help with the funeral, but he went to Chicago instead and met with a public relations specialist to help project him as the new leader. And everyone had agreed *not* to talk to the press.

I don't guess all this matters now because Jesse doesn't need King anymore. The media and his own intelligence have made him who he is now. But in those days, he needed to carry King's baggage around.

I heard rumors, too, that the monies he collected at the PUSH[75] Expos didn't add up. Hundreds of thousands of people paid three or five dollars to attend an exposition, but you later heard that PUSH had cleared only a few thousand dollars. I thought people had a right to know what the PUSH Foundation did with the money.

When I asked Jesse, he said, "I don't handle money. Go talk to the treasurer." The treasurer said, "Our lawyers handle it. Go talk to them." The lawyers said, "Talk to the foundation president." And the foundation president said, "You got to talk to Jesse."

In those days, Jesse made a big deal out of signing a covenant with a major company in Chicago to provide jobs for minorities and contracts for black businesses. The press was there for the announced deal. If he couldn't get a deal, he'd call for a boycott. We thought in terms of headlines. But we didn't go back to see how the covenant worked out.

I saw that black businesses got theirs, and Jesse received some kind of contribution from them. Or a representative from a targeted company would make a contribution to a church building fund. Then the campaign fizzled. And no one seemed to worry about the jobs people were supposed to get.

Jesse thought about the media night and day. He understood the media better than anyone I've ever met. Jesse was always good copy. He packaged himself brilliantly. On a slow day, if you needed a story, all you had to do was call him up. He packaged himself perfectly for radio. He could talk to you in a sixty-second second bite. His analyses were gifted. He could tear right through a situation, pull out the substance, and make it palatable and understandable. He was a very gifted interpreter. And he was safe as hell.

Everything he said was safe. His rhetoric was pure. That helped give him an excellent relationship with the presidents of the major media. I watched him come to the *Chicago Tribune* and sit down for breakfast with people so high up in the organization that I'd never see them. When he was talking to our bosses, he didn't bother with the reporters. And he talked to them on a first-name basis.

The press loved his campaign for excellence in the schools. So did the government. PUSH began to receive a lot of funds. He visited a school and told students to respect themselves, to undertake an emotional drive for excellence.

There was nothing wrong with that. But if you don't deal with teachers, deal with busing, deal with poor curricula—you aren't dealing with the whole problem. You are putting the focus on the child, as though he can do it all by himself. The parents loved it because they wanted their children to behave. The federal government loved it because nobody was talking about the real issues.

Everybody was happy. The kids were getting shortchanged—but the press had a catchy story.

Jesse had a special way of dealing with reporters, black and white, that won even the good ones over. I saw it happen. It happened to me. If you were a black reporter, he appealed to your nationalism, your racial pride.

He said, "We're in this together. They're out to get me. Brother, I need you because I'm weary of this struggle. If I only had just a few friends, you know what I could do."

So your heart went out to him. Here was a black man struggling for his race, in physical danger—you saw the retinue of bodyguards around him. He's sweating, preaching. "Hang with me, brother." Of course you're going to do what he wants! It appealed to *me*.

If you were a white reporter, he said, "I don't think you can understand what it is to be black, to know how blacks really feel. So when you go back to your office, you're going to be blinded, brother. But I understand the pressures that they put on you not to tell my story. Yet there will be a few people with the intellectual strength to resist the pressure they are going to put on you. But whatever happens, brother, I'm not going to hold it against you. I don't expect you to understand."

So he had the white reporter struggling with his conscience. The white reporter was thinking, *Am I really a racist? I'm going to prove that I'm not a racist. I'm going to really do it up for him.*

Yes, Jesse had us reporters wrapped. *I'm not going to write anything negative because I must prove that I'm black.*

I'm not going to write anything negative because I must prove that I'm not a racist.

It took me three years to research and write *Jesse Jackson: The Man, The Movement, The Myth.* It was published in 1975.

Black people didn't understand why I did it. Many thought it was something evil. Not many black women wrote books in the first place. Black people in general were not thought of as book writers, even by many blacks. And you were writing a book about a black man, their leader, and saying some negative things, what were they going to think?

What I heard from blacks was that somebody paid me off to do it. The CIA, or the FBI, or the *Chicago Tribune.* "Or," they said, "you're trying to set Jesse up, take him away from us."

You became a stooge of some kind of conspiracy. If you attacked the leader, you attacked black people. And to them, to analyze meant to attack.

I became the enemy.

I got threatening phone calls—death threats, actually. Someone would say, "I'm gonna get you before you get Jesse."

I had to have police protection when I lectured on a college campus. I had to have a bodyguard, donated by a black security firm.

A broadcaster discussed my book on his radio show.

"Hey," I said, "you forgot to invite me to be on."

He said, "No, I didn't."

When someone on the radio show tried to defend me, he was cut off. And I was accused on the show of writing the book because Jesse had rebuked me after we had been lovers. They said I wrote the book in retaliation for Jesse's scorn. That really hurt me.

I never publicly responded to the accusation because it didn't make sense. It was too simple. Coming from a place like Columbus, I never viewed Jesse in that way. We treated preachers as someone special in Columbus. Jesse was married. And I was a very good friend of his wife. I had put him way up on a pedestal. Becoming his lover never occurred to me. And he never approached me. He was my big brother.

I made a mistake when I told someone that we did interviews in his bedroom. But people who were close to him always came to his bedroom. That's where he was. He traveled all the time and was very tired when he got home. So he would be in his bed, surrounded by yellow pads, with aides all around him, as he received people like he was the Pope.

Certain black journalists, such as Ethel Payne[76] of the *Chicago Defender* and Vernon Jarrett, my colleague at the *Tribune*, spoke out in my defense, saying blacks had the right to write as they saw it.

When I spoke to black audiences across the city, I explained why they should analyze *anybody*, even me. I had learned through the Watergate affair that you can separate the president from the presidency. So you could separate the leader from black America, and black America could still be healthy.

I finally made my critics back off. I know the media the way I know Jesse. So everywhere I went, I raised the question: "Why? Why am I getting death threats? Why is my life in danger? Why do I have bodyguards?"

I covered the Mafia. I covered the street gangs. I covered the Black Panthers. But not until I covered the Christians was my life in danger.

When I started talking like that, the threats stopped. Nobody wanted anything to happen to me. I became one of the safest people in Chicago!

But the book never got a chance.

Four months after coming out, it hit the bestseller list in Chicago. The following week it disappeared from the list. Just like magic. The largest bookstore in Chicago cancelled an autograph party when they found out what was in the book. The local television talk shows would not have me on—even the ones with nationally known hosts.

And the publisher was telling me the book wasn't selling. If there was a demand, he said would put the book out. When I showed him affidavits from bookstores saying they could sell the book if they could get it from the publisher, he stuck to his story.

Finally, Dick Gregory[77] told me to move on to something else. He thought there was a national attempt to destroy the book. And he thought I was going destroy myself worrying over it.

After I spent a year at Harvard studying constitutional law as a Nieman Fellow,[78] I was transferred to the Washington bureau of the *Tribune*. There were no women in the bureau at the time. But after I arrived, I heard the men say, "I'll sure be glad when they get a woman in here."

How did that made me feel? It made me hostile. I'd say aloud, "I'd sure like to get some men in here, too."

They could never see me as a woman. They saw me as a black. Here comes Miss Token. Here comes Miss Affirmative Action. That's why she's here.

I wanted to learn the ropes as a journalist. But when I asked for help, I heard, "I'm not gonna do your work for you."

When they did get a so-called woman in the bureau, the men showed her around. They shared information with her, which they excluded from me. And they gave her stories that she could easily handle.

In 1980 I was sent to the Democratic National Convention to cover "ethnic" news. But I didn't get any assignments. I was told that blacks didn't have an important role, so I didn't have anything to do.

The "important" stories were given to whites. I asked to do something else, but they told me to sit this one out since I only covered blacks. I called them racists. I just went off!

In this business, most editors want a black to cover blacks, nothing else. You shouldn't think about covering space or energy. How about being a foreign correspondent? How many papers allow blacks to become investigative reporters?

It's not that you have to be that smart to do those jobs. They train you. They take young guys, put them under their wing, and in a few years they are winning Pulitzer Prizes.

It's surprising how incompetent are some of the white hotshots I've met in journalism. I traveled with one guy whose stories I'd have to write because he was drunk. He rose further on his newspaper than I could ever imagine rising.

American journalism, I believe, sold us a bill of goods by tagging us as a minority journalist. So they disrespect you. They don't think you can do the job. But most black journalists I know are probably overqualified for what they are paid to do. I used to wonder why many black reporters got out of the business around the age of thirty-five or forty. They *had* to. To keep their sanity.

Being in the Washington bureau was full of pain. But I survived because I always felt that I had a right to be there. I didn't care how foul they got. I had a right to be a journalist.

If Jesse Jackson were ever nominated by the Democratic Party to be president, I would vote for him. I think that even if he had that much power, he would still remember the poor people. He certainly would be more humane than those who have occupied the White House in recent years. And he certainly knows the issues.

Although he said I betrayed him in the book, I had no regrets about writing it. Because he was probably one of the most powerful black leaders that our country will ever have. And I thought he had to be analyzed like any great person, white *or* black.

We never reached the point where we really disliked each other. There was still something of the friendship left.

He called me a few weeks after the book was published, and said, "I think I can live with the book, Barbara."

Then he added, "I'm gonna have to bring you back into the family. I want to give you an award. I want you to come to PUSH."

"Well, okay," I said. "I'll come."

Then I received a telegram from his board saying, "Please don't come. We do not think you deserve this award."

"All right, then I won't come," I replied.

When Jesse heard about that, he called me again.

"I don't think I really want the award," I said.

But he insisted.

"I want you to come here to PUSH. I want to forgive you in front of everybody."

"I don't want to be forgiven," I said. "I haven't done anything wrong. I am a journalist. You can't forgive me for being a journalist."

Finally they sent the award to me in a box. It was a plate. I still have it.

I often recall how I felt when I wrote that book. I sat in my den writing at night. And I would be sweating a cold sweat. My blouse would be soaked.

Jesse was closer to me than any brother could be. And what I was doing was totally tearing down my role as his friend and his cheer-leader. I had to decide whether I was going to be a cheerleader or a journalist, and it was the hardest decision I ever made.

I cried all the time. One night, as I was crying so hard and loud, a little knock came at my door.

It was the four-year-old girl who lived next door.

She looked at me and said, "You big crybaby."

I stopped crying. And I never cried again.

C. SUMNER "CHUCK" STONE

Chuck Stone was a columnist for the Philadelphia Daily News, *when he suddenly found himself as a go-between for prison officials and convicts to negotiate an end to an uprising.*

———

I was nervous, so frightened, because I'd never done this before.

I thought I was going to cry I was so scared.

I kept thinking, *Who the hell are you? You're just a reporter. Just another person. What makes you think you can negotiate with four prisoners who have killed five people?*

This was Sunday afternoon, November 1, 1981, at the Pennsylvania state prison, about forty-five minutes northwest of Philadelphia. Since the siege began four days earlier, on Wednesday, everybody had been on edge.

Joseph "Jo-Jo" Bowen was serving three consecutive life sentences when he tried to escape. Three inmates were with him. They had four guns that had been smuggled in. When they tried to scale a thirty-foot wall, the rope broke, and they couldn't get out. So they regrouped in the kitchen, and took thirty-eight hostages. Three more inmates joined them. Then they let all but six of the hostages go—three guards and three civilian food service workers. They barricaded themselves inside.

Until that time on Sunday, there was no real communication between prisoners and prison officials. Jo-Jo said what he wanted to say. The prisoners couldn't get out, and the state troopers couldn't get in without storming the place.

You could feel the pressure. Two thousand inmates, about 95

percent of them black, had been confined to their cells since the siege began. Everybody was worried about starting more trouble. More than 130 heavily armed state troopers and prison guards were chomping at the bit outside, hoping to storm the place. They were filled with that white macho sickness this country suffers from.

I picked up a metal folding chair and started down the hallway from the command post. I had thirty yards to go to the kitchen, to face Jo-Jo and four guns.

An inmate yelled, "Chuck! Get this motherfucking thing going!"

I looked at the chair I carried. I said, *My God. I'm carrying my own execution chair!* I really thought I was going to die.

The night before, when I was getting ready to go to a party, I got a call from Dick Glanton, who was associate counsel to the governor. Dick's a brother, and we were old friends.

All this time, Jo-Jo refused to talk to anybody but Major Donald Vaughn, one of the prison officials who had the inmates' confidence. Vaughn was a terrific guy—another brother. But Vaughn was unable to learn what demands Jo-Jo was making to call the siege off.

There was talk about all sorts of folks negotiating with Jo-Jo. Somebody mentioned State Senator Milton Street. But Milt was very flamboyant, sort of controversial, a miniature Adam Clayton Powell Jr.[79] They didn't want the kind of publicity he would generate. So Richard Thornburgh, the governor, vetoed Milt.

"Chuck," Dick Thornburgh said, "how do you feel about going up to negotiate with Jo-Jo Bowen and the others?"

Bowen had said he was willing to consider me. But he had not agreed to it.

"Yeah, sure, I'll do it," I told the governor.

I figured I was going up there to talk on the phone. I didn't think I was going to be part of it.

"Okay, Chuck," Governor Thornburgh said. "State troopers will come by tomorrow morning to pick you up."

Why me?

Jo-Jo's mother mentioned my name. She had known about my

role as a congressional aide to Adam Clayton Powell. She said she had always admired me. She read my column in the *Philadelphia Daily News*, of course. And the wife of one of the guards they held hostage, said, "Why don't we send for Chuck Stone?"

Another factor in the decision was that the brothers trusted me. Almost from the time I joined the *Daily News* in 1972, I wrote about police brutality and prison reform. Then a few years later, people wanted for murder started turning themselves in to me.

I was with the Educational Testing Service,[80] when the *Daily News* called. The *News* wanted a black columnist. The other two Philadelphia dailies had columnists, and the *News* had more black readers than those two papers combined. I was getting restless. And since it was a presidential campaign year, I thought it would be nice to be back in the business.

I had always believed there should be more black columnists on white newspapers. And I knew the reason there weren't more was because white America feared black authority. Newspapers didn't mind hiring black reporters, up to a point. But they loved to hire black janitors and maids. The higher up you went on a newspaper, as in other white institutions, the more of a threat you became to the white power structure. That was why there were more black janitors on a white newspaper than anything else black.

In 1975, a lot of black people supported Frank Rizzo for another term as mayor. He went from black church to black church, trying to pick up support. In fact, he asked me to endorse him when we had breakfast at the Nineteenth Street Baptist Church.

"Mayor," I said, "you come out against police brutality, and I'll not only endorse you, I'll be your campaign manager!"

"I can't do that," he said. "The cops need my help."

Rizzo was charming, a helluva nice guy. I liked him personally, and I think we respected each other. I just hated his politics! I hated the fact that he did not do anything to rid the city of police brutality. I thought he was a brutal policeman when he was chief. I thought he was racist. And I always said that and gave him hell. We ended up being good friends. But I used to kick his ass regularly because he was wrong.

Under Rizzo, the Philadelphia police got an outrageously bad reputation as one of the most brutal police forces in the country. Johnny Carson used to joke about the Houston and Philadelphia police forces having a shootout because they were trying to arrest each other! So I wrote about police brutality all the time, because it just stuck in my craw.

One time, in the same month, police shot two handcuffed suspects, both black. Handcuffed! The cops said they were trying to escape. Both were killed.

Another time, a white guy ran a red light. The cops chased him to an all-white area. He was running away because he didn't have a driver's license. When he stopped, a woman policeman pulled him out by the hair and stomped him. And the other cops joined in. They had his picture on page one, with swollen face, black eye. When that story got around, the brothers said, "If they do that to a white boy, what are they gonna do to a nigger?"

Guys appeared in court all the time with bruises all over them. What happened? The police said the suspect fell down the stairs, ran into a wall, or fell off the toilet seat in the patrol wagon when it took a sharp curve going very fast. In the ghetto, we had an underground telegraph system, which put the word around, and the word was this: If you get arrested, the cops will work you over.

On a night in October 1977, I was in the office when I received a phone call.

"Chuck Stone?"

"Yeah."

"This is Chuckie Johnson. Robert Chuckie Johnson. I'm wanted for murder."

I said, "Okay. So?"

He said, "I killed a man a week ago, and I'm tired of running. I've been sleeping in the train station, in subways, backyards, and I'm tired of running. I want to turn myself in to you."

I said, "Why don't you go to the police?"

"No way, man. You know the police. I don't want to get banged around. If I turn myself in to you, they won't touch me."

Without grasping the enormity of what the guy was saying, I said, "Okay. Where do you want to meet?"

He mentioned a bar and said, "No cops. I'm gonna go with you. I'll go to your office."

"Okay."

I brought a photographer with me. We got to the corner where the bar was located. I was nervous. The photographer said, "Go on in."

"No," I said. "Screw you. We're going in together because in case he changes his mind and starts shooting, we're going to die together!"

We walked in together and saw him standing at the bar. He was huge, a big brother, about six feet three. What the white folks would call the perfect stereotype of your average black male.

I said, "Chuckie Johnson?"

"Yeah."

"I'm Chuck Stone."

"Okay. Let's go."

We got into my car. The photographer drove. I was writing the story. I asked Chuckie, "What have you done?"

He was an intelligent guy and had gone to college three years. But he came back to the ghetto and got involved in hustling on the street. The street guys were always teasing him, calling him college boy. One guy made him real mad. He was so angry he couldn't stand it. So he went to the guy's door with a shotgun, and emptied it into the guy. The police wanted him in the worst way.

We brought him to the paper. I called the cops, and they picked him up. We had a big front-page picture showing them handcuffing him. Within two weeks, a seventeen-year-old kid killed a man down near the projects. His mother called me.

"My son wants to turn himself in to you."

He was quite a bad little son of a bitch. He was walking through the projects, and some older guys were playing checkers. Remarks were exchanged. The kid went home, got a gun, and came back and killed this guy—a man old enough to be his father.

So I was standing in the projects waiting for this kid. I was by myself this time. I looked at the twenty-story building. *Somebody could take a pot shot at me*, I said to myself. I hid behind a tree and waited. About twenty minutes later, the mother came out, the sister, the kid. Then we all went down to the main police station.

Another time a guy called the paper at eight in the morning and asked for me. They said, "Mr. Stone hasn't come in yet."

The guy had been out with a chick in an all-night bar where you buy illegal booze. When he left, they ran into her old boyfriend, who beat the hell out of her. When the boyfriend came after the guy with a knife, the guy pulled a gun and shot him. We ran a picture of the victim, which the guy saw.

He called our people, "I killed the guy in the paper. I'm coming to turn myself in to Chuck Stone." The office almost went bananas.

When I got there he was sitting on the windowsill on the seventh floor, next to the main editorial offices.

I said, "Hey, how you doing?"

"Okay."

"You got your gun on you?"

"No. I threw it in the river."

"Cool. Then we can talk now."

I called the police to make sure he was wanted. They came to pick him up.

By the time I got the call from the state prison, a dozen suspects wanted for murder, shootings, or prison escapes had surrendered to me. As for the ones wanted for lesser crimes, I told them to call the public defender.

The odd part was that they knew I had firm beliefs about crime. I believed in the death penalty. And I believed in mandatory sentences for those caught with a gun. I wanted heavy sentences for dope pushers. Yet these people wanted it known to the public that they went into custody with no bruises, and that they were alive.

I wouldn't urge any journalist—anybody—to make a career out of doing this. I wish we had a police force that we trusted to treat anyone they arrested by the rules. But until that happened, I would continue to believe that when those people surrendered to me, I was helping save a human life.

That was the way I felt when the state prison called. The only way I would get involved as a journalist was to save lives.

They sent a black state trooper, a lieutenant, to pick me up. We took off in the car with the siren going, sixty-five miles an hour, all the way to the prison. I felt so important, so hip—sitting in the back, by myself, with the siren going.

We arrived at noon. We sat down and over the next three hours the authorities briefed me and brought me up to date. First, there was Jo-Jo, the leader. He was a car thief. If Jo-Jo had been given a car, or had a car to steal periodically, maybe he wouldn't have gotten into so much trouble. He loved to steal cars. When he was nineteen, he was finally sentenced to prison. Six years later, he came out a raging, angry man. His lawyer said he was the end product of a rotten prison system.

Two days after he was released, he saw an elderly couple enter their home in Germantown. He pointed a pistol at them. When the woman screamed, he shot and wounded both of them. When he tried to steal a car the next day, a police office spotted him. Jo-Jo drew his gun and killed him. He got a life sentence.

Two years later, he received permission to speak with the deputy warden at a prison inside Philadelphia. He and another inmate had converted to Islam and wanted to have religious services. An argument broke out. Jo-Jo produced a knife and killed the deputy warden *and* the warden. Now he had three life sentences.

With him in the escape attempt was Calvin "Pepper" Williams, a drug addict who murdered a college student over a couple of hundred dollars. There was Leroy Newsome who put a gun to the chest of a fourteen-year-old and killed him while he begged for mercy. And there was Lawrence Ellison, who was serving time for robbery.

All four of them were black, as were the three who joined them in the kitchen.

"We have two plans," Glanton said. "Plan A and Plan B. You're Plan B."

Although he never said so, I think Plan A was to storm the kitchen. You couldn't starve them out. There was no way. They had plenty of food and water. And I couldn't see how they could storm the kitchen without a slaughter. There were only two doors you could go through, and the inmates had pushed ovens against the doors.

Then, for the first time, I learned they had four guns. That had not been revealed by the press.

I said, "Oh, shit."

Vaughn repeated himself.

"They've got four guns."

"Major," I said, "are you out of your mind?"

He said, "You're not afraid, are you?"

"Do you think I do this every day?"

Then Vaughn called the kitchen.

"Jo-Jo, Chuck Stone is here."

"Put him on."

"Chuck Stone?"

"Yes, brother?"

"All right. Take your time. We'll be ready in a few minutes, bro'."

I could hear some thrashing about. It sounded like they were rearranging things.

Then Vaughn told me I would go down a narrow hallway with Jo-Jo's brother, Jeff. We would sit on the folding chairs we carried and wait for Jo-Jo to open the door. I would be so close that if Jo-Jo reached out, I could touch his hand.

It was 4:00. Time to go. But I wanted to talk about the guns. While we were talking, Jeff took his chair and walked down the hallway. He sat down and waited for me. I looked at him and said, "I guess I've got to go now."

I walked down the hallway and sat down. The door opened. It was Jo-Jo holding a double-barrel sawed-off shotgun. Pepper Williams had a .38. The brother on the left—Newsome—had a single-barrel shotgun. The other brother had the .22. Four guns were trained on me.

I sat facing death and thought, *God, that's a pretty gun. So shiny.* I looked up at Jo-Jo's intense, dark eyes.

"Assalaamu'alaikum, brother."

He answered with the Islamic greeting: *"Wa' aliakum salaam."*

I knew Jo-Jo was interested in Islamic religion. It was a fundamental tie among brothers in prison, more so than Christianity.

I'm a Christian and will keep on being one. But Christianity unfortunately has been a racist religion. It either approved of or never spoke out against the Ku Klux Klan and lynchings and the most horrendous massacres of the Indians and the blacks. The brothers in prison had turned away from Christianity because they knew that. They believed Christianity had failed them.

Suddenly, we heard some noise downstairs.

Jo-Jo yelled, "What are they trying to do?"

He cocked his gun.

"We're all going to die!"

"Oh, shit," I said. "What a way to go!"

Jo-Jo thought they were trying to storm the place, and they might as well shoot it out. He figured I might be a decoy. I started thinking, *If he starts shooting, do I dive to my left or to my right? If I dive quick enough, maybe I can save my life.*

Somebody had opened the door downstairs by mistake. Then they shut it and everything was okay. We just sat there for minutes, staring in silence.

My toes were curled in nervousness. And they stayed curled like that for three or four weeks. Whenever I'd stand up, my toes would automatically curl. I thought I was going to be like that for the rest of my life!

"Jo-Jo," I said, "where do we go from here?"

He launched into an unbelievable tirade. He talked about dignity and oppression. Of being called "boy" and treated like a boy. About the racist criminal justice system. About white inmates getting ten days in the "hole" for an infraction, but black inmates doing three months for the same offense. He documented incident after incident. And he quoted from Malcolm X and Marcus Garvey.[81] Then he railed against the Uncle Toms in the system.

His rage spewed out like a torrent. But I could see that he was smart, rational, logical, and well-read. He was just full of rage like so many brothers in prison.

My mind was turning. Should I seize on that point? Should I challenge this point? Should I keep quiet? I decided to keep writing, to keep listening to what he said. I let him talk for a half an hour. When I looked at my notes, I saw the same words: racism, oppression, lack of respect.

After he calmed down, he admitted that he was no angel. He had killed three people and was prepared to do his time. But while he was there, they had to give him his respect. That was why he had to get out.

"These pussies are driving me crazy," he said. "If I stay here, I'm gonna fuck up somebody."

I tried to ease the tension.

"Jo-Jo, I want you to know I haven't had anything to eat since breakfast. I'm hungry."

"Well, I just finished a big thick steak."

I said, "Thank you, brother."

They brought two hostages over for me to verify that they weren't being harmed—one white and one black, tied to each other with rope around their necks. *At least,* I thought, *they are equal opportunity hostage takers.*

Then I tried again.

"Jo-Jo, what do you want? What can we do?"

I convinced him to write it down. For psychological reasons, we called them points, rather than demands.

Pepper started to hand them to me.

Vaughn, who was watching from the end of the corridor, yelled, "Don't touch it. Don't touch."

So Pepper slid a metal clipboard across the floor. I, in turn, wishing to show goodwill, slid a copy of my novel, *King Strut,* to the brothers.

"You brothers may want to read this."

They thanked me.

"Jo-Jo," I said, "I'm going to take these twelve points with me, and I will be back tomorrow morning."

"I don't know, man."

"No. I'm coming back tomorrow morning."

What they asked for was reasonable. They weren't asking to be let off, not to be prosecuted. They asked for fair play—equal punishment for blacks in the prison. And they wanted to be sent to a federal prison. I had promised Jo-Jo that the demands would be kept confidential, nothing would be published in the press.

We didn't want any pressures to build up against them. People on the outside would start saying we shouldn't give in to convicts, and that would screw up the negotiations. All the officials—state, federal, and prison—agreed we should keep the demands out of the press.

Late that night, I stopped at my office to write my column about what I had gone through. But I said nothing substantive about the negotiations or the demands. I got home at one in the morning and had a big plate of ham and eggs. But I couldn't sleep, I couldn't stay calm.

About 4:00 in the morning, my city desk called me. The editor said there was an AP report that claimed to have some of the demands Jo-Jo gave me. It came from the *Pottstown Mercury,* the small-town paper next to the prison. Of the five demands he read to me over the phone, three were right on the mark.

"That's not true," I said. "They are absolutely wrong. They're lying."

I told my editor I couldn't publish anything, not even a hint of what the inmates were asking for because I'd given my word. *The Pottstown Mercury* had broken my word for me. Now my life was on the line. I had to go back and face this guy with a gun. If Jo-Jo found out it had been published, he would say, "Nigger, you lied to me. Fuck you."

And then he would shoot me.

When I took the demands to the command center, one of the office secretaries mimeographed copies for distribution to the officials. She must have given one to a reporter.

I was furious! When it came to my integrity versus the *Pottstown Mercury*'s integrity, my attitude was, "Screw the *Pottstown Mercury*." That paper had put my life on the line! It was typical, shitty, small-town journalism.

We didn't print a word.

At 10:00 A.M. the next day, I prepared to go back. I described the layout to Louise, my wife, and told her she couldn't tell anyone.

"Now don't worry," I said. "I don't think anything is going to happen, but you can never tell. I want you to know I love you. I love you and the kids."

Louise wasn't nervous, she was very strong. But sometimes she could be very sardonic and so irreverent. As I walked out the door, she gave me a half-smile.

"If those niggers kill you," she said, "I'll be so mad!"

I said, "Christ! I'll be mad, too, if they kill me."

We had had two hopeful signs during the night. The light had stayed on in the kitchen, and Pepper had called his family to say that they would be coming out soon. But the pressure was still tearing me apart. A war was going on in my stomach. I was popping Mylantas as if they were candy. I was beginning to disintegrate. I knew I couldn't last another day.

By 11:30, the officials had agreed to all twelve points. I knew that we had to settle it this day—or it wouldn't work. I sensed that. But I told everyone that it looked too easy. Jo-Jo wouldn't accept it. We decided to say that we could not promise a change of venue, even though they could go to a federal prison. That point would be out of their control.

When I returned to see Jo-Jo, he gave me six more demands—minor points, but new ones, in any case.

I said, "I'll take these back to the prison people but don't pull this on me again, please."

"Look," he said, "I'm tired of all this shit. I'm ready to go now."

This is some place to die in, I thought. *A corridor in the state prison, after we have put together the most fragile of fragile agreements.*

"Hey, man." I said. "I kept my word. I kept my end of it. I'll be back at 4:00 P.M."

He smirked at me. "You won't be back," he said.

"I'm coming back, goddammit, if I have to come back naked with nothing on, just to see your face when you know I keep my word!"

By now I felt I understood Jo-Jo Bowen. But I still feared him and the others. And when I got to the command center, Dr. Homer Keane, a white guy, a really lovely human being, the chief psychiatrist for the Federal Bureau of Prisons, actually began giving me therapy.

At 3:30 Jo-Jo called. "Where's Chuck Stone?"

I looked at the others, and said, "This is it. We're going to do it now. We're home free."

I went to the door and told Jo-Jo everything else was agreed to.

He said, "We don't think we ought to have to pay for the destruction."

"Damn," I said, "I don't know if I can get that for you."

"No, brother. We're not gonna pay for it!"

"Wait a minute. I'll be right back."

At first, Julius, the superintendent, balked. But then they called Washington. They called the governor's office to see if they could waive holding the prisoners accountable for destruction of state property.

"You have to do it," I kept imploring.

Finally, they agreed.

The federal official, the state official, and I initialed the last set of demands. And I went back to Jo-Jo.

"Jo-Jo, we agree. You're not going to be held accountable for the damage. It won't be deducted from your pay. Everything is agreed to."

"This is cool."

"You agree?"

"Yeah."

"Great."

I was so ecstatic I wanted to scream.

He looked up from the agreement and said, "Chuck Stone. I know you. I've read your stuff."

"Yeah?"

"Yeah. You write some heavy shit."

"Thank you, bro'. I wish you had told me that thirty-six hours ago."

Then he said, "What do we do now?"

"I don't know. I've never done this before."

We stared at each other.

He tried again. "How do you want to do it?"

I said, "I know the hostages have to come out."

Jeff said, "No, no. The guns have got to come out first."

I said, "I've got a better idea. Let the hostages bring the guns out."

Jo-Jo said, "All right."

But then he said, "I've got to get rid of my ammunition first. Empty the weapons."

We went back to the command post, and Jeff said, "Gentlemen, my brother is gonna fire these guns."

So they cleared the hallway.

Jeff and I went in the bathroom near the kitchen. Jeff stood in the corner, and I crouched behind the commode. Then they fired their four guns down the hallway and it sounded like World War II! Emptying the weapons was his last venting of rage.

I opened the bathroom door a little bit to dead silence. A voice said, "Chuck Stone?"

"Yeah, Jo-Jo?"

"We're coming out."

"I'm coming out too."

I thought, *Shit. I hope he's got no more bullets.* I stepped out in the hallway. "Here I am."

"I want to see you."

I moved to the middle of the hallway.

"We're coming out."

It was 5:00 P.M.

The hostages came out first and dropped the guns in a cardboard box by the door.

Then the inmates came out with their hands over their heads. They were stripped naked as they entered the corridor. They were taken to the command post and searched. Then they were given overalls and sneakers.

I sat there, writing furiously. A black lieutenant said, "Chuck Stone! You still writing? We done did the shit!"

When it was time to put the inmates in vans, I went to see Jo-Jo. He was in handcuffs. I put my hands up to his and clasped them.

I said, "Hang in there, good brother."

"Okay, man."

They took him to Lewisburg Penitentiary. The doctors said the hostages were in excellent condition. After the examinations, they were hugging and kissing their families. The relatives cried, telling me thanks, and shaking my hand. Meanwhile, news that the standoff had ended and nobody was hurt spread across the prison. The other inmates—all two thousand—were banging the bars on their cells, calling out, "Chuck Stone. Chuck Stone. Chuck Stone."

I held a press conference before leaving. There were reporters everywhere. It was an incredible experience. You were on center stage in this damn thing. You were both making the news and reporting the news.

When I got to the *Daily News* building, I saw a Channel 3 television crew. One of the guys said, "Here's the man of the hour. Here's the hero. We'll go upstairs and film now."

"You're not going to film me," I said.

He said, "We were told . . ."

"Well, you ain't asked me that."

"It's hot news," he said.

"Fuck hot news!" I said. "I'm not talking to anybody. I'm sorry."

He said, "But you're a reporter."

I said, "Kiss my ass."

I was really upset, wiped out. There was nothing left, nothing in me. I had to dictate my column. I didn't have the strength to type. I couldn't control my muscles. I was emotionally and physically exhausted.

I did only one interview, for a black reporter at *Newsweek,* as a personal favor to his editor, a friend of mine. I turned down *The Today Show, Good Morning America*, Ted Turner. The Canadian Broadcasting Network wanted to send a plane for me. I said no appearances. No nothing.

I told them, "All you son of a bitches always ignore these inmates, these brothers, and now you want to exploit them."

And what did the notoriety mean to me?

It was no big deal. As Horace Greeley once wrote, "Fame is a vapor, popularity an accident, and riches flee with the wind. Those who cheer today, criticize tomorrow. And the only thing that endures is character."

My colleagues at the *Daily News* were beautiful. They wrote terrific columns congratulating me for pulling it off. There was an editorial cartoon showing the Devil trapped in hell and saying, "Get me Chuck Stone!" The editors presented me with a miniature brass cannon to remind me of those moments I hid behind the commode in the bathroom.

There were journalism awards, of course. But the award that mattered most came from the Jaycees organization[82] at the prison. That was the brothers saying "Thank you."

But I also got some scars from that experience. People took pot shots at me. A journalist for the *Philadelphia Bulletin* tore me up. He said no journalist should ever get involved in making news. He said I was on an ego trip.

I agree that newsmen should stay out of news situations, except under one condition: Where human life is involved. If you're walking along the street and you see a guy jump off a bridge and you can swim, then you save him. You don't say, "Well, I'm going to sit here and write this story."

If you can save a life, you get your ass out there and do something! You have no right to remove yourself from a life-threatening situation. When the TV guys in Alabama filmed a guy immolating himself without trying to stop him, they were committing an immoral act, I believe.

Some black reporters and TV hosts said I needed to make a big play, to bolster my political career, to run for Congress. I went in to face four guns to bolster my political career? Incredible! I was fifty-seven-years-old at the time. I didn't need a political career. I was having a ball!

Since the prison uprising, ten more murder suspects have turned themselves in to me. I met one woman with her father in a restaurant. She made the city's Five Most Wanted Criminals list after stabbing a woman during an argument in a bar. And one guy suspected of battering his nineteen-month-old son to death called me after the cops killed a guy they had mistaken for him.

I really don't expect these folks turning themselves in to say thank you. Who wants to say thank you for going to jail? I just wanted to make sure they got fair treatment and were not abused.

But the novelty had worn off. It became a habit. No more pictures on page one. Maybe page eight or nine. And it was fatiguing. I didn't need this in the middle of the night! I didn't need that kind of worry at any hour.

I was flattered by the confidence the suspects had in me. But this was really about a lack of confidence in the police department. And although some of the cops started calling me Sam Spade or Sergeant York, I knew they had mixed feelings. They were glad I was doing the work, but it reflected on their job.

If my mother had been living, I'm sure she would have told me, "Charlie Boy, don't go to the state prison, that's crazy!" But afterwards, she would have said she was proud of what I did. And I would have told her that going there was the result of my Christian upbringing.

I would have reminded her of the passage she read to me so often from the Book of Matthew, Chapter 25, Verse 35:

"For I was hungry and you gave me food, I was thirsty and you gave me drink, I was a stranger and you welcomed me, I was naked and you clothed me, I was sick and you visited me, I was in prison and you came to me."

BERNARD SHAW

Bernie Shaw worked as a television correspondent for CBS and ABC and later became an anchor for CNN.

———

Walter Cronkite was staying at the Reef Hotel in Honolulu, just minutes away.

"Hmm," I said. "I think I'll call him."

This was 1961, and I was a corporal in the Marine Corps, stationed in Kaneohe Bay, working in the communications center. I was sitting in the barracks one morning when I came across a PR photo of Walter and Betsy Cronkite standing in front of the tail section of a jet.

When I was thirteen, I decided that I was going to be a CBS News correspondent. There were no black correspondents then, nor were there any in 1961. But that didn't matter. Edward R. Murrow was my idol. And the man next I admired the most was Walter Cronkite. So I rang his hotel several times that week. He was shooting scenes on the island for a CBS program. I tried at least twenty times, but couldn't catch him.

Finally he answered.

"Mr. Cronkite, my name is Bernard Shaw. I'm from Chicago. I'm a marine stationed here and I want you to know that I admire your work. You're my idol. And I'd desperately like to talk to you about the business."

He invited me to his hotel! I went to my commanding officer and explained what had happened. They let me off.

I met the Cronkites in the lobby. I told him how much I admired him, that, for me, he was right next to Edward R. Murrow. I wanted to know what I would have to do to become a CBS correspondent.

"Come on upstairs," he said. "Let's talk."

He looked at his wife, and she said, "No." They had a formal dinner engagement, so she went upstairs to get dressed.

"Let's stay down here and talk," he said.

I was very nervous. I was like a subject talking to his king. I took notes. My hand was almost too weak to write. At one point, I brought up color.

"You and I are aware of our number-one social problem," I said. "And I want you to know that no matter what you tell me about the conditions of the industry, I'm not going to allow what you say to dee-ter me."

With a smile, Cronkite looked at me, and said, "No, you shouldn't allow anything I say to *deter* you."

So I thanked him for that. Obviously, I have never mispronounced the word "deter" again in my life.

He was a deep source of encouragement in that first meeting. Occasionally, in the following years, I sent letters to let him know what I was doing. But I never asked him to intercede. I wanted to make it to CBS on my own.

I got out of the Marine Corps in 1963 and went back to the University of Illinois. In the fall of '64, Gordon McClendon, a maverick Texan and a millionaire broadcaster, was changing an R&B station, WYNR, over to an all-news format, WNUS. This was in Chicago, and I would go to pester them. I was just a college kid, but I told them I would like to work in their news operation.

"Fine. Do you have any experience?"

"No. But I'm a good reporter."

"How do you know that?"

I talked about my writing in college and the work I'd done in the Marine Corps.

"Well, you know, we need people with experience."

It was the classic story. Raw talent. You just need a break.

When the switch to all-news was completed, they looked for more people. I got my foot in the door. I went from changing paper on the wire service machine to running the copy to the anchors.

In 1966, Martin Luther King brought his campaign to Chicago. He lived in black neighborhoods, and marched into all-white neighborhoods. He was stoned by a white mob. There weren't many black reporters then, so I went in and sat down with the news director, Larry Webb.

"I'll make a deal with you. I will cover Martin Luther King for you day and night for only $50 a week."

He said, "Fine."

I didn't know anybody in the King operation. But I thought I had three things going for me. I was black, I knew Chicago, and I was aggressive.

I met one of the publicists in the movement, and she helped me get wired-in so that I knew what was going on before the reporters for the big papers. I got King's schedule immediately. And I went on the air with some new development every hour. King's people liked that. They could hear the results. I dogged King so much that after a while he started to call *me* "Doctor."

After some months, I moved over to WIND, a Westinghouse station, where I became the education reporter. Soon they brought me inside to anchor our prime evening newscast, *RADIO Newsday*, a fifty-minute program, sponsored by Chevrolet.

One day as I was closing the newscast a disc jockey handed me a bulletin: "Martin Luther King has been shot in Memphis."

It was April 4, 1968.

A cold feeling rushed through my head. I started to pant, the way you breathe hard when you run from the wire room to your typewriter, and you're late, and you're on deadline, and you're going on the air—and you fight to control your breathing, in order to come up sounding professional. That's how I felt.

I also felt a surge of anger. Yet I knew that I had to be a professional. I had to close out the newscast. A fight between emotionalism and professionalism was going on in my head. I was determined that professionalism would win. I read the bulletin on the air. Then a few other bulletins came in, and we moved them.

Within the hour, I was at O'Hare Field. A Delta flight was leaving Chicago for Memphis. The plane was overbooked, people were fighting to get on, it was total pandemonium. We turned the flight into a press plane. Photographers, wire service people—all of us crowded on the plane, standing in the aisles. The flight attendants couldn't make anybody sit down. So we made a deal that we would sit down for take-off. But as soon as we were up, everybody started frantically running through the plane, exchanging information.

When we arrived in Memphis the airport was deserted. No cabs, no porters. The ticket office was closed. We spotted a cab. Six of us—most of the Chicago reporters—paid the cabbie forty dollars to take us into Memphis downtown. Naturally, we wanted to go to police headquarters. As the cab approached, we saw that guys with shotguns guarded every door around the police station. These were scared-looking officers. We knew that King was dead.

We got out and showed our press credentials and went inside. I walked to the second floor. You could hear your footsteps on the marble. The corridor was darkened with night lighting. One florescent light beamed down ten yards away. I walked past an opened door, and then turned back and looked into the room. Under a light, sitting around a table were three guys, all alone. No other aides. No policemen or anything. Just in that room alone. Jesse Jackson, Ralph Abernathy,[83] and Andy Young.[84] They were still giving statements to the police. And tears were streaming down their faces.

I had covered them in Chicago, so they sort of knew who I was, but I didn't go into the room. I couldn't intrude. I didn't feel that I should walk in there.

Naturally, the next place we wanted to go was the Lorraine

Motel, where Martin was murdered. We went there and looked at the angles. We looked through the bathroom window across the alley, and then walked to where the shots were fired. For the next forty-eight hours, it was bedlam.

When Martin's body was ready for shipment home on the plane that Robert Kennedy had ordered, two seats were provided for the press. I was to have one seat, and the other would go to a reporter from the *New York Times*. The people in the King group knew me. They trusted me. And I was black.

But our news director in Chicago had gotten very uptight because the Washington office had ordered me to Memphis without asking him—which of course was petty. This was the most important story in the world at that moment, not just in the United States. He just bitched and bitched to Washington that Bernie Shaw had been taken out of his bureau without anyone asking him. He was adamant about my coming back to Chicago to help cover the riots in his city.

I had no choice. I stood next to Martin's coffin as it was loaded from the hearse onto the conveyor belt to enter the plane. It was the deepest hurt for me, knowing that I would not be on that plane going to Atlanta. I would not be there to report the final episode.

Later in the year, I was promoted and transferred to the Washington bureau as a national correspondent covering urban affairs. Six months later, I was assigned to the White House.

Westinghouse[85] put out a sheaf of screaming press announcements pointing out that I was the first black correspondent for a major network to cover the White House. I didn't especially like that. I have never liked a spotlight on me because I'm black. I believe that I'm a professional journalist first, a black second.

One day in 1971 I got a call from CBS. They asked me to do an audition. I didn't know it, but they had been watching me, talking to people who saw me working in the White House, or who had worked with me in Chicago.

CBS offered me a job. After a fight to get out of my contract with Westinghouse, I went aboard as a general assignment reporter. Lesley Stahl, Connie Chung, and I were the Class of '71. The three of us were hired within three weeks of one another.

I waited until I was officially on board before telling Walter Cronkite. He sent me a letter of congratulations.

I'd been on the job exactly three and a half weeks when I was thrown into one hellacious situation. President Nixon was going through the thing about wage and price controls. He had a huge blowup with the labor leader, Leonard Woodcock.[86] Labor was against controls being put on wages. It was the lead story on the Cronkite show that night.

And guess who the reporter was?

CBS had an elaborate editorial process. It was rare that something you wrote got on the air unedited or unchanged. But Walter Cronkite had a habit of waiting until the last minute to read copy from reporters in the field. Walter didn't see my script until twenty minutes to six, and our first feed went out at 6:30.

The script had been approved in Washington and New York by the Cronkite producers. But when he read the story, he didn't like the lead or the second paragraph. He didn't like the thrust of the story. Mind you, I'd been covering the story for a couple of weeks. I knew damn well what the story was. But there were instances when correspondents were not trusted as to their judgment.

Walter was an ex-UP reporter, and he always tended to lean toward what the wire service lead was. A comparison was always made between what our guy or gal in the field reported, and what the wires were saying.

The hotline rang. It had a funny ring in the Washington bureau. It sounded very pleasant. "Ding-ding-ding." But generally when you picked it up, you caught hell!

My producer said, "You gotta change your script."

"Why?"

"Walter doesn't like it."

We had a frantic argument. It lasted twenty seconds. There was no time to argue longer. It was now 6:05, twenty-five minutes from airtime.

"What doesn't he like?"

"He wants you to change the lead."

"What you're telling me is that he wants the UP lead. You know that the story is this. You approved it! The people in the corner office approved it! The people in New York approved it! But now Walter wants a new lead!"

This created a technical problem. I was supposed to do my report and then throw it to Richard Threlkeld in Los Angeles for a West Coast reaction. All of that was on tape. The tape was ready to go. But now Bernie Shaw's got to go "live," which was fine. We always did a lot of things live at CBS as developments warranted or facts changed. So I quickly sat down and rewrote the lead, based on my understanding of the way Cronkite thought it should be.

My heart was pounding. I could actually hear my heart pounding, like the story-high mock-up of a heart in the Museum of Science and Industry back home, which goes "boom-boom-boom." My fingers were trembling on the typewriter keys. I was sweating. My makeup was running. I was rewriting the first three graphs.

New York began to get concerned because they realized that they were putting intense pressure on a rookie reporter who had the lead story. They were also aware that they had approved the script an hour before. So now the question was whether Bernie Shaw— this new hire—would make it. I knew that my career was riding on what would happen in the next forty minutes. By now the technical people were running out the back door of the bureau, to string live cable up the street to the pay board lobby.

At 6:20 I got final approval. I ran down the stairs. Secretaries held doors open. I hit the street. A stopwatch bounced out of my pocket and shattered. I glanced at it and kept shagging. I had to get the camera positioned at the pay board. I was out of breath. I'd almost lost physical control.

I was there. I had to quickly cool down, put on fresh makeup, and try to memorize the lines. I was in front of the camera. The first time I tried it, I blew two words. No good.

The producer said, "We've got to do it over. You've got one more chance."

I took it all the way down to the sound bites. Labor chief Leonard Woodcock looked very angry. Then I said, "For more on this, we go to Richard Threlkeld."

This was "live" on tape. And it was now 6:29. A courier grabbed the tape and ran it back to the bureau to the control room.

The director yelled, "I need a time on this. I've got to know the length of Bernie's piece."

So they fast-timed it. And the show was coming on.

"Direct from our newsroom in New York, it's the *CBS Evening News with Walter Cronkite*. Bernard Shaw in Washington . . ."

They were still timing the piece.

Cronkite was saying, "This afternoon, President Nixon's pay board was disrupted when organized labor decided to walk off . . ." His writers had smartly written extra copy. Cronkite was into his roll cue—words leading to my report. The tape was retracked. He said, "For more, Bernard Shaw reports."

I came up talking—flawlessly. I don't know how I got upstairs to the control room to watch. I sat there, exhausted.

People started filing past, congratulating me and shaking their heads in disbelief. When somebody's crashing, you stand back and empathize with them. You don't interrupt them. You try to help them out.

A producer walked up to me. "I want to tell you something. I have never seen anything like that before. You're going to do well with this company."

People think this business is all glamorous. But after a while the glamour wears off.

To go into the Washington bureau as a reporter, thinking that you were going to make great waves, was difficult. Look at who was there—the brothers Kalb, Roger Mudd, Dan Rather, Nelson Benton,

George Herman, Eric Sevareid.[87] Some of those guys were originally Murrow's boys. You didn't make great waves, it didn't happen that way. CBS had a process for grooming people it chose to groom. And that process weeded out the people faint of heart.

Two years later, I was promoted to correspondent. It was a dream fulfilled. I passed the word that I would like to cover Latin America. I was fascinated with the area. And I had learned to speak Spanish. But I was told the whole area was already spoken for.

After four years, I was convinced that I would not be sent to Latin America as a CBS correspondent. About this time, George Watson told me that if I came over to ABC, I could cover Latin America. "We'll make you bureau chief." I joined ABC in April of 1977, based in Coral Gables. Goodbye CBS.

One night in November of the following year, I was in a Miami Beach hotel. I was to pick up an award for an ABC entertainment program. Nobody in New York wanted to spend a weekend flying to Florida to pick up a trophy. As the bureau chief, I got the call. It was a boring banquet. I was anxious to get back home. I had been out of the country for three weeks, and it seemed that I was always away from Linda and the kids 85 percent of the time.

When the banquet was over, I started driving across the causeway. I turned on the radio and listened to the NBC News on-the-hour. I heard a report that a California congressman named Leo Ryan was missing or had been killed. There was something else about four others being killed, but I didn't quite catch it all. So I decided to stop by the office to check the wires and see what was in the mail.

In a small bureau, you tended to turn the wire machine off on the weekend. So I was waiting. And before anything came up I called my wife.

"Where have you been?" Linda said.

"I'm in the bureau. I just stopped off from the hotel to check the mail, to see what's going on. I'll be home in a few minutes."

"They have been looking for you. You've got twenty-five minutes to get out to Miami Airport. There's a Lear jet, and the crew is waiting for you."

"What's going on?"

"You better call New York."

I called New York.

"We want you to get down to Georgetown, Guyana, right away. Not only is Congressman Ryan dead, but other people are dead too."

I grabbed my bag and went to the airport. When I got there, it was like a convention of Latin American correspondents. But what I was told was not happening. Our jet was not there, it had mechanical problems. The other networks took off before me. I finally got my jet around two in the morning, which didn't amuse me at all.

People were asking, "Can we get a ride on your jet?" I gave a ride to Peter Arnett of AP.

"You can go down with me. Just don't say anything to anybody."

Peter sat on top of some equipment. We went wheels-up at three. When we were airborne, I asked Peter, "Would you like a drink?"

"Yeah, sure."

I pulled out the drawer and saw some Chevas.

"I'll be damned," he said. "You network guys!"

Our pilot was getting reports on what was going on. New York was trying to fill me in on the People's Temple. I had never heard of it. It was an obscure cult in San Francisco run by a half-mad self-appointed messiah named Jim Jones. Apparently he had convinced a thousand of his followers to set up a commune in the middle of the jungle. He called it Jonestown. Congressman Ryan had gone there on a fact-finding mission, concerned for some in the Jones group who wanted to get away.

We landed at Georgetown's International Airport. Guyana was a steamy South American country. I had never been there. The first thing I noticed were helicopters going in and out of Jonestown. We were frantic. We ran from person to person trying to learn something. There were Guyana government officials and American embassy officials at the airport.

"No! You can't go to Jonestown."

Everybody was stopped cold from going. Physically. The pilots from the choppers passed the word: "Something really terrible is out there. It stinks."

We knew the story was in the jungle. But we couldn't get there. The frustration was mind-blowing. The Lear jets kept coming in. Off popped Karen DeYoung of the *Washington Post.*

"Bernie, what's going on?"

I gave her a fill. I always gave people—even if they were the competition—a fill. In a situation like that, you wanted to be helpful because you never knew when you were going to need help. I did the same thing the following days. I carried out film for the wires, for *Newsweek* and *Time.*

There were no satellites in Guyana. So New York had to erect a feed point for the story. And it was not anywhere close to where the story was. The feed point was San Juan, Puerto Rico—two-and-a-half hours away by Lear jet. That was the closest thing we could get. This was Sunday in the United States. So the first news would be the 6:30 evening news.

We were still frustrated at the airport. Then we heard that we would get an eyewitness account to the shooting of Congressman Ryan from an NBC producer. He said a NBC crew was at a dirt airstrip. Ryan was trying to take off with some people defecting from Jonestown. A tractor showed up pulling a trailer filled with assassins who opened up. Ryan was killed. So was Greg Robinson, a reporter for the *San Francisco Chronicle.* Also killed was an NBC reporter, Don Harris and his cameraman, Bob Brown. Both of them had survived Vietnam.

We heard how Bob Brown had continued to roll his camera even though he was being shot to death. Steven Sung, the NBC soundman, was connected to Brown by a cable. The gunmen shot Brown point-blank. Sung played dead and survived. It was horrifying.

We had our first story. The race was on. Communications at most airports were terrible. But here it was abysmal. I found a Pan

Am ticket office. They were closed, but I bribed a couple of custodians to let me use the phone—gave them $25 each, probably a month's salary for cleanup people. They let me in the manager's office, and I was able to use his phone.

So now I was doing two jobs. I was trying to keep the radio network off my back by filing for them. And I had to make sure the TV people got what they needed by monitoring what I was giving the radio guys.

A producer had arrived on our second Lear. I wrote the script, recorded the track, did a stand-up close, and then passed him the cassettes. He was off to Puerto Rico. The race was on, but it was not as competitive as we thought.

CBS's man decided to fly to Caracas to try to feed from there. New York had already told me the only place to feed from was Puerto Rico. Caracas was down. When he got to Caracas, the CBS guy found that out, so he left for Miami. But in his frenzy he forgot his tapes in the airport terminal. When he got to Miami, he literally did not have a story.

I almost cried when I heard it. I really felt sorry for him. That was a terrible thing to happen to anybody.

The competition actually started the next day. We're talking about Monday. The networks really cared about their evening news programs, Monday through Friday. That was their bread and butter.

We went into town after the feed was ready and checked into our hotel. As soon as I got to my room, I walked downstairs and saw three black women on the switchboard. I went behind the counter and gave each of them an envelope—$50 each. It assured us that we would have it easier getting our reports out, as well as talking to our TV people ahead of anyone else.

By this point we had been working for ten hours and hadn't even seen the capital city. So we'd been awake for thirty-six hours. But we went out on the streets anyway. The American embassy was a complete zero. We pestered the government people, the police headquarters, and the military service.

"What's going on?" we begged.

You had to blanket the city, talk to anyone. We began to understand that something awful had happened out there in the jungle.

We got a word or two here, a raised eyebrow there. I began to realize there were hundreds of dead. They had committed suicide. Most of them were *black!*

I got the same feeling I had when I received the bulletin that King had been shot. I felt a cool rush in my temples. *This is incredible,* I told myself. We had never known that black people were prone to take their own lives. There had always been a racial pride in the fact that no matter however much blacks were mistreated in their history, one thing that they had never done was to act crazy and kill themselves. I was sweating. I was depressed.

The next morning the interior minister announced that there were hundreds of bodies out in the jungle. A gasp went over the news conference. In his paranoid madness, Jim Jones has forced or induced 912 followers to die with him. Most of them drank or were forced to drink a cyanide-laced FlaVor-Aid fruit drink.

Jones told them, "Everyone has to die. If you love me as I love you, we must all die or be destroyed from the outside."

He had promised the unwanted—the poor, the old, blacks, other minorities—they would live in a jungle paradise. He gave them a hell instead.

By this time on Monday morning, Guyana time, *Good Morning America*, *The Today Show,* and *CBS Morning News* were still on the air. I didn't wait for the news conference to end. I crawled across the floor to the cameraman.

"I want you to keep rolling. Roll on everything."

Not a single word of the press conference had been broadcast. I ran out to the hall and stood in the middle of the street. I waved down a cab.

"I'll give you $10 to take me to the hotel right now!"

He rushed me to the hotel. I ran into the lobby.

"Give me an outside line!"

I ran upstairs, laid down my tape recorder, and got everything squared away. The operators punched me through. I did a live radio bulletin that nine hundred bodies had been found in the jungles of Guyana. The radio editors were incredulous. They knew it was factually true because I was reporting it. But it was just incomprehensible.

I stayed on the line and Steve Bell debriefed me for *Good Morning America*. And ABC radio network had the story from the press conference out so fast that the wire services started quoting us!

The news conference had ended when I got back. My camera crew was taking notes and catching highlights. Those guys were reporters, too. We tried to bribe our way into Jonestown. We had only a precious few hours.

Meanwhile, I talked to New York constantly. It became clear that the World Series of journalism was on for this story tonight.

I asked myself, *What do we have?* The news conference. The crew took the only footage of Leo Ryan's body being brought back in a rubber bag in a station wagon and taken to a mortuary. They must have paid somebody some money because they shot it in a restricted area.

I kept looking at my watch. I had it set on New York time. No matter what was happening in Guyana, you had to know the time in New York. It was a two-and-a half hour flight to San Juan. I had to be wheels-up from Guyana no later than two-thirty. That meant I had only an hour and a half to do whatever else I was going to do with the story.

New York told me they were flying an editor and equipment to San Juan to edit whatever I had. Besides worrying about the story, I had a horrific headache. I needed sleep.

"What is important to the American people in this story?" I asked. "Factually, hundreds of people have been slaughtered or committed suicide. But what do I leave them with?"

I realized that I should show the American audience the mood in the capital. Otherwise, they would think the whole country was coming apart. I did a stand-up in front of the American embassy with the flag at half-mast. Life still goes on. But out there in the jungle, it's a different matter.

I jumped in the car, and we raced to the airport. We were waiting for a second crew to come in. I said, "You can have the best pictures and interviews in the world, but if you don't have time to edit the stuff, your story's not going to get on the air."

I told the crew, "You guys, I want you to go with me on the plane to Puerto Rico."

They were as exhausted as I was. This meant they would get some rest, besides helping me edit. I was really concerned about their rest. If you've got an exhausted cameraman, he might make serious mistakes with focus or other technical matters. If the soundman is not alert, he could ruin a whole interview for you.

The other networks didn't understand what I was doing. They said, "Why is Bernie's crew going to San Juan?"

When I got on the plane, I told Bruce, "Set up the camera so that I can put a cassette in the deck and look through the viewfinder." I wanted to look at every piece of tape that we'd shot. Once we were airborne, Bruce said, "I think we should try to get aerials from Jonestown."

"You know it's almost three o'clock ," I said.

A few seconds later, I decided to chance it. While we worked in the city, our pilots had talked to the helicopter pilots who were bringing bodies back. So they had the coordinates of Jonestown. We cleared the tower quickly. When we were about two miles out, we made a turn. We didn't get permission or anything, which was dangerous. First of all, we were flying into airspace which we had not been cleared for, and other planes could be operating in that area. But our guys were being very careful.

Jonestown was a little more than a hundred miles away. We got there fast. We went in and made one pass. It was eerie because you saw the bright speckled colors—blues, reds, yellows, greens, oranges. I wondered, *What the hell is that?*

From the air, with the bright South American sun beaming down, the colors were exaggerated. They just sort of exploded. We wanted to go down closer. And we needed to go slower. A Lear jet flies fast, so we did something that was very, very dangerous. But we were working under the gun. We were on deadline. And we were competing.

Bruce, who was very tall, situated himself in the cabin. He held the camera steady. We took the Lear down as close and as slow as we could go. We were bordering on stalling. But we got good shots. Then it occurred to us what those bright spots were. It was the blankets and brightly-colored clothing of dead people. Dead people stacked up in the sun.

I said, "Bruce, we've got to get the fuck out of here. If we don't, we're gonna miss the bird."

So we took off. For the next two-and-a-half hours, sitting at my little typewriter, I structured in my mind what the story was. How are we going to begin? In effect, I was producing my own story.

I opened a Coke and poured it over ice. For a moment, I looked out the window. I thought, *The whole network is riding on my shoulders with this one story.*

"Damn," I said aloud, "that's a lot of pressure!"

I went back to writing. I screened every piece of tape. I made notes of where the interior minister was in the cassettes. Where the picture of Ryan's body was in the rubber bag. The aerial shot. I was writing very tightly. When you cover a very full story like this, you tend to overwrite.

It was 4:00 Eastern time. We were halfway to San Juan.

I didn't know that ABC had an editor in place, a producer there, and a truck waiting at the airport. And there was Mr. Fixit, a local guy who knew every policeman and all kinds of shortcuts. So when we arrived in San Juan, we cleared customs quickly.

We came out of the side door, and Mr. Fixit said, "Bernie Shaw, ABC?"

"Yeah."

We jumped in the back of a freight delivery truck, and a tarp was thrown over us. The guy was going fifty-five miles an hour during rush hour, on the wrong side of the street, with a siren and red lights flashing. And we got to station WAPA, the ABC affiliate, in twenty-five minutes through rush-hour traffic.

The producer held the door open. I ran into the entrance. A phone line had been opened to New York. Av Weston and Tom Capra[88] got on the line.

"What do you have, Bernie?"

I told them the major elements.

"Let's do it. Now, get off the phone! We'll let you work."

It was now 5:30. I was hyper. I turned to the editor who had flown in.

"Look, first of all, we track. You've got to lay down your picture here. I want you to go ten minutes into this cassette. You'll find this picture."

In effect, I was producing the piece. Only I knew where all the pictures were. We got the piece laid down, and we were ready to bird.

It was ten minutes away from airtime. We told the show that we were going to make it. The last shot was being laid in. We put the piece on the bird, and that piece came down in New York.

When the competition arrived in San Juan, they tried to screen and edit in twenty minutes. It was impossible. They couldn't figure out how it was that I was able to arrive in Puerto Rico with a complete spot ready to go. The trick was simple. Take your crew along so you can screen on the flight. That's why we beat them.

I heard later that when the opposition saw the piece coming down in the control room at CBS, they said, "Bernie Shaw is kicking our ass in Guyana."

That night Walter Cronkite called a meeting at CBS and chewed ass. "We got beat by one of our own people." He was so angry he sent a top producer down from the Washington bureau. Roger Mudd told me, "I hear you handed us our head on a platter."

I didn't physically get into Jonestown. It was always a pool situation. And I felt that it was more important for my cameraman to get there than for me to walk through it. What was important was to make sure that ABC had good pictures.

I depended on Jack Clark. And Jack suffered through it. He dealt with the stench of the bodies, bodies melting, literally melting, in their own oil. The stench affected him so much that he could only hold his shot—keep the subject in focus—for six or seven seconds at a time. He put a handkerchief over his mouth. He fought back the tears. Then he was crying. He could only shoot in short bursts.

After about a week, I got some help. I was completely run down, physically and mentally. By now, CBS had four producers on the scene. We were overtaken. I was later chewed out. I was told that I should have asked for more help. I shouldn't have waited so long. I didn't mind that so much. We excelled when it counted—in the first couple of days.

A few months later, I was in Nicaragua covering the unrest there, the opposition to the dictator Samoza. In June, I finished the assignment and prepared to leave Managua. When I left they sent in Bill Stewart. He was in New York, working general assignment. They decided we had better keep Nicaragua staffed.

Every afternoon, at 5:00 P.M., the network sent material to all their affiliates across America. Some of it could be used for their early evening newscasts. On this day, the feed from Nicaragua was obviously going to be the top news going out to our affiliates. I was in the Washington bureau watching the afternoon feed with Frank Reynolds.

We saw it unfold.

The film showed Bill Stewart walking up to a guardsman to try to talk to him. The guardsman waved him off.

But he goes back and kneels down to show that he means no harm. Then he pulls out his press pass.

The guardsman walks over with a rifle. He orders Bill to lay prone on the street in the gutter.

Then a guy walks up and squeezes off one round. Bill's head and body plop up off the pavement and then fall back down. Obviously, he's dead.

Jack Clark, our cameraman, had the presence of mind to sit in the van and keep filming all this.

Frank Reynolds got up. He turned and slowly walked into his office, and slammed the door. I started crying uncontrollably.

I'd known Bill Stewart for two years. We played the scene again. I felt intense guilt. I knew that it was not my fault that he was there. But I felt guilty because a good correspondent, a good human being, was murdered on my beat. I felt that I should have been there.

I know that had I been there, it wouldn't have happened. My skin color was the same as the skin color of the guy who squeezed off the round. I spoke Spanish, Bill didn't.

The whole tone of my work in journalism began to change. I began to think that ABC didn't pay me enough to take such risks. I loved my wife, my kids, and myself too much to keep taking the risks.

I told New York, "It's been fun until now. I realize you're not going to have somebody to replace me next week or next month. But I want to tell you formally that I would like a transfer."

After a few months a reporter was sent to take my place. And the family and I moved back to Washington.

I felt good. I had been promised a major candidate for the presidential campaign, George Bush. At the beginning of the New Year, I picked him up. We did our first special out of Des Moines, at the Iowa Caucus. Frank Reynolds came on the air and threw it to me. I asked Bush how he had done with the caucus and if he thought he could keep up his momentum.

A couple of weeks later I ran into ABC executive Dick Wald in Washington.

"You know," he said, "I thought that was a very mediocre interview you did with George Bush."

"Dick, I'm surprised to hear you say that."

I continued, "Did you know that the two questions I asked Bush had been decided on a week before the special? It was a heavily scripted show. The structure of the show required that I ask two questions."

I was saying that Bernie Shaw didn't decide what would be asked.

A couple of weeks later, I went back to Washington. When I got to the bureau, I told a desk assistant I would be going out to New Hampshire for the primary campaign there.

"You're not going to New Hampshire," he said.

"What are you talking about?"

"Brit Hume is going to New Hampshire."

I wasn't officially notified by anybody in a ranking position that I was being pulled off Bush as the primary correspondent. Later I found out that I could stay on to do radio and the *Good Morning America* spots. I asked people why I was taken off, and nobody could tell me anything. There was not one word of criticism from anybody about my work.

I decided that unless I remained the primary correspondent on George Bush, I would have nothing to do with the campaign, absolutely nothing. I would just do general assignments out of the Washington bureau.

Brit Hume felt awful. He said, "I don't like what they're doing to you. Nobody likes what they're doing to you."

Of course I was embarrassed when I told Bush that I was not going to be covering him. His aides seemed shocked. He had a quizzical look on his face.

"Why?"

"I don't know. They just want to make a change."

"I didn't always agree with what you said, but I thought you were doing a good job."

This was one of the few times in the business that I really had to ask myself: *Is this a legitimate journalistic decision being made by management, or is this the result of racism?*

I decided that I certainly wouldn't charge racism publicly. And I decided that I had no grounds on which to charge it privately. But I suspected that it was there. What bothered me, what frustrated me, was that I could not prove it. If I could have proved it, I would have confronted management privately, not publicly. But I couldn't. And that aggravated me more than anything else.

The 1980 presidential campaign went right past me. I sat it out. My contract ran out a few months later.

I joined CNN and became an anchor.

AUSTIN SCOTT

Austin Scott covered the civil rights movement for the Associated Press in New York. "How should a black journalist consider himself?" he asked. "As a black first? Or a journalist first?"

———

I never found being black a disadvantage in the news business—unless you wanted to get hired.

When I graduated, I couldn't find a job with anybody. This was 1961. I had a degree in journalism from Stanford. I had done one summer as a vacation replacement with the Associated Press, and I had worked part-time at the *Palo Alto Times*. Despite all that, I couldn't get hired.

Finally, I took a job as a copyboy at the *Oakland Tribune*. I was sharpening pencils and getting coffee for a drunk editor who would come-to long enough to yell, "Boy!"

Oh, sure, being black can be an advantage in covering some stories because you can get in places that white people can't unless somebody black knows them. It ranges from black caucuses, at political conventions, to a black neighborhood that has erupted into a riot.

If you believe that the job of the news media is, as Bob Maynard[89] says, to try to be an instrument of community understanding, then we need a lot of different kinds of stories. That means stories written by people with different perspectives. And sometimes a radically different perspective is needed to penetrate the hidden stories about the experiences of different groups. A lot of groups certainly didn't get fair treatment in the news media ten, fifteen, twenty years ago, and they sometimes still don't even today.

I got into journalism rather innocently. Until college, my only connection with journalism had been as a newsboy delivering the *Philadelphia Bulletin* at Lincoln University. I rode around with huge stacks of papers that overbalanced my bicycle so much I couldn't let it go because it would tip over. It never occurred to me to wonder how the words got into the paper. I just carried it because I needed to make some money.

I was a physics major my first three years in college. But I discovered that physics was mostly math, and I decided that I didn't really love it. So I was looking for something else when I joined the school paper at Stanford, which I did because I had to have an activity credit. I discovered I liked reporting. It was a license to ask a whole bunch of nosey questions and expect that I had a right to get answers. And I was discovering more about the world.

I picked Stanford rather than some other school because Stanford was the only university we looked at—and we looked at several—which had a brochure with a specific statement that people were not hazed because of their color, age or academic status. My friends were white, in part because that was what was available in my class. There were only three or four black students at that time, and the others were either above or below me in class, so there was no real cohesion. There weren't any racial incidents as such, because there weren't enough of us around to be threatening.

The newspaper guild began to put pressure on the Associated Press because the AP didn't have any full-time blacks. Never had any, and the guild was threatening a discrimination suit. My name came up because I had applied at the San Francisco bureau. The bureau chief told New York that I was easy to check out because his daughters had gone to Stanford, too. He said he would talk to the journalism dean. So I got a Good-White-Folks-Seal-of-Approval and three days later, the AP called and said, "We have an opening now."

I went to work that summer doing odd jobs and the night radio wire. I was the first full-time black at the AP. But this was a temporary summer fill-in, and at the end of the summer, they had to send me some other place because whoever was on summer leave came back. I turned down their first offer, which was Chicago. I took the second one, and went to Sacramento as a political reporter to cover state government.

After three years I grew restless. I decided to change jobs. I applied to *Time* magazine, so I had to fly to New York. When AP got wind of that, they said, "We'll send you to New York." I said okay and got transferred to New York in May of 1964.

Harlem erupted in flames a few weeks later. It was the first of the great urban riots of the Sixties. And it was a real eye-opener, because I didn't realize how deep the anger and rage ran in the black community.

I never had the feeling of having lived in a large black community as a full-time participant. I was eight years old when my family moved from the south side of Chicago to Lincoln University in Pennsylvania. My dad was an administrator at Lincoln under Horace Mann Bond,[90] who was Julian Bond's father. He was hired as business manager and later became vice president.

My mom raised me and my brother. She didn't work. I grew up two doors away from Julian Bond, who became a well-known civil rights leader. Despite that it was a black university, I had a fairly sheltered experience. Lincoln was a very artificial atmosphere. The school was out in the country, away from everything except some real Ku Klux Klan–type towns, which my parents kept me away from. I didn't hang around so much with the students as I did with other faculty kids.

My parents were upward-looking, middle-class–oriented blacks, who felt that their kids didn't need to learn a lot about ghetto problems. Their children needed to have self-confidence and to be determined to get ahead, to learn all the values that you needed to move ahead in white middle-class America.

So I found myself in the streets of Harlem for AP.

We had a number of years of riots, or "urban rebellions," whatever you want to call them. Scores were killed. Hundreds were injured. Whole neighborhoods were gutted. Some people saw it as the next logical stage growing out of the civil rights movement, which began in the South with the sit-ins in 1960—a nonviolent pressure movement that said essentially, "We are being wronged, and we will take whatever measures we have to take to point this out until you come to your senses and stop wronging us."

Black folks in the North were so fed up that they lashed out in riots. The question raised was: "Why would people bring down their own neighborhoods?"

The answer was because they were mad and weren't going to take it anymore. That kind of expression didn't emerge in the most rational form. It just came out as rage.

I was taught in journalism school and by the editors at AP that the goal was objective reporting. That was constantly drummed into me: Good Reporters Are Objective. They tell both sides of the story, and they don't favor one side or the other.

But by the time I got into the streets of Harlem and Chicago and Cleveland and Buffalo and Rochester and watched them burn, it was clear to me that this was a story that you could not be objective about. Because objective reporting, in the terms of the mainstream white media, meant writing something they found believable. And they did not know enough about black communities to find what was going on in the streets of America believable. So they automatically discounted a certain proportion of what a black reporter told them.

Thus black reporters could not tell what we *actually* saw in the streets. The white media wouldn't believe us. Or we were accused of being biased, of reporting in favor of black interests, all of which was taboo at that time.

Sometimes the editors said, "This is too extreme." Or, "We don't want to offend our readers." Or they used some euphemism that really meant, "I don't believe that is really going on out there."

I soon learned there was no such thing as objective reporting. Everybody has a point of view. If someone tells you that you're objective, they are probably saying that you have met their biases in terms of what you are reporting.

I decided that my role in covering the riots would be to get as much of what was really happening onto the AP wire as I could. That is, what black people were feeling. Somebody else could cover the police department. Somebody else could cover the politicians. But nobody was going to cover the streets if I didn't do it.

Right away, as I found myself on the streets in tense times, I learned that white folks couldn't read black folks' faces. Every crowd that developed was always described by white reporters as "menacing," "angry"—you name it. It might have been just folks who came out on the street to see why there was a commotion in their neighborhood. But the white reporters couldn't tell the difference.

The white guys stayed behind police lines. They weren't out where I was. But there were times when I needed to watch what was going on in the streets, with the community and the cops, too. I found there were certain places in the streets of black America where you could do that without actually being a part of either crowd.

From time to time, I'd make sure that I was in one of those places, where I could get an overview. Sometimes it was up on a fire escape. Sometimes it was in a window. Sometimes just on a different street. You watched the horizon, waiting for the red plume at night, the smoke circling by day. And you'd head there.

The Harlem riots broke out when a white policeman shot a black kid. He said the kid threatened him with a knife. But the kid was shot in the back of the head, and the cop had prior commendations for disarming criminals armed with knives *and* guns.

Some witnesses said he put the knife in the dead kid's hand.

The cops had formed helmeted lines and were advancing with guns and clubs against the crowd in the street. All the white reporters were back behind the lines—partly because they were afraid, partly because it was the way they reported stuff, partly because Harlem to them was like a foreign country.

I didn't want to get pegged that way by staying behind police lines. So I was in the streets running with the folks. And I felt comfortable there.

In Mississippi and Alabama, cops could get away with anything. There was a lot of fear of police officers. But in Harlem and in other places in the North, folks would stand their ground and holler and yell and scream, "You goddam racist motherfuckers! Why don't you leave us alone!"

Women, no more than four feet eight inches tall and thin as rails, would bend double and yell and scream epithets at the cops. And seeing that triggered something in me, because I knew people wouldn't do that without an awful lot of provocation. I was amazed by the depths of their anger and the sorrow. When I walked the streets, I saw obvious reasons for that anger and rage—the poverty, the exploitation. The stores were owned by whites. The rackets were controlled by whites. The police were mostly white.

And everywhere were huge amounts of open white hatred, something I'd never encountered before as a sheltered kid.

I never got hurt or even threatened during a riot, except one time, in Jersey City, not long after Harlem. The cops had formed a skirmish line a couple of blocks from a big housing project. They decided that the way they would deal with the crowds on the streets, who were yelling and threatening them, was to herd everybody inside a cyclone fence and pen them up inside the housing project.

I got herded along with everybody else, as did several other black reporters. Folks began to get mad and tempers started to boil. Somebody in the crowd figured out that I was a journalist. It was probably easy to tell. Suddenly, a couple of other journalists and I were surrounded. Some articulate young dudes began verbally attacking us.

"What the fuck are you doing here? How come you work for the white newspapers instead of the black newspapers? How come you never tell the truth? Why don't you ever report how *we* feel?"

The crowd began to stir against us.

I was doing my best to talk my way out. I don't know exactly what I said because these were hard accusations to defend against. But we managed to talk our way out.

I was in for more fearful times. In 1966, on the West Side of Chicago, I was in the streets with the people again. A line of cops formed just like in Jersey City. Naturally, the crowd gravitated in that direction. Then the cops started advancing with their clubs and suddenly broke into a run towards us.

I found myself running with kids who were in much better shape that I was—thin, wiry, athletic teenagers. It was all I could do to keep up with them. The crowd started to scatter in various directions away from the cops. I stayed with a core group. We turned a corner and ran a half a block into an alley.

It was getting pretty dark, about twilight now. I got halfway down the alley and saw that there was a boarded fence across the way, it was a dead end. The fence was probably no more than ten feet tall but it looked eighteen to me! One by one the wiry guys jumped up, grabbed the top and crawled over. I couldn't possibly do that. I probably weighed two hundred pounds. I was five feet eight inches tall and had never been athletic. What was I going to do?

The alley ran between two brick tenement buildings. There were narrow indentations, maybe half a person deep in the brick wall. I figured I could get away with it. It was dark enough now. I wheeled into one of the indentations and flattened myself against the wall.

The cops came to the head of the alley. They opened fire. I heard the bullets whizzing by. Some of them ricocheted off the wall just past me. They filled that board full of holes. None of the fire hit me.

When the cops left, I stepped out. I didn't go around the other side to see if anybody got hit. I'd had enough.

Detroit scared me, too. That was 1967 and forty-six people got killed. Just like before, I was phoning in little snatches of stuff all the time. And some rewrite person in the office took it and shaped it into a story. You were really the eyes and ears of the AP bureau.

I was using a pay phone after curfew. A National Guard tank rolled down the street. The lead tank, which had a mounted machine gun, saw me and bumped over the median strip, rolling straight toward the phone booth.

I was talking to my office. The tank rolled up to the open door of the phone booth. Then it slammed into the booth. I held up my press card. The machine gun was right at my throat. It seemed like an inch away.

Scared? Yes, I was scared!

Somebody in the tank said, "What the hell are you doing out here?"

Earlier that week, a supermarket had been torched. When I came around the corner in my rental car, I stopped and looked at the burning supermarket, amazed. This was an integrated neighborhood. White folks were looting, running into the building empty-handed, and running out with boxes of food. Black folks were doing the same thing. Everybody seemed to be real friendly, pointing out to each other stuff that hadn't been taken yet.

I dictated a story about how Detroit wasn't an all-black story. These were poor folks of both races, looking for a chance to get some of the stuff that they felt had been denied them. That was the kind of perspective I tried to put in my stories.

There were other times when my editors didn't believe my reports from the streets—or didn't want to believe them. In 1968 the Republicans were meeting in Miami Beach far from any black folks, and I got sent away from the convention to cover Northwest Miami—black folks in the streets again.

I was in the phone booth, and somebody on the second floor on the motel balcony across the street started shooting at the cops, who were behind me somewhere. The cops returned fire. I was describing on the telephone to the AP bureau what was going on. The firing back and forth.

The guy I was dictating to interrupted. "You filed a lot of this kinda stuff yesterday. You filed a lot this morning. And we're getting queries from newspapers in other parts of the country saying that they don't believe our copy, because no one else is reporting from Miami the kinds of things you're reporting."

He paused for a minute.

"How do we know that this is all happening?"

I said, "Just a minute."

I held the receiver up outside the booth. A whole series of gun-shots went by!

The guy said, "I believe it! I believe it!"

At times I withheld information on stories because I felt that my editors or the news organization was incapable of dealing with it. Or they wanted me to run with the information in a direction that I didn't think was responsible. Under the circumstances, I knew I couldn't win a fight with them. So I didn't talk about what I had learned.

For example, I might hear that some black nationalist was talking about blowing up the Empire State Building. I understood—and this is really an important point—I understood that he was probably blowing off steam. He didn't mean it. It was the equivalent of a guy on the corner saying, "You motherfucker, I'll kill you," and you know he doesn't mean it. But if I told my editors about this threat, they would want a story, and I would get in trouble if I couldn't produce it.

Once I got to Harlem, I quickly learned that the white media by and large had no understanding of and no tolerance for other people's different way of doing things.

A community do-gooder group or a corporation would call a board meeting in mid-town Manhattan. White folks would show up in droves. There was a parliamentary procedure. Everybody respected the chair. Nobody shouted. They got their business done. Then they adjourned and went home.

But you could go to a meeting in Harlem, and it was in total dis-array. There was no parliamentarian. Folks were fighting over who had the right to speak. The chair was shouting back at everybody else. It was total turmoil. But eventually everybody got his say. The meeting was over, and stuff had gotten decided.

A white reporter would go back and write, "After a disorderly meeting in Harlem today, such and such was decided."

I realized it was not disorder. That was the way we did things. We didn't have access to white institutions and their calm way of doing things. So we did it our way. And it was not the worst way, nor the best way. It was a way that lent itself to certain kinds of things, and we got our business done.

You shouldn't judge the process by another culture's terms. But the white press did that all the time. That's when you started withholding information. You might not report that the meeting was disorderly. You understood that in our terms it wasn't any more so than a church service on Sunday, which might seem loud and boisterous to white people. That's not loud and boisterous. That's normal *for us*.

But this was the kind of thing you couldn't talk about in the newsroom. And you found yourself having to deal with it on your own, unless there were other black journalists around. That was one reason why I came to believe that black journalists should be organized. And there were a lot of other reasons, too.

One. The most important reason was that the people who tried to keep our beliefs and our concerns out of the media were themselves organized in a de facto way. They talked to each other. They reinforced each other's point of view as a daily part of the way they did business. If we took them on as black individuals, it was too easy for them to dismiss us as being preoccupied with a narrow point of view.

Two. We were split ourselves. We saw that in the negotiating that went on among black reporters before they filed the EEOC complaint against the *Washington Post*.[91] If we didn't talk among ourselves and reach some agreement on what our collective priorities needed to be, then we made it easy for our opponents to divide and conquer us. The folks who hired and supervised the media tended to see us first as a group of blacks.

Three. We were in the business of information. We needed to hear other people's positions on race, on economics and politics. If we didn't organize ourselves, we wouldn't know the diverse points of view that we brought to an issue, let alone what other racial groups might bring.

Four. People with the power to hire preferred to hire people they felt comfortable with. And almost everyone who hired felt most comfortable with people who shared their culture and their points of view. Although media managers sometimes learned to be comfortable with a fairly wide range of viewpoints, they seldom learned to be truly comfortable with a wide range of people.

Five. In every country around the world, the media primarily served that nation's established institutions. It was true regardless of the type of government. Even in the U.S., where the media occasionally took pride in doing hard-hitting exposes, in the day-in-day-out-bottom-line bulk of the words, in the bulk of the pictures, there was a tendency to unquestioningly parrot what we were told by crafty PR people and various spokespersons. And if, as is true in this country, the institutional point of view is not to rock one's own boat, then we black reporters needed the strength of numbers to get our points across.

Six. In nearly every media institution, the tendency was to hire a few minorities and then stop.

Seven. Look at the numbers. The media were one of the last major opinion-molding institutions in this country to remain overwhelmingly segregated. Over 50 percent of our newspapers had no minority news staffers. That was primarily smaller papers, but, still, they reached a lot of people.

Eight. It was generally *not* true in the news business that people were rewarded in proportion to their talent. People who made the bosses feel uncomfortable were penalized unless their talent was so overwhelming that management was willing to put up with a lot of shit to get their product. And a lot of us blacks still make management feel uncomfortable just by voicing our opinions, or even by showing up for work!

Nine. Organizing would give black journalists much greater contact with the broader spectrum of our communities. Then we could teach black folks about access to the media, and provide more reliable contacts than if they depended upon only those minority journalists they happened to know.

Ten. As I have said before, there is no such thing as an objective news reporter. All news is filtered because it's shorthand. The most important decisions are not what to put in, but what to leave out.

How then should a black journalist consider himself?

As a black first? Or as a journalist first?

Black people deserve the same chance as anybody else to do the kind of reporting they want to do. So if you want to be a black first and a journalist second, that's great. You ought to get the kinds of stories that you do well as a result of that. If you want to be a journalist first and a black second, you've got a right to do that. And you might want to select different kinds of stories. Management should be sensitive to what you want in terms of how it assigns you.

The more racially oriented the story was, the more I became a black first and a journalist second. But I don't see a lot of contradiction there. Because until relatively recently, you couldn't depend on anybody but black journalists to deal with stories that were very black-oriented. You had to become a black advocate inside your institution, or a large chunk of the truth would never make it into the paper. If I'm covering something that's not particularly racially oriented, then I won't be thinking in terms of race. So I probably go back and forth.

I don't think it was an accident that when the doors to the white media were opened by the civil rights movement, the black people who filtered through tended to be those who had adopted white community attitudes and ideas, and could speak that lingo, talk that talk. They were the ones the white media wanted.

But there are other media managers who really like a damn-the-torpedoes-full-speed-ahead attitude. Still, aggressiveness is considered a good point in black journalists *only* as long as he doesn't cross whatever line management finds threatening.

You can see the difference in mainstream newspapers. The *Washington Post*, because of Ben Bradlee, liked aggressive people who talked back, who were uppity—to a point. You had to know where that point was. If you were going to cross it, you'd have an interesting time there.

The *Los Angeles Times*, though, wanted above all, journalists who were obedient to the wishes of the newspaper and would not get into fights or cross words in the newsroom. They didn't care too much about what happened to you on the streets. Both papers used to call in important and powerful people for meetings with select groups of editors and reporters.

At the *Washington Post*, when I attended some of those meetings, there was a can-we-get-'em? attitude. "Let's get this son of a bitch to really admit some of the things he's been hiding." When the *Los Angeles Times* held the same type of meetings, there was a very clear rule: Don't embarrass the guest.

The white media *has* changed and grown. But it has not changed enough and grown enough. There is a lot more reporting of who we are and what we do than there used to be. But there is still a fair amount of stereotyping, and there are areas that just don't get covered. Blacks tend to get reported about these days in terms of people who are successful—sports figures, entertainers, people who are terribly well-off. We don't get covered in terms of the problems most of us face that have to do with either racism or poverty.

There is a pervasive notion out there that people who-can't-make-it is because of something they're doing wrong. This ignores, for instance, the changing workplace. We live in a time when corporations are demanding more efficiency. One way to be efficient is to have computers and machines to replace people. So we produce more and more with fewer and fewer jobs. The highly skilled jobs remain while others are frozen out of the job market. That is not something poor people, unemployed people, can do a lot about.

Overall, the media does a much better job today covering the minority community than it used to. We still don't get the same kind of fair shake as middle-class or as rich folks. Some of that stems from the fact there aren't enough of us black journalists out there yet to keep the screws on.

So, to me, it means that we are still on the journey.

EARL CALDWELL

Earl Caldwell covered the Black Panthers for the New York Times, *and was involved in a press freedom issue that was taken to the U.S. Supreme Court.*

———

My big trouble started in December of 1969. That's when the FBI asked me to spy on the Black Panthers.

I had been tagged as the *New York Times* reporter who covered radicals and militants. Now this was weird because here I was, this colored kid from the small town of Clearfield, who knew little about the civil rights movement. I grew up in the middle of two mountains in central Pennsylvania, and you would have had a hard time counting twenty-five black people in my town.

But I was a reporter, and I was colored, so white people assumed I must be an expert on everything concerning blacks. One editor asked me for James Baldwin's telephone number. When I told him I didn't know Baldwin, he got irritated because he thought I was holding out on him. So I became a black specialist almost by accidental circumstances.

Wally Turner, an editor at the *Times*, said to me, "Go try to make contact with Eldridge Cleaver."

Eldridge Cleaver was a leading Black Panther who had spent time in prison for attempted murder and had written a book called *Soul on Ice*, which had become a national bestseller. Of course I didn't know him. But I heard that his wife, Kathleen, had been in the same organization as my good buddy, Ivanhoe Donaldson.[92] My plan was use my connection to Ivanhoe to interview her and get to Eldridge Cleaver that way.

I flew to San Francisco and went to their house on Pine Street, and asked to see Kathleen. I was told to wait in a room. A woman came in and propped up a big photo of Kathleen against the wall. She was wearing a black outfit, with black boots, and looking like a radical. Pretty soon Kathleen came into the room. She looked like the picture—black outfit, boots.

I said, "Ivanhoe Donaldson is a very good personal friend of mine—"

She interrupted me. "I hate Ivanhoe. I've never liked him."

I tried the name of another friend. Everybody I named, she dumped on.

I said, "Jesus Christ!"

Then Eldridge came in with an entourage. He didn't even say hello. He walked past me like I was dirt.

"I've got to go somewhere," Kathleen said to me, "but you can stay here."

She went to a closet, reached in, and pulled out a blue case. She unzipped it and took out a rifle. After pulling back the bolt to make sure it was loaded, she put the rifle back in the case and zipped it up. Then she went out with some people.

I was thinking, *Jeeeesus Christ!* At that time I had been covering the riots, and although blacks kept talking about it, I had never seen anybody pull out as much as a pistol. And Kathleen had that rifle!

Cleaver came over and said, "Where are you going?"

I said, "I've got to go to, uh, Oakland."

"Can I get a ride with you?"

"Sure."

I had written a story about the riots that had taken place in Boston, and Abe Rosenthal, the managing editor, had sent me a note saying I had done a great job. I told Claude Sitton, a well-known white reporter who covered the civil rights movement, how I got the Boston story.

I said, "These kids from the riot were in a parking lot. So I gave them a ride and interviewed them."

"You mean you were riding rioters around in a *New York Times* car?" Sitton asked.

He cussed me out.

So here I was at it again. Not just Eldridge Cleaver, but a whole boatload of Panthers wanted a ride. They all piled into my car—my *New York Times* rental car.

"We want to make a stop," they said. "Okay with you?"

"That's fine," I said. My idea was to hang out with them, get to know them. Then I would be on the inside and learn the whole deal.

We drove to a house, and I pulled off the street into a parking space. We walked upstairs and went into a room. The people in the room were whispering to each other. I saw a couch. A guy went over and pulled it away from the wall. It had no back on it.

Behind the couch I saw boxes filled with every kind of weapon known to man!

I said to myself, *I'm a big* New York Times *man. I've got to stay cool.* But another voice was saying, *You better get your ass out of here.*

I went to the kitchen to pull myself together. I didn't want to know anything about what was happening. I just said, *Get the hell out and be cool.*

Pretty soon they said, "You ready to go?"

"Yeah."

"Well, we're going to take these boxes of books here over to Oakland with us, so we'll put them in your car."

I could hardly see out the back window. Mind you, this was when Huey Newton's trial was going on for killing a cop, and the Panthers were talking about "the sky's the limit"—meaning they were ready to take up arms.

We crossed the Bay Bridge. A cop started following us.

They told me, "Turn down this street!"

I didn't know where I was. This was the first time I had been to San Francisco.

"Go down this way! Turn down this street!"

The cop stopped following us.

"Pull up over there at that house!"

We had hardly stopped at the house when those fools started flying out of the car, grabbing the boxes. I turned around and looked.

I saw guns on the back seat of my automobile! My *New York Times* rental automobile!

"Open the trunk!" a man said. "Open the trunk!"

I was trying to cuss these people out. But I was so scared I couldn't get the words out of my mouth. I opened the trunk. Books slid out. And guns!

A guy ran from the house and yelled, "You got to put them back in the car. The doors are locked!"

I hollered, "Y'all not putting that shit back in my car!"

A guy started calling to me, "Brother, Brother, Brother."

I said, "Brother?!"

He said, "Let us steal this car."

"Look," I said. "I'd love to let you steal it, you know? But it's not rented in my name. The white boy at the *New York Times* got it. Wally Turner. It's in his name. And if I don't have this car when I get back over there, it'll be a lot of trouble."

You know how it is, when something horrible happens, just after it's over, it's almost like you fall apart. I was *so* nervous. Lord! Scared! I went back to the bureau and wrote my story saying that that Panthers were threatening that "the sky's the limit." I said the Panthers were seen moving guns, that they were moving large numbers of weapons from San Francisco to Oakland.

I was so angry at what they had done to me!

When the story came out, I was scared to go back to the Panther office. I said, *Boy, when these guys see this stuff you wrote, it's gonna be your behind! What are you gonna do?*

I thought about leaving San Francisco for New York. But Wally Turner said, "Go back over there, Earl."

I went back to the Panther office. No one said anything to me. *Didn't they see the story?* I wondered.

Come to find out, they did. The Panthers *wanted* people to know what they were doing. They *wanted* me to write in the paper about them having guns.

I made three mistakes. First, I said they were moving the weapons from deep in the Fillmore slum to Oakland. The *Times* challenged me on what "deep in the Fillmore slum" meant. I didn't know. All I knew was we were in an area called Fillmore, and I figured we were deep in it.

I said, "Believe me. I saw some of this with my own eyes."

I didn't tell them everything that had happened. I wasn't about to be *that* crazy!

The second mistake was that I tried to describe the weapons. I said they had rifles, handguns, and automatic weapons. That was the beginning of my troubles with the FBI.

My third mistake was to think the Panthers didn't understand what my role was—that I was a reporter, and when they did stuff around me, it was going to be in the paper. They understood perfectly. They wanted it in the paper.

I stayed in California a couple of weeks and then returned to New York. The FBI came looking for me my first day back at the office.

The FBI agents said, "We've got to know more about this."

I said, "I don't know any more. I can't even take you to the building where I saw anything. Everything I know is in the paper."

They asked what I knew about the weapons. I told them I didn't know the building where the weapons had been picked up or where they had been dropped off. I couldn't find either one of those places again because it was my first night in either of those towns—San Francisco or Oakland.

The FBI argued that if this was a white group, they would be here asking other reporters, and the reporters would help them with the story. I argued that there was no other information. I had nothing else to tell them.

I was speaking to them in the lobby. I sent word by a receptionist for another reporter to come help me.

He arrived and said, "Do you have anything else to tell them?"

"No."

He pulled me away from the FBI agents, and said, "Come on, let's go." We returned to the city room. I knew, though, that my problems with the FBI were not over.

But my parents had raised me to deal with anything. They were of modest means. My father was versatile. He was a stone mason. He was a carpenter. He could do a lot of things with his hands. What he had most going for him was that he didn't believe in making bills. He believed that if you made a dollar, you saved a dime. This man couldn't have been tougher.

The area where I grew up was noted for two things—coal and clay. The clay was used for making sewer pipes and bricks. Coal was the biggest thing. But blacks couldn't get into coal. And the brick plant didn't hire many blacks either. So most of what our family ate, I raised or grew. My mother used to do people's ironing, and I delivered it to their houses.

I was probably the smartest kid in my class. I was an excellent reader. The teacher called us her "blue-chip readers." I was partly showing off—and acting a little bit. After I got out of high school, my father asked me what I was going to do. It was a rule in our house, you had to do *something!*

So I went Buffalo to work in a steel mill, and I made a lot of money. While I was there, I enrolled at the University of Buffalo. In my second year, a professor took a liking to me because I was doing well. He got me a job interview with a Philadelphia company.

The guy interviewing me said, "Of course, you'll be working in the South. Nobody will hire you in the North." Well, to me, the South was the Land of the Bogeyman. After that interview, I was finished with business school. I signed up for the air force. But before I was inducted, a buddy of mine who was sports editor of the local paper, said, "You've got to be crazy. I'll get you an entry-level job on the paper." When he left, I became the sports editor.

I was crazy about sports writing. The year Pittsburgh won the World Series, I went to a press banquet. Someone introduced me to the big-time sports writers, Shirley Povich and Bob Considine. Being a little hick kid, I announced that I thought Shirley Povich had written the greatest sports story of all time about Don Larsen's no-hitter. I said I had memorized it.

Bob Considine said, "You did what?"

"I memorized it."

"I don't believe it."

"Yes, I did."

"Well, if you memorized it, let's *hear* it!"

I recited Povich's story.

They cracked up! They said, "You sit down right here with us." They gave me some tips on how to get a better job. From that point, I worked on several small papers. I was the Jackie Robinson of every place I worked until I got to New York.

The Rochester paper was a great experience. The city editor told me when I arrived, "People say there's a lot of discrimination in housing and that blacks have trouble renting homes and apartments. You're looking for an apartment yourself, so why don't you write about your experience?"

I went searching for an apartment. Another reporter, who was white, followed on my heels. I wrote a story about how I couldn't rent an apartment in Rochester but the white guy could. That was how I was introduced in the Sunday paper. I was the black reporter who couldn't find a home.

Jimmy Breslin came to Rochester in 1964 to cover the riots. He was my favorite writer. I took him around and introduced him to people. In the course of our conversations, Breslin said, "What do you want to do?"

I said, "Oh, if I could just get a job on the *Herald Tribune*."

He told me to call the editor. The next summer I thought the *Tribune* had hired me. Actually, they said they were *going* to hire me. I came back to Rochester and announced that they *had* hired me. Hell, I went through that until the end of 1965, but I never got the job and they never called me.

The editor of the Rochester paper said, "We want you to stay here. But you you've got to withdraw your resignation. What're they saying in New York?"

"I haven't heard anything."

It became an embarrassment.

There was a big black-out in New York. The *Herald Tribune* called Rochester to find out if it was also blacked-out there. It was. They wanted somebody to cover the story, and they called *me!*

That was my big break. The editor said he wasn't going to let me hang any longer. As soon as the strike was over, they would hire me. Then when I got to New York, the *Herald Tribune* folded. I had waited longer in Rochester for the *Herald Tribune* to call me to New York than I had actually worked on the paper. So I was broke and out of a job in New York.

Jimmy Breslin said, "I can get you a job. Call an editor at the *New York Post.*" I phoned and they said, "We'll hire you but you have to come to work tomorrow morning." I went to work the next day.

I hated it!

I had always worked at a morning paper, and the *Post* was an afternoon paper. And I didn't know how to do straight reporting. Ted Poston—he was a big-time black person in the business— taught me. He took me under his wing. Ted taught me how to work in an organized way, how to report and write and rewrite. When he saw I didn't know how to do it, he didn't tell anybody. But I still didn't like the idea of an afternoon paper.

What I liked were the people I was meeting. There was a whole cadre of black reporters in New York. Gerald Frazier was at the *Daily News*. Tom Johnson worked for *Newsday*. A couple of guys worked for radio stations. Every organization seemed to have one black, and they all were in a pack covering the news. And I ran with them.

New York was really exciting for me because I had grown up in an area where there were no black people. I was seeing and learning all this stuff for the first time—about the civil rights movement and everything that was going on.

I called the *New York Times* and asked for an interview. I got Abe Rosenthal on the phone. He said, "If you had come over here right away we might've hired you. But we've already hired so many people that we don't even have a desk for you. But I tell you what. Call me in six months and we'll see."

As it turned out, six months to the day, I was riding to work. I was reading the *Post* and saw my byline on a story. It was a story I hadn't written. I'd never seen this story before. "By Earl Caldwell." I couldn't wait to get in the city room to tell the city editor that somebody had made a mistake.

"Look at this," I said. "Somebody really goofed up. *My name is on this story!*"

The city editor said, "You hadn't had a byline for a while. We figured you wanted to see your name in the paper, so we put your name on the story."

That scared me. It was *unthinkable* that they would put my name on anything I hadn't written. That might get me in all kinds of trouble. My instinct told me to be scared of that. I called the *New York Times* the same day.

I started at the *Times* in the middle of March 1967. That made two blacks at the *Times*. Tom Johnson and me. They loved Tom. We called him "Big Black." Newspapers had the attitude back then that they needed one black person. Tom was their black. I was the new guy. They wouldn't let Tom go out of town to do anything, because they always wanted him there in case something happened in New York.

Maybe at no time before or since was it ever like the summer of 1967, the summer that cities exploded across America. The *Times* being the *Times* said, "We're going to cover this story differently. We're going to assign two reporters, and they will go everywhere to cover the riots." They assigned Gene Roberts, who was the Atlanta bureau chief, and me.

Automatically, I became a national reporter within a few months of being on the paper! The idea was that Gene Roberts, who was white, and I would go to a town and cover the story together. But things started happening so fast that Gene would be going this way and I'd be going that way. It was an incredible summer. That was what really started it for me, and it never stopped.

I was in Memphis when Martin Luther King was killed. Claude Sitton sent me down there with instructions to get any information I could on the FBI and how they were feeding malicious rumors to newspaper editors about King.

I thought I'd run into the Ku Klux Klan. I wondered what I was going to do about a cab. "You're gonna have trouble with the cabbies. They're not gonna want to take a black anywhere."

All the cab drivers were black! The cab driver who took me—I couldn't get rid of the guy. The second night I was there, King was killed. Not really knowing anything about the civil rights movement, I found it was a heavy, emotional thing being in Memphis at that time.

After King's death, I was in the Washington bureau. Scotty Reston[93] came up and said, "I just want to shake your hand and introduce myself." He complimented me on how well I was doing on the paper in such a short time. Another reporter said, "Your name has been on the front page more in the last month than the White House reporter."

So civil rights became my beat, and I started covering the Black Panthers at the tail end of 1968.

The *New York Times* was always asking me, "Who is in charge of the Panthers? Who's calling the shots? How do they operate? Where do they get their money?"

I went to see the Panthers carrying a tape recorder, and they allowed me to use it. They understood the importance of having stories written about them in the *New York Times*. So I was able to capture a lot of what they said.

I wrote a long story in the *Times*—and I had it all on tape—quoting David Hilliard[94] as saying that the Black Panther Party recognized the government of the United States as being oppressive to blacks, and as black people they had not only a right but a duty to take up arms against that government. I described what it was like at night at the Black Panther office, which had bullet-proof plates around the walls and guns in the corners.

The FBI showed up again. This time they wanted me to be an informant, to spy on the Panthers.

I told them that not only could I *not* do that, I told them I couldn't even *talk* to them because somebody would think that I *was* doing it. I said my sources would dry up, and it could get me in a world of trouble. I could be physically harmed if I presented myself as a reporter to the Panthers and then ran around being some kind of spy for the FBI. In any case, I said, I wrote everything I knew about the Panthers in the newspaper.

The FBI began to call the office every day and ask to talk to me. They were pushing it. I told Wally Turner. It was decided that I would stay off the phone. When a call was for me, the secretary would say, "He's not here."

Then the weirdest thing happened. The FBI had women call me. The secretary would put the woman through, and she would say, "Hold on just a second, Earl." And the FBI agent would come on the phone.

One day the FBI called the office and said, "You tell Earl Caldwell we're not playing games with him anymore. If he doesn't want to talk with us, he can tell it to a grand jury in federal court."

That was on Friday. On Monday, a U.S. marshal showed up at the office. I wasn't there, but Wally Turner was, and he called me, and said, "Listen, you'd better get over here right away. There's a marshal with a subpoena for you." I hustled to the office. Wally said the guy was coming back later in the day.

Wally said, "Do you know what a subpoena means?"

"No."

"It means they want to subpoena you and everything you've got in your office. They're going to want to see it. My advice to you is to get the hell out of here. Get on a plane. Go to Alaska!"

His next question was, "What're you going to do with all that material you've collected on the Panthers?"

"I don't know. Maybe I'll pack it up and put it in a crate and ship it to my parents in Pennsylvania."

"No, no," he said. "You don't want to get your parents involved in this kind of business with the FBI. You don't want to do that."

"Well, what am I going to do?"

We started discussing my alternatives. So I made the decision that if I thought anything might be questionable, I would destroy it. I got two large garbage cans and filled them up with my material on the Panthers. I shredded the stuff by hand.

To this day, if there's one thing I regret more than anything else, it was getting rid of my material. I destroyed the transcriptions of tapes, the actual tapes, and documents. I saved some stuff but 90 percent of it I got rid of right then.

It's funny because when we went through the court proceedings—and it went all the way to the Supreme Court—we were arguing about things that didn't exist. And no one ever knew that but me and the secretary and Wally Turner.

But I had the right to destroy the material at that point because I hadn't been served with the subpoena. I kept some files that I thought belonged to me. I was going to try to write a book on the Panthers through the eyes of one of them. I did a lot of tape recordings with him, and never published any of the material. I always kept him out of the story. I also kept every newspaper and every flier I'd collected. I felt that belonged to me.

It never occurred to me that the FBI would say they wanted this material. Or that they would even know about it.

It was 10:00 in the morning. I had got rid of the material and was ready to leave. I didn't know exactly where I was going, but I intended to go home and figure out a plan of attack and then take off.

But instead of leaving, I stayed. I had destroyed stuff I had spent a whole year collecting. I had lost my desire to run. I was so angry.

The U.S. marshal returned. I was standing by the secretary's desk. He said, "Is Earl Caldwell here?" She looked at me. I looked at her. And I burst out laughing. I assumed they knew I was black.

He gave me the subpoena. It called for me to appear before a grand jury with all my note books, tape recordings, and all information pertaining to the Black Panthers, especially anything that involved David Hilliard and the subject of my intended book.

The subpoena effectively stopped me from writing about the Black Panthers. It also changed my status. It turned me into a celebrity reporter. My name would appear on the front page of the newspaper from then for maybe a year or so.

The media saw this as an attack on press freedom by the Nixon administration. Abe Rosenthal said, "The *Times* supports Earl Caldwell completely." The paper enlisted one of the most prestigious law firms in San Francisco to represent me.

But the first thing the lawyers told me was, "We want you to bring all of your information on the Panthers down here so we can go through it. We've got a tremendous problem of law and order, and maybe some of this material should be given to the FBI. But we can't advise you until we go through it and see what you've got."

That scared the hell out of me. Never in my wildest imagination had I thought that anybody was going tell me that I should turn some of my stuff over to the FBI. I told the lawyers that I didn't have the material, anyhow.

The New York office of the *Times* sent Harding Bancroft, one of their vice presidents, to San Francisco to assist me and the lawyer, and to develop the *Times*'s course of action. The night before I was supposed to appear before the grand jury, I had dinner with the lawyer and Wally Turner and Tom Wicker,[95] who happened to be in town.

My black buddies in journalism were working on a strategy for me, too. They had formed an organization of black journalists from New York to California. One of them called with the name of a lawyer in the Bay Area that I could get, Anthony Amsterdam.[96] I didn't know him. As it turned out, he was a real heavyweight.

But we had no time! I was supposed to appear before the grand jury the next day. It was late at night, and Amsterdam lived on the other side of Stanford in one of those fancy towns near Palo Alto. We started driving and found his house around midnight. We woke him up—his wife made us coffee—and we talked until 3:00 in the morning. He already knew the case. My buddies in New York had told him everything.

The first thing he said was, "You have a legal right to refuse."

Those words came like a bolt of lightning. *A legal right to refuse!*

I told Amsterdam that the *Times*'s lawyer had scared the hell out of me when he said I should bring my stuff in. Amsterdam said, "Let me handle this. Don't show up at the meeting with the lawyers. I'll go. I'll explain the position you're in. You should arrive later in the meeting."

The subpoena was against *me*, not the *New York Times*. The *New York Times* was not mentioned. When we left there that night, I was very happy and relieved, but still nervous.

I said to myself, *The vice president of the New York Times is out here and you're not going show up at the meeting, but you are going to have some lawyer there that he doesn't even know!*

Early next morning, I called Harding Bancroft at his hotel and told him I was worried that my name was the only one on the subpoena. It was against me *personally*, and I didn't know what was going to happen. I told him I'd engaged an attorney, who advised me that it would be best if I stayed away and showed up later after they all had a talk. I said I'd like to do it that way, and hoped he would understand.

He said, "Yup. I understand. That will be fine."

Harding Bancroft turned out to be a wonderful man.

They all met at the office of the law firm. I sat in the waiting room. Soon Harding Bancroft came out.

He said, "This fellow Amsterdam is terrific! Bringing him into this case was the best thing that has happened to us so far."

So then I knew I wasn't an ass for doing what I'd done. Everybody understood it. The first thing they did was to get the subpoena postponed. And they began to move to limit its scope.

That's when the court fight began.

Anthony Amsterdam turned out to be a guiding light. We were trying to figure out how much we could afford to pay a lawyer. We couldn't get the money from the *New York Times*. We had to raise the money ourselves. The black organization of journalists was trying to raise funds but said they couldn't make Amsterdam any promises.

Amsterdam said, "No, no, wait a minute."

He refused to accept any fees. He said he only did pro bono work. He only worked without a fee.

It was like a miracle!

We not only got a man who turned out to be a brilliant constitutional lawyer, but I learned that he was widely known in law circles, and that I was indeed fortunate to be able to get him.

The federal court judge's ruling was considered to be in my favor. The *New York Times* published an editorial saying I'd won. His decision said that every citizen had to appear before the grand jury when called—including me—but that any information I had that I received on a confidential basis was protected. He also ruled that I could bring my lawyer, but he couldn't go into the grand jury room, although I could come out and talk to him.

The *New York Times* went to court and argued for a right to have a standing in the case because it was their reporting activity that was involved. It was really them more than me. When the *Times* was given a standing, they wrote an editorial saying that it was a great victory. It was a great ruling for everybody.

Except for *me!*

I had to go to court to testify before the grand jury against my news sources. I told Amsterdam that I was in a bind. We decided to appeal. So there was a split. Abe Rosenthal posted a famous memo on the bulletin board in New York: "We all sympathize with Earl Caldwell in the difficult position he finds himself."

Rosenthal felt that every citizen had to appear before the grand jury, including me as a reporter. If I made the argument that I shouldn't appear, the *Times* couldn't support me. So they sympathized, but they didn't agree. And though they later came back into the case, the *Times* really sort of cut me loose at that point.

If I appeared before a grand jury, I would only verify my news stories. So we argued that if I went before the grand jury and put on the record what was already on the record, it would be a barren performance. The FBI wouldn't learn anything. But it would be destructive to me as a reporter.

We argued that there were only a handful of black reporters with the major newspapers. We brought all my stories to show that I was able to get on the inside of the Panther operation to write effectively about the organization. Even the FBI said that everything they knew they learned from the *New York Times* and other newspapers. But the very action they were taking against me would make sure there would be no more stories. No more enlightened stories.

Tony Amsterdam argued that I still had a legal right to refuse because if the government would not gain anything they didn't already know from my appearance, then why were they doing it? Why were they pushing it? To embarrass me? To destroy my reporting?

So we appealed.

The appeal was denied. I was called to appear before the grand jury. I refused.

A court hearing was called. The judge said, "Do you still refuse to appear?"

I said, "Yes."

He said, "Did you read the order of the court?"

"Well, no, I didn't read it."

The judge said, "Wait a minute. We're going to halt these proceedings until you read the order of the court!"

I sat down next to Amsterdam and read the court order. It said that if I refused, *I would go to jail at that moment and stay there until I agreed to abide by the order of the court!*

I was stunned! I was ab-so-lute-ly *stunned!* My car was on the street! My apartment wasn't locked up! I was not prepared to go to no damn jail right at that moment.

It was the first time it dawned on me that this was *serious!* The Justice Department had an attorney who was famous because he had prosecuted Axis Sally[97] in World War II. He argued that I should go to jail "right this moment."

The judge said, "Do you still refuse after you read the order of the court?"

Tony Amsterdam was beside me. He said, "Don't worry. If they lock you up, we'll go tonight into federal court. We'll appeal to Supreme Court Justice William O. Douglas, who is in charge of this circuit. We'll get you out. You won't be in jail more than a day."

I stood up and said, "I refuse to testify."

The Justice Department lawyer argued that I should be taken into custody and put in jail right then. Amsterdam argued that I should be allowed to be free until I had a chance to appeal, that I should be given a chance to exhaust the legal process in this case.

The judge ruled that I could remain free on my own recognizance until we had a chance to appeal.

I didn't go to the hearing because I was beginning privately to feel that race was involved. I thought it was better if they didn't see me there as a black person. You always want to be strong, but you never really know how strong you are going to be. I was determined to refuse. But other things started going through my mind. I was thinking that maybe I should flee the country like Eldridge Cleaver and other Panthers had done.

All of a sudden this became a national story. My parents began to call me. "What are you doing out there? Why are they trying to put you in jail?"

The Panthers ran my picture in their paper: CALDWELL REFUSES TO ATTEND. FACES IMPRISONMENT RATHER THAN TESTIFY.

The whole thing was taking on a life of its own. I didn't know what to do.

Anthony Amsterdam always said—and it made me feel good—that my news stories were part of the best argument that he had. He said, "Look what Earl Caldwell was able to do by not having to have the government watching over him. Look at the access that he had. Look at the kinds of stories that he was able to write. Look at the information that he was able to give to society. And we're a free society. We need this. We must have this freedom."

Then the most stunning thing happened. We won the appeals case unanimously. Nobody believed it! The *New York Times* jumped back in the case because they were in a very strange position. People were saying that the *Times* had abandoned me. The *Times* said that while they couldn't join in as a partner, they agreed to pay all the expenses in the case. They even wanted and tried desperately to put Tony Amsterdam on the payroll. Tony refused.

The position of the Court of Appeals was that I should not have to appear in what would be a barren performance. The Court said the Justice Department had to show that I had information about the Black Panthers which they couldn't get from anybody but me. If they could show that, I would have to answer the subpoena. The Court said to have me appear only to put on record information that was already on the record would have a chilling effect on my right to function as a reporter.

That was the thing I was most proud of. I hadn't kept anything secret. It was all on the record. I had fulfilled my duty as a reporter. I was consistent with that from the very first when I saw the guns and right to the time David Hilliard said, "Yes, we believe that we should pick up arms and try to violently overthrow the government."

We had a victory celebration. Tony Amsterdam said, "You know they're going to appeal." To me, the victory belonged to Amsterdam and the black journalists because everyone was down on us for pursuing it. Wally Turner was with me all the way. He tried to keep the best relations possible between me and New York. They were very good about giving me time off and helping me prepare for the case.

I didn't have time to cover anything. I was running around making speeches. I had become a celebrity and in demand on news shows to discuss the case.

Tony Amsterdam was right. Less than two days after our victory celebration, the Justice Department announced they were going to appeal to the Supreme Court.

I flew to Washington to hear the case argued. I felt should I be there. *This was the Supreme Court of the United States!* I didn't feel race would make any difference to the Supreme Court. The civil rights movement took issues to the Supreme Court. That was where you went to get justice.

At one point, the *New York Times* said to me, "We don't want to get a specific court decision on your case. We want both sides to assume certain rights. The government assumes certain rights, and the publishers assume certain rights. We don't want it defined. We don't want you to get a court decision because we're likely to wind up getting some bad law written, and we will all suffer under it."

So instead of this being my case only—the *United States v. Caldwell*—they took two other cases involving journalists[98] and pulled them all together to make one ruling.

Justice William O. Douglas wrote the most exciting minority opinion. He was our advocate. God, he was *fierce* for us! He said that the constitutional defenses that had always protected the press were being torn down, and if what the court was ruling on became a settled wrong, then tough times were ahead for the First Amendment. Reporters would be reduced to dealing only with hand-outs from the government, because a reporter was no better than his sources.

The decision came down in 1972. The vote was 5-4 against us.

I thought it was unfair to combine the two cases with mine. But Tony Amsterdam said that was the way they did it. When the Supreme Court made law in an area, it was standard for them to take a variety of cases and use all of them to make the law. I thought that the other cases were very different because they involved actual law breaking. The Justice Department could never show in my case that there was any violation of the law.

But we had fought the good fight. And in a sense we had won because we were the first of our generation of black journalists of any significant numbers to work at major newspapers. Serious questions were raised as to how we were going to act as reporters. I think we came away from the case with the good will and respect of our black communities, of our peers and for me.

The decision didn't mean much to my subpoena or to the Panthers. Watergate was about to begin, and Nixon and his Justice Department had enough trouble on their hands without trying to put a reporter in jail. And by then, the Panthers that I knew were either in jail, out of the country, or in the graveyard.

Much of what the Panthers said was rhetoric. They were not in a position to take up any arms against anybody. They were just trying to stay *alive!* But they were perceived as crazy and violent—as something that had to be destroyed.

There were two white Americas then. There was one white America that responded to the Black Panthers, especially young white college kids. One of the reasons the government came down on the Panthers so hard was because they were effective in influencing young white people. They'd call a rally and get ten thousand people and ninety-five hundred of them would be white.

I don't know if they could have rallied ten thousand black people, because a lot of the black community was afraid of them. They kept them at arm's length. They were sort of like the bogey man in the black community.

The Panthers had a kind of poetry to them. They had these sayings like "Right On." Right on what? They didn't say. Just "Right On." They taught the kids their slogans and had them shouting "Power to the People!" What kind of power? How?

But beyond the rhetoric, they also had an effective breakfast-for-children program. At 5:00, in poorest neighborhood in San Francisco, they served breakfast to all of these kids every morning. Free!

When you really got down to it, the Black Panthers weren't asking for earth-shaking change. They were asking for fairness. They wanted to expose racism. They wanted to expose brutality. They wanted to expose the mistreatment and murder of black men.

But the way they operated put them into a conflict that became a virtual war with the police. And they were never able to get beyond that. There were police raids on their offices across the country—Seattle, Sacramento, Chicago, Detroit. They were being jailed. They were being killed. They were fleeing the country. They became weary from being under constant attack. They just got torn up.

You had to understand how I felt watching and being part of all this. I was a colored kid from Clearfield, Pennsylvania, who grew up, basically, in an all-white town. My parents were hard workers up there in the mountains, and I was the first of my family to get the chance to go to college and to see a larger world.

And I wound up working for the *New York Times*, covering the most important stories in America.

It was amazing.

CAROLE SIMPSON

Carole Simpson was a reporter in the Washington bureau of NBC-TV who experienced, as she put it, a "double whammy" of being black and female.

———

I worked on the student newspaper at Hyde Park High School in Chicago. According to my teachers, I was also quite good in English. They encouraged me to write. And I decided I wanted to be a journalist. I guess I envisioned myself as a colored Lois Lane or Brenda Starr. We didn't say "black" in those days.

My parents thought I was *crazy*.

My father was a mail carrier. My mother took in sewing. She had not even gone to night school, and my father had only finished high school. But I grew up in a home in which achievement was expected. They were very concerned about their two daughters getting good educations. They wanted me to go to college to become a teacher. Then I would be assured a job. The idea was that if some man couldn't take care of you, you would be self-sufficient. That was the black middle-class ethic back then.

I told my parents I didn't want to teach. I wanted to write. I wanted to go to journalism school. They had never heard of journalism. They didn't even know what the word meant. A newspaper reporter? This was 1958. They didn't know that anybody black worked for the white newspapers.

"What are you going do?" they said. "Work for *Ebony* magazine? The *Chicago Defender*?"

"Yes, if that's what it takes. I want to write."

I told them I wanted to go to the Medill School of Journalism at Northwestern University, outside of Chicago. I knew its reputation.

We had huge arguments. My parents insisted I get the teaching degree first, then try this "crazy journalism." I finally convinced them, and they were supportive even though it all sounded very alien to them.

When I applied to Northwestern, I had a B plus average— everything in terms of academic credentials and desire. But an admissions counselor told me not to try to get in because I wouldn't be able to find a job after graduation.

"Why not?"

"Because you're a Negro. And you're a woman. Nobody's going to hire you. You would be much more sensible going to the Chicago Teachers College. You can write then."

I was shattered.

Sure enough, I got a letter saying, "We regret to inform you that you cannot enter Northwestern."

So I decided to apply elsewhere. I went to the University of Illinois. After two years, I transferred to the University of Michigan. At graduation time, I was the only black among sixty finishing in journalism, and I was the only one who didn't have a job. When I went to the placement bureau interviews, I got the same story. You're black. You're a woman. You're inexperienced.

I felt terrible. I thought, *Am I stubborn? Am I too idealistic? Am I crazy? Did I waste all this time?* Then I got angry. I said, "What they're doing to me is crazy. I'm good. I can do journalism. All I need is a chance to demonstrate it." I knew something would happen sooner or later. But without a job, I had to go back to work at the Chicago Public Library, where I'd worked every summer from the time I was sixteen years old.

Wesley Maurer, the chairman of my department, felt terrible, too. He tried all summer long to find me a job. And then, in August, he called to say he had lined up something at Tuskegee Institute.

"Tuskegee Institute? I have never heard of Tuskegee Institute."

Professor Maurer said, "It's in Alabama. A black college in Alabama. You know, Booker T. Washington."

In the back of my brain, the name Booker T. Washington struck something. "What kind of a job?"

"You would be editor of the information bureau. Do all the press releases for the school. You would teach journalism, and they want you to be advisor to the student newspaper."

It was doing journalism, and I didn't have any other job.

Tuskegee was quite a change for a young black girl who grew up in a big city like Chicago. I was going south to a little town of five thousand people. What surprised me was that everybody spoke to everybody. In the big city, you didn't speak to strangers. I was considered stuck-up in Tuskegee until I learned Southern ways. And I came to like the friendliness. When I started stringing for the Voice of America,[99] doing interviews with African students on campus for broadcast overseas, I got my first radio experience.

After two years, I decided that if I went to graduate school to study journalism and got another degree, surely somebody would hire me in the profession. So I went to the University of Iowa, mainly because I got a fellowship there. But after one semester, the only thing that fit into my schedule was a radio and television workshop. I still planned to be a newspaper reporter. I had never thought of broadcasting as a career.

While I was taking the course, I auditioned for the campus radio station, which was heard throughout Iowa City. They had never had a woman to do news on the air, and I became the first. Then everything started to fit into place. I was reporting. I was writing.

And I was using my voice, which I had been developing by doing a lot of theater in high school and college. I was projecting my voice, speaking clearly, enunciating properly.

One of my professors said, "Why don't you think about a broadcasting career? I think the time is right."

This was 1965 and the civil rights movement had taken off.

"This may be the time for a black and for a woman," he said. "You ought to consider it. Plus, I think you're good."

So for the first time, I thought about broadcasting instead of newspapers. When I began looking for a job, it was as if America had suddenly discovered black people in the media. They needed black reporters to go into riot-torn neighborhoods. White reporters were too conspicuous; they were too scared.

My sex and color, which had been disadvantages, were suddenly in my favor. I had newspaper job offers from all over the place. And from radio stations. I turned down everything to go to radio station WCFL in Chicago, which was my hometown and was a big market. The station was affiliated with the Mutual Broadcasting Network.

Women in Chicago did talk shows and celebrity things, but did not work in hard news. I was going to be *the* pioneer—the first woman, black or white, to broadcast news in Chicago. And it was really tough.

WCFL had a good and very large news department. But there was a lot of resentment of me. I was not only the first woman hired, but also the first black. And the men knew that I'd been hired without any commercial broadcasting experience, in the second biggest market in the country.

The news director, who went out on a limb to hire me, was in my corner and tried to help me. But, otherwise, I was made to feel very uncomfortable, very unwanted. I got the bare amenities of hello. And I was almost totally ignored. It was as though I wasn't really there. I was a kind of a nonperson.

And I got no real help. Nobody would tell me how to do anything. So I didn't know what I was doing right when everything was happening. Mayor Daley.[100] The civil rights confrontations. The student protests. The antiwar rallies. It was a turbulent period in American urban history. And I was stuck in the middle of it. I had to educate myself. But it was a very lonely time.

After the men saw that I was capable of doing the job, they started to become a little friendlier. But they took every opportunity to rattle me—to make me blow my lines on the air, to try to drive me crazy.

They snatched my script from my hands while I was on air to see if I could keep talking. My copy was set on fire. They threw a big rubber tarantula on my desk. Can you handle it?

I even had guys come into the studio while I was doing the newscast and drop their pants, underpants, everything, mooning me while I was on the air. They did anything to try to rattle me.

But I always felt I had to do a good job, not only for Carole Simpson, but for black people and for women. I was determined that they would accept me not because she's pretty good for a woman or pretty good for a black. I wanted to be accepted because I could do the job.

I tried so hard to prove myself that I took dares when men said I couldn't do something.

One time, after I had joined WMAQ-TV, the NBC-owned station in Chicago, a pet snake got loose in one of the western suburbs. They found a skin, which they thought to be that of the escaped snake. They took it to the Brookfield Zoo. At first it was incorrectly identified as belonging to a cobra. And that sent a terrible alarm through the western suburbs. A poisonous snake was loose!

Later on, it was determined that the skin actually belonged to a perfectly harmless snake. So we went out to the zoo to talk to the herpetologist and prepare reports assuring people they had nothing to be afraid of while the snake was loose.

The herpetologist brought out a snake like the missing one. It was huge, about six feet long!

The guys from the other stations decided to do their stand-ups with the snake. I wouldn't touch it. I was terrified. I hate snakes. *I just hate snakes.*

But the guys taunted and teased me. "You're scared. You're just a woman."

They made me so mad that I was determined to do my stand-up holding the snake.

I asked the zoo guy to help me with the snake. "Is he gonna bite me?"

"No. He's perfectly harmless. Just touch him."

I was surprised to find that it was soft and smooth, not cold and scaly. And I was going, "Nice snake. Nice snake."

After I got acquainted with the snake, I said, "Could you just kind of coil him up in my hands?"

"Okay, but be careful. Don't drop him. Just hand it back if something happens. Just don't drop the snake."

So they coiled it in my hands, and I was trying to look comfortable. By now, there were a hundred people around me, besides the TV crews, waiting to see what I could do with the snake.

My cameraman intended to start tight on the snake and pull back to reveal me holding it, this way emphasizing to the public that the snake was not dangerous.

"Are you ready?" I asked. "We're only going to do this one time. I'm not going to hold this snake anymore."

The cameraman said, "Let's roll'em."

I start talking. I was thinking, *This snake is totally harmless and you don't have to be afraid of it.*

Suddenly, I felt something wrap itself around my waist. I was looking at the camera, so I didn't see what the snake was doing.

"What is this thing doing? Stop it! Stop it! Come get this snake!"

The zoo guy said, "Don't worry."

The crew was laughing.

"We knew you couldn't do it. We knew you couldn't."

So I tried again. I start talking and I felt it curling around me again. I said, "Take this snake!"

But I decided to give it one more try. And that would be it.

They coiled him up again. I got him. Everything was going fine. I was about to finish with my sign-off, "Carole Simpson, NBC News, Brookfield Zoo."

At the point where I was about to say Brookfield Zoo, the snake, which was slowly crawling up in front of the camera and facing me—

which I didn't know—came directly into my view. I saw this thing staring at me with its forked tongue darting out. I couldn't say Brookfield Zoo. I just pitched him to the zoo man.

So they ran it on the air just like that.

I got harassed by the TV guys at WMAQ like I was by the radio guys. One day I came back from covering the trial of a former governor of Illinois. I was going to do a voice-over as we showed sketches made in the courtroom. Then at the close, I would come on live during the newscast. I was standing the whole time.

Throughout the entire live program I was doing, one of the anchormen was crawling along the floor behind me. Then he started goosing me. Goosing me the entire time I was on the air!

When we went off the air, I said, "Are you crazy?"

He laughed.

"Why would you do something like that?" I asked.

He kept laughing.

I didn't complain to the news director. I had to make the point that I didn't like it, but I couldn't antagonize the anchorman so much that he would keep me off the air. I would wind up on the street without a job. Just like the episodes at the radio station, I had to keep my composure. There was always the danger that you might anger someone in power.

In 1974 I accepted an offer from NBC to be a network correspondent, and I moved to Washington to cover human resources. That seemed an okay assignment for a black woman. It was about welfare and pregnant teenagers. It was about school desegregation. You can handle that, they were saying to me.

But the important assignments like the State Department, White House, and Capitol Hill—that's not for you. Nobody was giving me anything. When I did get to Capitol Hill, after three years, it was because I fought long and hard for the opportunity.

I was covering the Hill when Hubert Humphrey died. It was cold, very cold, when they brought his body back to Washington to lie in state in the Capitol Rotunda—mid-January 1978. After a memorial service, his body was to be taken to Andrews Air Force Base and shipped back to be buried in Minnesota.

We had a television position on the House side of the Capitol called the "elm tree site." My job was to interview some congressmen, and to describe what I could see of the procession from my vantage point.

I was quite a distance from the steps of the Capitol. So I had to rely on a little monitor to see what people at home were seeing as I talked about it. One of our directors called me on my earphone. "Carole, we want you to talk till the hearse and the funeral procession drive out of sight."

My little monitor was rolling but wouldn't hold the picture. So I couldn't see what our cameras were seeing.

The director said, "Carole, you've got to talk the casket down until the procession moves out."

There was no time to argue about it.

"Standby. Standby. Go, Carole, Go."

I vaguely saw the casket coming out of the doors from the Rotunda. I ended up talking about twenty minutes nonstop. I talked about everything I could ever remember about Hubert Humphrey. The night before, I had read all this stuff. Not to prepare myself, because I never thought I'd have to do anything like this. I was just interested.

But thank God I had read the stuff. And fortunately, I had covered his campaign in '68. I knew about his battle with cancer, about the possibility that his wife would take his place in the Senate. I was talking about the weather, talking about the trees. I was almost reduced to having to read the label in my coat.

The director was saying in my ear, "It's beautiful, Carole. Keep going. You're doing fine."

He knew I was straining. I couldn't tell our viewers that I was unable to see the pictures they were looking at.

Then I heard music. "Faith of Our Fathers." I started to break up. I was touched by this man who had wanted to be president so badly. I started talking about how hard he fought for civil rights platform at the 1948 Democratic Convention. He never stopped fighting for civil rights. I was moved. My voice started to crack.

Finally, I recovered. But it was tough. I got tremendous accolades from the president of the news division. People talked about how moved they were listening to me speak about Humphrey.

No matter how high I think I have climbed in this industry, or how important I may think I am, I always remember that I'm a black woman. Don't get too big now. Don't forget what and who you really are.

I know I have some name recognition and some respect around the country. Yet I'm always aware that I'm black and that I'm a woman. Racism will rear its ugly head when you least expect it.

One day I took a young black woman assistant with me to the White House. It was a rainy day. One of our technicians went to get a sandwich. I didn't want to leave, because it was pouring rain. And I had some radio reports to do.

So I said, "If you go out someplace where they have take-out, would you mind bringing us back some sandwiches?"

He was standing in the middle of the White House press room. "What kind do you want?" he said. "Collard green sandwiches?"

As loudly as I could, I said, "Collard green sandwich? I don't know what you're talking about. What is a collard green sandwich? Do *you* eat them? I've never heard of anything like that. Why would you suggest that we would want something like that?"

He turned very red. I looked around the room.

"This man wants to know if I want a collard green sandwich. Have any of you ever had a collard green sandwich?"

I kept talking to him very loudly. And you know, that guy can't look me in the eye even today.

Another time, a network held a going-away party at their Washington bureau. One of the executives walked up and said, "Where's your apron and cap? Aren't you going to serve?"

I didn't start in this business yesterday. I think I have some stature. I was appalled. And I never let anything go by.

"How dare you?" I said. "What are you talking about? What do you mean, 'Shall I serve?'"

"Oh, it's just a little joke, Carole."

It's always just a little joke. Just a little joke.

You hear more and more of those kinds of things. I remember a period when nobody would say anything like that to somebody black. But slowly, ever so slowly, this stuff is coming back. It's creeping back in.

I think I operate under a double whammy of being a black and a woman. There are people who don't like me because I'm black. And there are those who don't like me because I'm a female. I had hoped that at some point in my career I would reach a point where people would see me as Carole Simpson. That's it. I'm just Carole.

I may place more value on my talents and ability than I should, but I keep thinking that if I weren't black, I would be doing as well as Lesley Stahl.[101] Maybe I would be further along, with a plum White House assignment, or a Sunday talk show. But I couldn't just be white and talented. I'd also have to be blonde and blue-eyed and very beautiful.

The feeling is prevalent. If you're black, if you're a woman, you're not quite as good as that white man. You may be good but not quite as good as Sam Donaldson. Not quite as good as Brit Hume. And I feel I am.

But even once you get an opportunity to demonstrate what you can do, you still have the ol' boy network to deal with. And nothing will change until that changes. Until women and blacks make some of the decisions about what goes on the air, about who gets hired, who we cover.

All that is decided by white, upper middle-class, middle-aged men. They are not interested in black issues or women's issues, Hispanic issues or poor people's issues. They'll deal with it only when they have to. When the president sets up a hunger commission, they will do a report. But we arrive late on all issues like these.

If there were more diversity in who makes the decision in network television, there would be a better representation of the multicultural nature of our society in what we see. Unfortunately, I don't see any changes coming anytime soon. I don't see any women on a fast track in management at any of the networks that will someday make them president of CBS News or NBC News or ABC News. I don't see any blacks on a fast track either.

Jesse Jackson has helped a lot. Without him running for president, there wouldn't have been anybody on television talking about blacks. Ronald Reagan made it clear what the country should feel about minorities. And that has had an impact on the men who run the networks. They have other things to talk about. Not blacks. Not women. We are not stylish anymore. We are not in vogue. No matter how good we are.

One day around 1970 I tried to be the best, to beat them all. I was years into my broadcasting career, it was September of 1969, and I was to cover what would be known as the Chicago Seven trial. It attracted worldwide attention. The BBC was there, Reuters, all the wires, and all the networks. I was not only filing for Chicago but for CBS stations in New York, Los Angeles, Cleveland, and Washington.

This was the case that grew out of the riots during the Democratic Convention in Chicago in 1968. The Yippies[102] and Bobby Seale[103] and Dave Dellinger[104] and the peace activists were on trial for inciting the riots. When the trial started, I found out I was three months pregnant.

When Bobby Seale was bound and gagged in the courtroom, I was having morning sickness. I alternated runs to the telephone to file, with runs to the bathroom to throw up.

The trial wore on. I got bigger and bigger. I was eight months pregnant. I wasn't sure what was going to come first, the baby or the end of the trial. When the defense rested and the jury went out to deliberate, my office decided that I would be better off in a hotel close to the courthouse. The jury deliberated for four days. I was having a terrible time. I was sick and hadn't been able to sleep.

At 9:00 in the morning, I got a call. My office said the jury had reached a verdict.

"Not today," I said. "I just feel terrible."

My producer said, "Look, we've got to be first."

I said, "I'll do what I can. But I'm not going to have a miscarriage trying to be first for WBBM."

The office had paid somebody to hold a pay telephone open for me near the courtroom. On the other end of that line was somebody who, with the flick of a switch, could put me on the air simultaneously on five CBS radio stations. It was all set. The important thing now was for me to get out the courtroom and to the location to file the verdict before anybody else.

The courtroom was jammed. I positioned myself at the back so that I could avoid the crush when everybody ran out. They had locked the door. Then they read the verdicts. Five of them were guilty and two of them were acquitted. I was writing my story while the judge polled the jury asking, "Is this your verdict?"

Suddenly, one of the deputy marshals got up, came to the back, unlocked the door and went out. I got up and went right behind him.

The other reporters looked up and saw that I had left, and they all started to leave, but the judge said, "Bolt that door."

I was out. I was gone—the only reporter out.

I made it to the telephone and called in the verdict. I got a five-minute jump on my nearest competitor. The CBS television correspondent was locked up in the courtroom, so CBS had to use my radio report as a special report on TV.

I had scooped this huge press corps. Me, a black pregnant woman.

Two weeks later my little girl was born.

Ed Bradley, later a correspondent for CBS's 60 Minutes, *began his career as a math teacher by day and a disc jockey at night.*

——

CBS asked if I'd go back to Southeast Asia. This was early 1979.

I said, "Sure, I'll do anything to go back."

I loved it over there—Vietnam, Cambodia, Laos, Thailand, Malaysia.

We flew from the United States to Frankfurt and then to Kuala Lumpur, Malaysia. We spent the night and got up early the next morning and flew to the other side of the peninsula. That's where the "boat people"[105] came ashore, the refugees from Vietnam.

We arrived and were driven to a hotel. A press contingent was already there. The government was asking reporters if they wanted to see a refugee camp.

I said to myself, *Well, hell. We didn't come here to see what everybody else is going to see. We're all jet-lagged, so let's just take a nap and we'll figure out what we'll do tomorrow.*

Everybody else left. We went upstairs to sleep. I was asleep maybe ten minutes when somebody banged on the door.

"Hey, there's a boat coming in!"

I put on my shoes and ran down to the beach. Sure enough, there was a boat foundering offshore, just coming apart, twenty or thirty yards out.

God knows how long they had been at sea. Or how little they'd had to eat, how much they were dehydrated, how weak they were.

Then we saw somebody trying to bring a kid in. And the villagers weren't helping them. They just stood around, watching.

I walked right out there, in chest-high water. I met them halfway. I grabbed the kid. Then I returned and helped some more people. When I went back out, a couple of villagers came with me.

Our cameraman was filming all this, so I became a part of the story, I guess. It wound up on *CBS Reports,* a show called "The Boat People."

I acted from instinct. The thought never crossed my mind that, *Well, you're just a journalist and you should stay put. You should be an observer.* I saw people in trouble, and I went.

But *he* crossed my mind. Again. The man running with the suitcase in one hand, holding his wife's hand with the other. The man in Saigon. The day Saigon fell. He was running to catch us, and he couldn't. I can see him. I can see him so clearly.

I got to Vietnam almost by accident in the first place. I never planned it.

My parents weren't surprised that I became a foreign correspondent or a network anchor. They didn't have middle-class money, but they had middle-class goals and values. And I was always told, "You can be anything you want."

My parents were divorced. My father lived in Detroit and owned a business of vending machines. I lived with my mother in Philadelphia. She worked in a restaurant at night. She didn't want me running the streets unsupervised, so they sent me to a boarding school in Woonsocket, Rhode Island. I played football, basketball, track, baseball, and hockey.

I made it for three years before the money ran out. My father stopped paying the tuition. My mother was able to rake and scrape enough for another year. But he wouldn't pay it and she couldn't afford it. So in 1958 I came home and did my senior year in Philadelphia. But I had to work after school so I couldn't play ball anymore.

I wanted to go to college but didn't know where. One day a neighbor invited me to a sports banquet at Cheney State University, a predominantly black school on Philadelphia's outskirts. I fell in love with it.

They said, "This is a teacher's college."

"What does that mean?"

"They teach you to become a teacher."

"Okay," I said, "I guess I'm going to be a teacher."

My senior year in college I met a disk jockey in Philadelphia named George E. Woods. He was also the program director at WDAS. I grew up listening to Georgie Woods, he was the most popular disc jockey in Philly.

My classmate, a woman, had invited him to talk to a class we called "School and Community." The purpose of the class was to teach us to relate to the kids we would meet in poor communities. It was to get future teachers involved, to go where the kids were, rather than saying, "You have to come to me."

George Woods was very impressive. He said, "Hey, everybody. Hi y'all?" That's the way he used to open his radio show. "What I do is communicate with kids. As teachers, that's what you'll have to do."

I was impressed with his approach. The other college kids snickered. I think George was insulted, but he continued on.

I went to him afterwards and apologized for my classmates. I thought their attitude was reprehensible. I was embarrassed by what happened. So he and I sort of hit it off. We went to the snack bar and had a sandwich. And he invited me out to the radio station.

I went to the station and took one look at the microphones and dials, and said, "Hey, this is for me!" I was hooked. I knew I was put on this earth to do something in radio. I'd go to the radio station after school every day, just hang out.

Then in January 1964 I graduated, and I was assigned to C. W. Henry School in Germantown to teach fifth-grade math. Eventually, through George, I met Del Shields, who was a disc jockey on FM. He did a jazz show.

Del took me under his wing. I volunteered four nights a week at WDAS-FM to do unpaid sports and an unpaid hourly newscast.

Eventually, I became a jazz disc jockey. If there was anything I could do that wasn't being done, which would get me on the air, I did it. I did news, sports, play-by-play—anything.

I used to listen to the CBS affiliate in Philadelphia. I used them as a classroom of the air, listening to the way they delivered the news and covered stories, because I had no journalism background. I'd never had a journalism course or a journalism professor.

When I finally got a chance to do live radio news, to cover stories around Philadelphia, I watched the CBS reporters and then listened to how they reported the same story, to see if there was anything I could learn. But more than that, I listened to the CBS network. If you grew up when I grew up, *everybody* I knew watched Walter Cronkite. I knew Roger Mudd and Eric Sevareid, Daniel Shorr and Peter Kalisher. I used to pattern myself in their manner—the CBS manner.

By 1967 I'd reached a point where I had to make a decision about my career. I had been teaching for three years. At the end of three years, you had to have so many hours toward a graduate degree, or you didn't get another pay raise. I didn't have any hours because while everyone else was doing graduate work at night, I was working as a disc jockey. And in the summers I taught summer school. Either I had to get some graduate hours, or I had to get into radio news full time.

I saw a survey that showed the average salaries after "x" years in communications and after "x" years in teaching. There was no comparison. My future in education looked fairly limited. I had also reached a point where the classroom bored me. It was too repetitious, the same lessons, the same numbers—just different kids.

I'm the kind of person who can't take confinement. I don't do well in an office environment. I like to have the freedom to go outside. So I started looking around for a way to get out of teaching.

I was reading a broadcast magazine and saw a notice that WCBS, the flagship station of the CBS network, was changing over to an all-news format. I knew WCBS because my girlfriend had moved to

New York, and I used to go up to see her on weekends. So I fired off a letter registered "Special Delivery" to Ed Joyce, the news director, asking for an audition.

Then I called and asked if he had received my letter. And, of course, he couldn't have gotten it because I had just put it in the mailbox!

I said, "This is Ed Bradley, WDAS radio in Philadelphia. I know you're changing over to an all-news format, and I'm interested in having an audition. I'd like to see your operation. And I'd like you to see me, to see what I can do."

"We don't have to wait for a letter," Joyce said. "We can set up an appointment now."

So we set up an appointment for the following Monday. I came up early and listened to the newscast, hour after hour, to see how they did it. I put in many hours of listening to WCBS. Plus, I was aggressive anyway. So when I went in for the audition, I was ready.

Unfortunately, they had scheduled another guy from my station for the same day. Joyce apologized. "This is embarrassing."

I said, "No, not really. I'm sure you have more than one job. I don't feel embarrassed at all."

"Okay, what we'd like you to do is write a five-minute newscast."

I knew their format. And having listened to their news before coming in, I knew what the top stories were as they saw it. I sat down and read the wire copy and wrote with that guideline in mind. Then they wanted me to record it. But I had to badger the technicians to get it done.

Finally, this guy got tired of hearing me say, "Can we do this now?"

"Yeah, come on," he said. "I'll do it." He was just trying to get rid of me.

They asked about my average day. My average day was teaching school. I wasn't even doing news anymore. I embellished what my day was like. In other words, I lied. But I didn't fake anything. I told them things that I did after school. I'd check with the newsroom and see what was needed. I'd go to sports events. I'd interview ballplayers. I'd interview people in the news. I'd cover breaking events. Which were all things that I *had* done.

"Would you send us an actuality?"

I didn't know what the hell an actuality was.

I said, "Um. Well, I'm not really sure I can."

"You must have some interviews you've done with people."

I said to myself, *Actuality. That must mean tapes of interviews.*

I said, "You know, we're a small station and after we do an interview, we erase the tape."

I was going to Atlanta the next day, so I didn't have time to go back to Philadelphia to interview somebody and send it back to them.

"Let me borrow a tape recorder," I said, "and I'll get you some actuality here."

Ed Joyce told me later he thought I was a little crazy at that point.

Joyce said, "We don't want any man-in-the-street interview."

"What do you mean, man-in-the-street? I'll go out and do a real in-depth interview."

He gave me a tape recorder, and I left. The first thing I did was buy the *New York Times* and look for a story. I looked for the biggest local story of the day that I thought I could handle and for which I could find people to interview.

The top story was a meeting of the city's antipoverty agency that had erupted into a brawl. I said, "Hell, it doesn't take much homework to do this. All I have to do is find the head guy." He happened to be H. Carl McCall. So I called his office.

"Mr. McCall is not in."

"I'd like to see him at noon."

"He's got a lunch."

"It won't take long."

"I'm sorry. He won't be able to see you."

I went to his office anyway, around the corner from CBS on Fifth Avenue. And I sat there. When he came in, I knew what he looked like from his picture in the paper. I threw the microphone in his face and asked him a couple of questions.

"This will only take five minutes. I've just got a couple of questions about the meeting. It's no big deal."

"Well, okay. I've got five minutes before lunch. Let's go on back to my office, and we'll sit down and do it properly."

"Fine."

So we sat down.

"I haven't seen you around town," he said. "This isn't your first day on the job, is it?"

"No, it's my second."

I did the interview and went back to CBS. I listened to the tape and wrote the script. Then I badgered another technician to record it. I recorded my wrap-arounds and took them to the news director. He looked surprised.

"I'm going to be in Atlanta. Here's the hotel where I'll be staying."

And I was out the door.

My competition from the station in Philly still sat there twiddling his thumbs. He had written his newscast, but the technicians kept telling him, "We're busy right now. We'll let you know when we've got some time." So he just sat back and waited for them to come and tell him. As opposed to me, who kept saying, "Look, can we do this *now?*"

Just on the basis of aggressiveness, I shot him out of the water. The next day I got a call from Joyce.

"We'd like to offer you a job. Not as an anchorman, but as a street reporter. We think you have some problems. But if you can take constructive criticism . . ."

At that point, we got disconnected.

I thought, *Oh, shit. He's going to think I hung up on him.*

I was so nervous I was shaking. I got down on my knees between the two hotel beds, praying! This was a job that paid minimally, *minimally* four hundred dollars a week. Between the two jobs I had in Philadelphia, I was making a hundred and eighty. So I was going to more than double my salary!

I called Joyce back.

He said, "Gee, I asked you about constructive criticism, and you hung up.

"Oh, nooo. I didn't hang up. No!"

He repeated the offer.

I said, "Fine."

"When can you start?"

Well, I need to give them two weeks' notification. Then I'll be there."

Being black was probably an advantage at the time. There were riots everywhere that summer. People who had always excluded blacks were making a move to include them. WCBS had one black technician and one black secretary. That was all. So I was the first reporter. But they made it clear to me that they weren't hiring me as a black reporter.

Joyce said, "You will go into the mix like everybody else."

It's okay if somebody wants to specialize in black stories, but that wasn't what I wanted to do. I wanted to do everything! I wasn't going on board to become the minority affairs specialist. You get painted into a box. It'd be like teaching school again. Or like being a beat reporter.

I wouldn't want to cover the State Department today. And I hated covering the White House. It was the same every day. You went to a cubicle office. I always had a broader horizon than that.

I started working a regular shift but did many more stories on my own. Hours meant nothing to me. There was one editor who would look at the "day book" and see a black story and assign me to it. I called him on it.

"Look, how come you always pick out a black story for me? That's not why I was hired. I don't mind covering black stories. In fact, there're some I will bring to you that other people here won't even be aware of, because of the contacts and knowledge that I have. But I don't want to be in a position where you look at the 'day book' and think 'Aha, a black story—Bradley.' If that's the way you want to work, then you and I need to talk to the news director."

He went mumble, mumble, mumble. But he got the message.

In 1971, I quit the job with CBS radio and moved to Paris. I felt like I was on an assembly line. A sign in Times Square showed a man running, looking at his watch. He was going nowhere. That scared me.

I had gone to Paris in 1969 to take a break. I fell in love with the city and decided that I wanted to live there one day. That was another reason I had been put on this earth—to live in Paris. And I would write the Great American Novel.

After I ran out of money, I caught on as a stringer in the CBS Paris bureau. It was the best way I knew to make enough money to live in Paris without having to answer the bell every day in a career pattern.

Sometimes I covered the major story in Paris at that time—the peace talks to end the Vietnam War. I spent a lot of time on a stake-out outside the Hotel Majestic, watching the arrival and departure of the four parties. They included the U.S., South Vietnam, North Vietnam, and the National Liberation Front—the Viet Cong.

During the day, Le Duc Tho, the chief communist negotiator, might have something to say. Or Madame Nguyen Thi Binh, the Viet Cong leader. Or Ambassador Porter for the Americans.

Peter Kalisher generally did the television piece. I did the radio. For the major broadcast, the editor in New York always preferred Kalisher. It had nothing to do with ability or competence. It had everything to do with Kalisher being the CBS News *correspondent*. I was the CBS News *stringer*.

There were the formal talks and the secret talks. By the summer of 1972, Henry Kissinger had gotten well into the secret stuff with Le Duc Tho. He took elaborate precautions, with French coopera-tion, to fly in and out unnoticed. They were talking about putting a cease-fire in place in return for the complete withdrawal of U.S. forces and the exchange of prisoners.

When Kissinger came out of one of his meetings with Le Duc Tho, we were standing outside the house.

"How did you find me?" he asked, surprised.

Our cameraman had received a tip. The week before, I had done a piece that New York loved about American blind kids touring Europe. They were going to the Rodin Museum in Paris. Kalisher didn't want to cover the story.

"Geez, this isn't going to go anywhere," he said. "Blind kids? What the hell can they see in a museum?"

I decided to find out.

The kids were allowed to touch some of the sculpture. One kid climbed up the big statue of "The Thinker" and described how it felt to the other blind kids standing below. I had a wonderful little story. And it was the end-piece on the evening news with Walter Cronkite.

As a stringer, you're not in it full-time, but you're not out of it, either. And that used to bother me. It also bothered me that whenever you signed off as a stringer, you didn't say "Ed Bradley, CBS News, Paris." You'd say, "Ed Bradley *for* CBS News, Paris." Most people wouldn't even notice that. But it got to me. It made me feel like I was a second-class citizen.

I decided I couldn't continue as a stringer. My ego couldn't take it. I needed to go back to New York, talk to CBS and decide my future. I returned with the record of having discovered Henry Kissinger coming out of a secret meeting, and having done a nice little film piece about the blind kids.

The first thing I did in New York was to have lunch with Bob Little, the foreign editor.

"We don't have much to offer you in the way of a job," he said.

I always loved New York. But I decided I didn't like New York as much as I thought. It wasn't time for me to return there.

"I know you don't want to go someplace like Chicago or Atlanta. And I don't think we have much to offer you overseas."

New York, then?

I started trying to think of the worst place in the world to live.

I said, "I'd rather live in Vietnam than live in New York."

It was a totally innocent remark.

"Are you volunteering?"

"No. But would you want me to go to Vietnam?"

"I don't know, but I'll let you know tomorrow."

The next day he asked me to have lunch with Sandy Socolow, the director of news. I figured, *Hell, Sandy wasn't going to have lunch with me to tell me he* didn't *want me to go to Vietnam.* There was no other reason for him to have lunch with a stringer.

He made the offer.

"I want you to take twenty-four hours to think about it."

"I've been thinking about it the last twenty-four hours. I'll go."

"No. Take another twenty-four."

I knew there was a risk in going. You could get killed. Or worse yet, you could get maimed, which I think frightened me more than getting killed. But, still, you say, *It's not going to happen to me. This bullet doesn't have my name on it.*

I called my mother.

She said, "Why do you have to go?"

"Mom, I *want* to go."

"Son, it's going to be dangerous."

"Nah. It's not going to be dangerous. It's no big deal."

I made it seem as inconsequential as covering a fire in Chicago. "The war is winding down. It's not going to be dangerous."

So I was off to Saigon—almost by accident.

Kissinger would soon be saying peace was at hand and that American ground forces would be gone.

In Saigon, there wasn't much to do except wait for the "Five O'Clock Follies," as we called the daily American press briefing. There was a lot of office time. If there was fighting close to the city, we'd jump in the car and drive up the road until we came upon some "bang-bang" and filmed it.

In those days, you produced the story on the scene yourself. I used to call it the "Three S's." We shoot it, script it, and ship it. The producer was someone in Hong Kong or Bangkok, who received the film with the narration and suggested shots. He cut the piece depending on the shots. Then he put it on the bird, the satellite. I was my own producer.

I heard stories about correspondents who carried weapons. My sense was, first, I didn't know how the hell to use one. I was not a country boy, I didn't grow up hunting and fishing. In Philadelphia, no one went hunting on my block. I had a cousin who lived out in the country. He had a gun, and we shot at a bottle on the lake. Other than that, the only time I ever shot a gun was at a penny arcade gallery at a fair.

Second, I figured, "How could I explain carrying a gun if I ever got captured?" The first words I learned in Vietnamese were "Journalist! Don't shoot!"

One day I started thinking that if the war does end, what happens to the American guys who deserted? So we started looking for them. I figured they had to be living on the Vietnamese economy. They had to have a Vietnamese connection in order to survive. So we sent out a Vietnamese reporter to make contacts and to see if we could ferret out deserters. He found three and persuaded them to talk to me. Then I convinced them to go on camera.

One agreed to speak from the shadows, and one from the back, with nothing showing of his face. The third guy said, "I want them to see my face! I want to tell them what's wrong with this war. I want them to look into my eyes, whatever the risks might be."

At the time, the average piece on the *Evening News* was about a minute forty-five, two minutes maximum. Take-outs—long pieces—were three-and-a-half, four minutes. This piece ran six minutes and forty-seven seconds. People just fell out of their chairs. And the "attaboys" started coming in—messages from New York that meant a pat on the back. It was the first TV coverage of any deserters.

I had been in country only a couple of weeks when I met the Viet Cong. We went to a village and the interpreter learned there were some VC in the area. We soon ran into a Viet Cong patrol. They were friendly.

We sat down, and they offered us fruit. I thought, *I go halfway around the world, run into my first Viet Cong, and what do they serve me? Watermelon! No! No! I'm sure they don't know the stereotype.*

I sat there and ate watermelon with six VC. They didn't want their pictures taken. They said they would get permission from their commander to take us out to their unit. But it never happened.

Vietnam got the most attention, but I liked Cambodia better. Phnom Penh was one of my favorite cities in the world, the other being Paris, of course. Phnom Penh was a wonderful city, I just loved it. The people were different. I found the Vietnamese to be cynical and hard. I attributed that to what they had gone through. They had been at war for over thirty years. There were Vietnamese who'd never known a day without war. Practically everyone had some member of his family who had been killed or wounded.

The Cambodians had been at war less than five years. The toll by then had not been as harsh as it was on the Vietnamese.

There had been a black American presence in Vietnam for years when I got there—black soldiers. So I was just one more black American to them. It was, "Hey, soul brother."

Cambodia was different. There had been incursions but no continuing American troop presence. What struck me were the similarities I found among Cambodians to black people I knew in Philadelphia, Detroit, or in New York. Blacks come in all complexions and facial types, from full round eyes to narrow, almost oriental eyes. One of my best friends in college was a black guy whose nickname was "Fuji" because he looked Japanese. His real name was Levi Bowman. Even his mother called him "Fuji" because he had eyes that looked Asian.

And blacks have nose shapes that vary from thick and broad to narrow and aquiline. The same with lips. So in Cambodians I was seeing facial characteristics of people back home. And many Cambodians are darker than Vietnamese. I can't tell you how many times I saw someone who looked like—gee, there was a woman who looked like my friend Ann in New York. Another one looked like my cousin Geneva. It was really striking.

A full-scale war was going on in Cambodia between the government troops and the communists, the Khmer Rouge. It was easy to find war in Cambodia. Most days you could just drive out a little ways and find it. There was always this fear that went with you. But at first you didn't know how to react.

I mostly worked with Norman Lloyd, an Australian cameraman, who is to this day one of my best friends. And Sophan, a Cambodian, was our soundman. We worked very well as a team.

There were times when Sophan said, "I had a dream that we shouldn't go down the road today."

Well, you couldn't say, "You've got to go down the road." You can't make a guy go down the road if he thinks he's going to get killed!

There were days when I'd say, "Hey, not today." If you're scared, you're scared. Fortunately, I never had those days when there was a story that had to be done and I had to go down the road to get it.

It was easier to be a correspondent in Vietnam, when there was a heavy American presence, because you knew if you got hit, they'd medevac you out of there. But if you were in Cambodia, shit, you might die out there, waiting for somebody to come get you. They didn't have medevac choppers. You'd better have a car on the road waiting for you. That was the only way you could get out. And the only medical treatment in the field was a Cambodian medic.

Norman and I didn't do things in a conventional manner. We got up at 5:00 in the morning and hit the road. We'd spend a couple of hours checking a different sector. We knew all the commanders. They were glad to see us because we brought goodies for them—a big bag of rice, a couple of cases of sodas, coffee, tea. They didn't have this stuff. It didn't cost us much. And we got good information in exchange. They would show us a map. The commander was not going to lie because that was where his soldiers were. Then we'd return to the hotel in Phnom Penh and meet everybody else for breakfast.

The journalists gathered for breakfast at a little hut with a table. We called it the "Groaning Board." The head of the Cambodian public affairs office, Colonel Am Rong, usually gave us a briefing. Most of the time he read from a piece of paper and said that nothing significant had happened. Or he gave us some casualty figures. Sometimes we knew it was government bullshit, because Norman and I had just been in the field and knew what had happened. We knew that the government forces were getting their butts kicked.

On Easter Sunday 1973, we had been in the field with government troops for two days. There were a hundred and fifty of them, with a half dozen armored personnel carriers outfitted with recoilless rifles and 50-caliber machine guns. We had film of all of the elements of the story. It was time to go. But we needed an editorial end to the story.

The Khmer Rouge were still in the tree line. Were the government troops going to sit there? Pull back? Or try to go in and get them?

We stopped shooting film until they made up their minds. We changed all the film in the magazine, so we would be ready to move, because we felt they had to attack. They couldn't just sit there. They were getting mortared now, and taking machine gun fire. They couldn't stay in an open field like sitting ducks.

As I stood behind an APC,[107] I saw a shady tree. The film bag I carried was big enough to sit on. I decided to move over to the shade and sit down. Rounds were hitting thirty or forty yards from our position. Then one landed right where I'd been standing a moment before.

A soldier in front of me fell with a hole in his back so big I could put my fist through it. Shrapnel peppered my back. A big piece sliced through my arm above the elbow.

The first thing I thought was *Oh, my God, they're going to cut my arm off!*

I always had a fear of being maimed. If you're dead, there's nothing you can do about it. But if you're maimed, you have to live with that the rest of your life.

Norman caught a piece of shrapnel in his arm that later got infected. Sophan, our sound man, escaped with a scratch.

Right away they loaded us in the personnel carrier and pulled out. They took us as close to the road as they could. Our Cambodian driver was there with the car. He always waited for us where he dropped us off. So he took me to the hospital.

The doctor, a Cambodian, stitched my arm. He said he couldn't get at the shrapnel in my back because the holes were too tiny. It would work itself out or dissolve in the body.

"Don't worry about it," he said.

I still wonder about the shrapnel when I go through metal detectors.

They used to say that when you get thrown from a horse, you've got to get back on as soon as possible to overcome the fear. After we got wounded, Norman and I felt that we had to go back into combat, to put ourselves in a dangerous situation just to get over what had happened, so we could be normal about it again.

So we went out and kept asking, *"Où est la première ligne?"* Where is the front line?

All the Cambodian officers spoke French. They directed us three miles down the road.

"Excusez moi, mon capitaine. "Où est la première ligne?"

"Á trente mètres." Thirty meters from here.

It got hairier and hairier. More and more shooting the farther we walked.

Now we were crawling facedown in the dirt, next to an officer.

"Capitaine, où est la première ligne?"

"C'est ici, monsieur."

We were right there.

"Okay," I said. "Let's fan out and get some pictures."

It got hot and heavy. There was a lot of small arms and machine gun fire. Rocket-propelled grenades were coming in. Norman would pop up behind a tree, shoot and go back down.

I was pinned down. A bullet whizzed by. Another kicked up dirt right by my arm where I'd been wounded before.

"Norman, I think we ought to get out of here."

"I'm glad *you* said it."

We turned around and started crawling back.

"Geez, that was dumb!" I said.

But it got us over the fear. We dealt with it. We could return to covering the war without feeling we had to do something ridiculous to prove we were over the fear. We'd done it.

I left Southeast Asia in the summer of 1974. I was back in Phnom Penh early the next year, on the eve of the collapse.[106]

One morning Norman and I were making the rounds of the command posts. We saw two guys walking down the road. They were carrying a pole, which had a sling attached to it, and there was a guy in the sling. They were bringing him out. He was bleeding profusely, hit in the leg.

We could see the stump thrashing from side to side. The guy was in so much pain. They called for a helicopter. But there was no helicopter for soldiers because the Cambodian officers were running shuttles to carry people who could pay to get out of the country. And there was no medicine to give this guy because his officers were selling that, too.

We stopped a truck, loaded him on it, and followed it to the hospital. They operated on him and cut his leg off. We went back next morning to see him. He had died.

So in the next day's story we asked, "Where's the medicine? Where are the helicopters? Where are the supplies sent from America?"

We took pictures of the soldiers and their families leaving on the helicopters. We went to the medical warehouses and found no medicine. It was being sold on the black market or to the Khmer Rouge.

Fighting took place every day now. It was like a noose around Phnom Penh. Every day it tightened. You could see it. It was just a matter of time. And then came the day of evacuation.

Norman and I thought we'd better leave. If we didn't, the fall of Phnom Penh was happening so fast that we wouldn't be able to get the story out.

It was strange. There was no fear that day. We weren't leaving because we were afraid. We had to get the story out. There was never a sense of danger, whereas later in Vietnam, there would be. There was a fear for your life when Saigon fell—which was unfounded, as it turned out. If there was a true danger, it was in Cambodia.

We figured we probably would be able to come back the next day. At the very most, two days. We could charter a plane. We were at breakfast that morning and somebody yelled, "They're gonna evacuate!"

We had a charter coming in to take the CBS equipment out. It was due in about noon. So we got up and went over to the American Embassy. A press officer lost his composure. He was ranting and raving about CBS embarrassing the American government by having a charter coming in to evacuate equipment.

Then he told us we could take one bag. I had to leave behind my clothes and camera equipment. We were trucked to a soccer field. The Cambodians—monks, everybody—were lined up, waving peacefully. There was no panic. There was no shooting. The helicopters landed and the marines got out, with weapons locked and loaded.

I looked into the face of a black marine. I could see his fear.

I thought, *Shit, he must see something I don't see.*

"Norman, what the hell is going on?" I said.

"Shit. I don't know."

We found out later they had been told that some of them wouldn't come back from the mission.

The kids kept waving. It was like a circus. Then a rocket landed on the other side of the river. It wasn't even close. The Khmer Rouge were just tightening the screws, heightening the level of tension.

I sat next to Neil Davis[108] on the helicopter. He was killed a decade later covering an aborted coup in Thailand. Neil and I were both crying as we lifted off. Cambodia was so special to me and to him. It was hard to leave people behind. You didn't know what their fate was going to be.

I couldn't have imagined in my worst nightmare what eventually happened. Out of a population of seven million, the Khmer Rouge, proclaiming the Year Zero,[109] massacred or starved to death nearly two million people. Another quarter million became refugees. No one knew *that* was going to happen.

In my last hours, our driver vanished. He was such an amazingly gentle man. He had served as one of Jackie Onassis's guides when she went to Angkor Wat.

Sophan was still shooting film with Norman. He had the sound box around his neck. He took it off and gave it to us. Tears filled his eyes. We left him.

Sophan died. Probably the driver too.

Dith Pran, the Cambodian who helped the *New York Times* and later survived the killing fields, told me he saw Sophan on the road when they were forced to leave town. Sophan was naïve, not as savvy as Pran was. Sophan thought that he could talk and reason with the Khmer Rouge.

Sophan said to Pran, "Let's tell them that we speak English. We work with journalists. They will need us."

Pran said, "Don't say a word. Don't say anything."

Sophan talked. Pran remembered the day they took Sophan out of the line with other people. That was it. They took him off. Pran never saw him again.

I looked at Neil Davis as we helicoptered from Phnom Penh. I thought about how futile it all was. Why did this happen? Why?

We were evacuated to a helicopter carrier. From there we went to an air force base in Thailand and on to Bangkok. When we got to Hong Kong, we bought some new clothes, and continued to Saigon.

A number of people had stayed behind in Phnom Penh. Later, we chartered a plane and flew back and circled the city. When we radioed the embassy, they told us what was going on.

"Don't land because the airport's not secure."

By this time, the Khmer Rouge had taken over. The last pockets of government resistance were falling. The remaining Westerners had moved into the French embassy. We figured there was no easy way for us to get back in.

In a matter of days, Saigon came to an end, too. We knew it was coming. We were told to stay tuned to the armed forces radio station. They were mostly broadcasting Muzak. But every hour they had a satellite newscast from the United States.

They told us that when the evacuation came, an announcer would break into the programming and say that the temperature in downtown Saigon was a hundred degrees and rising. Then they would play Bing Crosby's "White Christmas." That meant evacuation.

I don't know who cooked that up. Probably the same guy who decided that the code name for the American embassy officer running the evacuation was "Wagonmaster." It was pure D-grade American West fantasy. Round up the wagons in the corral.

An earlier advisory said that if you were with CBS, you should go to a particular location. UPI would go somewhere else. Then a bus would pick us all up and take us to the Saigon airport, where we would take a plane out.

I saw people walking down the street with suitcases. I knew the evacuation was on. Communist troops were minutes away.

We went to the first location. Nobody was there. We looked at the paper which gave the directions.

"Let's go to the second location."

We got to the second location. Nobody was there.

By this time, thousands of people were in the streets. The Vietnamese now knew it was going down. They saw all the "round-eyes" walking the streets. This must be it. So the Vietnamese were packing their suitcases and trying to get out, too.

We got to the third location. Nothing. Someone said, "Maybe we should go to the fourth location."

I said, "Unh-unh. Stay here."

Nobody was in charge. So I just took command.

"It's obvious the evacuation is running behind," I said. "They haven't sent a bus to this place yet. Instead of wandering through the streets, let's just stay here. We know this is one of the evacuation points. Sooner or later, somebody will come here."

So we stayed there. Finally a bus came.

I told people to get in line, and I put them on the bus. The Vietnamese who showed up had no identification to get on the bus. The ID to get on the bus was to be a "round-eye." One Vietnamese who said he worked at the embassy, so I said, "Hurry, man, get on the bus!"

The guy they sent to drive didn't know how to operate a bus. He didn't even have a key, so if it stalled, we had to jump-start it. He could have taken wide streets like Nguyen Hue and Tu Do, but he decided to go down the narrow streets. They were lined with soup stalls and little restaurants that were just cook pots and benches, with a poncho liner thrown over them to keep the rain off.

When the driver turned a corner, he wiped out three restaurants. But we were headed for the airport.

When we got to the airport the Vietnamese—our guys—shot at us. *Shot at us!* I said, "We're not going to make it."

So we ended up going down to the Khanh Hoi district, near the port facility. The guy parked the bus and radioed the embassy. Wagonmaster was on the other end. There were three buses now. The driver told us to get out. He said the helicopters would pick us up. You could see the Chinooks five-thousand feet up, circling.

Ten thousand Vietnamese were out there now. Boats were pulling away from the dock. People jumped into the river, trying to catch the boats.

I said to the driver, "Are any security forces coming to protect us?"

"No, the helicopters will land, and you'll just get on."

"Wait a minute. The helicopters are going to land here? And all these Vietnamese who are jumping into the water because they are so desperate are going to stand back and watch us climb on to the helicopters? And they're going to wave to us goodbye? Nah, I don't think so."

I turned around and said, "Nobody get off the bus."

I told one Vietnamese family, "Don't get off the bus."

"Must go," they said. "Must go."

"Look, the helicopters are not going to land here," I said. "Don't get off the bus because there's no guarantee that you'll be able to get back on."

I was afraid the crowd would turn ugly. But I couldn't keep them on the bus. They got off. People started milling around. Somebody put a suitcase down. A Vietnamese boy snatched the suitcase and ran. They started after him.

"Hey, let it go, man," I yelled. "Whatever was in the suitcase, let it go. You'll never get it back."

"I guess you're right," he said.

Then it started getting ugly. I went to the bus driver.

"I want you to put all these people back on the bus. We're pulling out of here."

He said, "You gotta stay here."

"Get your ass on the bus!" I said. "If you don't drive it, I will. And I'll leave you here. We're going back to the embassy."

So we put the people on the bus.

And this one family, I'll never forget. The man was running with the suitcase in one hand, pulling his wife with the other hand, trying to get to the bus. I can see him so clearly.

We headed back to the embassy. When we got there, thousands of people were trying to get in. We went to a parking lot across the street. Keyes Beech of the *L.A. Times* called somebody he knew in the CIA. They told him to come to the back of the embassy. So we went to the back to a wall.

Marines on top of the wall were beating back people who were trying to climb over. We were ten or fifteen yards away. But it took us an hour to get that far. There was a crush of people, a mass of humanity. You couldn't take your passport out for identification because somebody would snatch it. It was madness.

Our cameraman, Keith Kay, was taking pictures. I said, "Keith, we've got enough pictures. I think we ought to try to get over this wall."

I worked my way toward a black marine. I hoped the brother would recognize that I was black and wouldn't mistake me for a Cambodian and knock me down. They were slamming most of the Vietnamese back with rifle butts.

Finally we got over the wall.

People squatted on the ground. Fires burned in fifty-five-gallon barrels. Barrels of money were being burned—whole barrels full of twenty-dollar bills. Then a guy came out of the embassy. He had an armload of money, stacks of new bills.

"Are you going to burn that?" I said.

"No," he said. "Takes too much time. I'm going to shred it."

Geez, I wanted to say, *I'll help you! Oh, man!*

We went into the building and up some floors. Americans and Vietnamese were crowded together. An American guy was married to a Vietnamese, and she had her whole family there, including aunts and uncles.

The ambassador's conference room was at the end of a hallway. I heard elevator music. I looked into an office. Press clippings were posted on the wall, giving a history of the war. There were photos of Nguyen Cao Ky,[110] William Westmoreland, Lyndon Johnson—headlines: "Rolling Thunder." "Search and Destroy." "Light at the End of the Tunnel."

A light shone from the ambassador's conference room, filtering over the people waiting for the helicopters to land on the roof. I said, "Maybe *this* is the light at the end of the tunnel. Maybe peace *is* at hand."

I reached the roof, and we were lifted off by a helicopter. We had started out at 9:00 that morning. Now it was dark.

319

I thought about that face again, the face of the guy running with the suitcase. His suitcase was in one hand. He was pulling his wife with the other hand. She held two kids. They were running to get back to our bus at the river.

Two Vietnamese boys ran alongside of him. Pop! They hit his arm and took his watch. Pop! They hit the bag and the suitcase flew open. Clothes and money spilled out.

He was trying. But he never made it. I'll never forget the look on his face as long as I live. I can see him so *clearly*. He never made it.

I told him not to get off the bus.

WALLACE TERRY

Wally Terry, who graduated from Brown University and was editor of the school's daily paper, worked as a reporter for the Washington Post *and* Time *magazine, and was the author of* Bloods, *a bestseller about black servicemen in the Vietnam War.*[111]

———

I first went to Vietnam on assignment for *Time* magazine in March of 1967. This led to a cover story dealing with the performance of the black soldier in our first fully integrated war. When I didn't wilt under fire, *Time* asked me to return later that year.

For many reasons, 1968 was not a good time for me. Eight years into my profession, I had seen too much death, covering the civil rights movement and the urban riots. Close friends like NAACP leader Medgar Evers and a white minister, Jim Reeb, had been murdered in the South. Dr. Martin Luther King, my son's godfather, would be next. Now I would be back in Vietnam. When, I wondered, would God lower the curtain on my play?

Saigon, 1968. I am living at the Embassy Hotel. I am hungry for a guide to Vietnamese culture, and I find one—John Cantwell, a *Time* correspondent from Australia. He loves Asia, its people, its languages. He can speak three dialects of Chinese. We are like roommates because we are the only *Time* reporters staying at the hotel.

One night, John and I take a bagful of hamburgers up to the roof of the hotel to watch the rocket attacks and flare drops around the city. We decide this is one war we don't want to lose our lives in.

"What would happen to my wife and kids," John says to me. "It would be bloody stupid."

For both of us, Vietnam is making less sense each day.

Once a champion weight lifter, John still stuffs himself with vitamins, drinks only fruit juice, and carries around a portable chest expander. He relishes guns but not as much as the birds he keeps in our office at the *Time* villa. He loves to stand at the top of the stairs whistling at them, trying to coax them to sing.

May 4.

The Communists have stopped shelling for a few days. In that brief respite, I decide it is safe enough for my wife, Janice, to make her first visit to Saigon from Singapore where we've rented an apartment for her and our three children. Her plane arrives in the afternoon. John and I take her to dinner. Johns spins us tales of his journeys to Phnom Penh and Vientiane.

May 5, 4 A.M.

Saigon is shaken by rounds of mortars and rockets. It sounds like the Tet offensive all over again. John and I agree there's nothing we can do while it's still dark. We decide to meet at 8:00 at the *Time* villa.

8 A.M.

We don't have much time before the deadline on this story. One of us has to get to a military briefing at the public affairs office, and one of us has to see what damage has been done to the city. I tell John to go to the briefing. I will look around the streets.

"No, man," John says. "Janice is here. She'll be frightened. You should stay with her. I'll go out."

He insists.

"Okay," I say. "But whatever you do, stay away from Tan Son Nhut and Cholon, the Chinese sector of the city."

"Sure, sure," he says.

8:20 A.M.

On his way out, John runs into another journalist, Frank Palmos. Palmos asks if he can come along. Then three more reporters— Bruce Piggot and Ronald Laramy of Reuters and Michael Birch of the Australian Associated Press—want to come too.

All five pile into the Mini-Moke, a small jeep, and set out, following the Saigon River. John drives straight into the Cholon sector.

9:30 A.M.

Frank Palmos, visibly shaken, his clothes torn, staggers into the villa.

"They're all dead," he cries out.

I'm stunned. I call Janice. I need help. I can't find anyone to help me go get John.

Worried, Janice puts in a call to Zalin Grant. He and I had worked together in *Time*'s Washington bureau, and he has just returned to Saigon as a correspondent for the *New Republic*.

Zalin—we call him "Zip"—had done his military service as an army intelligence officer and was then hired by *Time*, one of the few newsmen who could speak Vietnamese. In 1967 he came back home and, in one of his first stateside assignments, stood up to black rioters in Newark. That's when I met him—at the *Time* Washington bureau.

Gutsy little white dude, I thought. He wore handmade Italian suits and drove a Porsche. *Cocksure of himself, too,* I thought.

Zip had picked up his nickname playing football. We played some touch together. He wasn't bad. But he couldn't play basketball worth a lick. And when he opened his mouth, out fell the grits. A Southerner! From South Carolina!

I had grown up in Indiana, afraid of the South. And after I saw the former slave markets on a trip to Charleston, I had nightmares. But it was Zip's character that made me forget his accent. He was tough, brave, and fair.

When Janice phones Zip, she says, "Something has happened to Cantwell. Wally needs you."

"Where is he?" is all Zip says.

Palmos's story.

When Zip arrives at the villa, I pour some scotch into a paper cup, put it in Palmos's hand, and ask him to tell his story.

They had driven five miles from the center of downtown Saigon into Cholon, he says, after they caught sight of two helicopter gunships rocketing against an enemy force. They left the main road, Tran Quoc Toan, for a side street, Minh Phung. John then turned off onto a dirt road, No. 46. There, they ran into scores of Vietnamese fleeing.

"We drove against them," Palmos says.

An old lady shouted, "VC! VC! Go back."

John drove fifty more yards. Two figures holding rifles moved to the center of the road. Another figure appeared from behind an oil drum with an AK-47 assault rifle. John stopped the Mini-Moke, turned off the engine, and raised his hands in surrender.

He kept saying, *"Bao chi. Bao chi."* Press. Press.

It was a Viet Cong suicidal strike force. They opened fire point-blank. Palmos says he jumped free and ran for cover. When he thought their clips had been spent, he leaped from his hiding place and ran for his life.

Zip and I exchange glances. We are thinking the same thing: *How much did he really see?*

Zip is not convinced they are dead. I don't want to believe it, either. All I can think is, *I have to find John. I let him go there. If he is alive, or dead or captured, I have to know. I owe him that.*

11:30 A.M.

Zip and I climb into another Mini-Moke. We look for an army unit that is supposed to be going into the Cholon area. We find it, but it's stalled. A tank had thrown a tread. It would be hours before it was moving again.

"We'll have to go it alone," Zip says. "John could be bleeding to death."

I think to myself, *I'm with the right man. Zip speaks Vietnamese. He can handle this.*

We stop a few blocks from the intersection of Tran Quoc Toan and Minh Phung. We can hear bullets whistling close by. We get out, walking in a crouch. We approach some Vietnamese sitting on the sidewalk. They are very polite. They offer us a seat and some tea.

Zip speaks to them in Vietnamese. Yes, they say, the Viet Cong are in the area.

Despite the gunfire, we are anxious to get through. Zip spots a police precinct station. He thinks they can help us.

We are ushered into the commander's office. He is wearing a flak jacket and sitting down to breakfast.

Zip loses his cool. How can this man be so nonchalant while his neighborhood is being overrun by the Viet Cong? Zip curses the commander in Vietnamese and English.

Amazingly, the commander does not get upset. He knows Zip is telling the truth.

"I've got an armored car," he says. "I'll get my jeep, and we'll go out and see what's happening."

He seems almost friendly.

We follow his jeep and armored car like a convoy. But when we come to the intersection of Tran Quoc Toan and Minh Phung, the police dare not go further. We are on our own again.

1:00 P.M.

We hire a cab, a little yellow and blue Renault, and offer the driver $10, a king's ransom, for each block he will drive us on Minh Phung. He drives two blocks into the sound of automatic-weapons fire, then waves us out of the cab.

We start walking down the street side by side, like gunslingers on the way to the O.K. Corral. Suddenly it becomes so damn quiet.

Along the sides of buildings and in doorways, South Vietnamese paratroopers smile knowingly at us. They aren't budging. We start walking past them. The street is absolutely deserted now.

We are walking on the edge.

Zip whispers, "This is impossible."

There is no way of getting to John and the others until the U.S. Army units move closer. The Viet Cong are everywhere. It would be suicidal.

We drive back to the *Time* villa. Central Saigon is surreal. There is fighting going on a few miles away, yet here it is absolutely calm—almost lovely.

3:00 P.M.

Zip talks to some refugees who tell us that they have seen some bodies and are pretty sure the white men are dead. We are still hopeful that they are only unconscious. We climb back in the Mini-Moke.

The Americans are now pushing into the area. We are finally able to drive down Minh Phung. At road No. 46, we spot a demolition team. They tell us it is still too dangerous to go farther. When we say we are going to try anyway, they give us each a carbine. We walk down the dirt road.

There, we find them.

I am too overwhelmed to cry.

Laramy is sitting up in the Mini-Moke, his arms still upraised. The others are on the ground. Their bodies are full of holes. Caked in blood. Covered with flies. Bloated from the heat. John has been shot twelve times.

I want to touch John, but Zip waves me off. "Don't touch anything," he warns. "There might be booby traps."

We walk back to Minh Phung. The demolition team has called an ambulance, but the driver refuses to come closer. The area is still hostile. We are going to have to bring the bodies out ourselves.

Finally, the demolition team offers to drive us back in. But when we get there, they keep a safe distance. Only Smitty, a black sergeant, is willing to come up and check for booby traps. He separates the bodies.

Zip and I start loading the bodies into the back of the Mini-Moke. I raise John's shoulders gently. I don't want to hurt him any more than he has been hurt already.

"This is no time for a show of reverence," Zip says. "We've got to toss them in there and get out of here as fast as we can."

Suddenly, nearly thirty young men about sixteen to twenty-five years-old wearing black pajamas, run right by us, in formation. They look at us with pure hatred. They are clearly Viet Cong. Probably they are John's killers.

Why don't they kill us? Perhaps it is their rush to get out of the area.

Zip gets into the driver's seat. I slide in beside him, holding the bodies. We drive back to Minh Phung and load them into the ambulance.

5:00 P.M.

Zip goes back to his hotel. There is blood all over his pants, but he doesn't care.

I go to our hotel to meet Janice. All that I found on John's body was a whistle the Viet Cong had no use for, the one John played for his birds. It is all that is left of him. I slip it into Janice's hand. We cry together.

The next day, when I walk into the daily press briefing, the press corps bursts into applause. I look to see who is coming in behind me, but there is no one there. The applause is for me. And for Zip. And, I will always feel, for our comrades who died doing their job.

Today Zip lives in Paris with his wife, Claude. He is working on his fourth book on the Vietnam War. I know Zip took those risks that day as much for me as he did for John.

All the absurd distinctions society would make between us—black and white, North and South—vanished that day. Zalin Grant and I found what many soldiers were discovering at the same time in Vietnam. A bonding took place, as much for us as it did for the soldiers who risked their lives to pull their comrades out of the line of fire.

In one solitary moment, in the horror of it all, we discovered what Dr. King dreamed of: The sons of slaves and former slaveholders could sit at the same table. We found a better vision of ourselves and of our nation.

We became more than friends. We became as brothers.

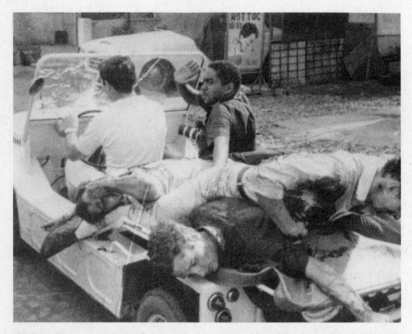

Wallace Terry and Zalin Grant recovering the bodies of four journalists killed by the Viet Cong on May 5, 1968 in Saigon, Vietnam.

EPILOGUE
Janice Terry

My husband of forty years, Wallace Terry, had been complaining of a cough that wouldn't go away. He was seeing physicians and specialists who were treating him to make sure an old case of pneumonia had not recurred. Yet the cough persisted. One day at noon when I arrived to take him to a scheduled appointment with his doctor, he suddenly collapsed as he was putting on his coat. An ambulance quickly took him to the nearest hospital where he was immediately put on a respirator and sedated into a medically-induced coma.

It was then established through exhaustive blood tests that he had a rare vascular disease called Wegener's granulomatosis, which strikes about one in a million people. The disease can be treated with drugs, but in his case it was diagnosed too late. He did not emerge from the coma and died on May 29, 2003.

Wally's close Vietnam War friend, Zalin Grant, who came from Paris for the services, suggested that I publish what he had written on *Missing Pages*. I knew that my husband planned to write a two-volume work and that the first volume had been completed. But I was unable to muster the emotional strength that I needed to go through his files until more than a year had passed.

When I located the manuscript, I asked Zalin Grant to adapt a piece Wally had written for the July 1, 1990, issue of *Parade* magazine entitled "A Friendship Forged in Danger." This was one of Wally's favorite articles, because it captured his optimism about relations between blacks and whites, and I knew he intended to include it in this book. The photograph that accompanies the piece illustrates the truth—and proves the mendacity of the British journalist—as Wally recounts in his opening Author's Note, about what really happened in Saigon on that Sunday morning in May 1968.

I would like to express my appreciation, on behalf of Wally, to the following people and organizations: Phyllis Westberg of Harold Ober Associates and Keith Wallman of Carroll & Graf for seeing this work through to publication; Bill Takes for his corporate understanding; the John S. and James L. Knight Foundation, the Gannett Foundation and the Henry Luce Foundation for their support. My most notable appreciation to our children, Tai, Lisa, David and his wife, Serda, and my sister Gayle Jessup White. Many others gave their support and encouragement to Wally, and I would like to express a spiritual thanks to all of you from both of us.

EXPLANATORY NOTES

Janice Terry

Carl Rowan

1. **United States Information Agency:** Established in August 1953 and terminated in October 1999, the USIA was an agency devoted to "public diplomacy." Its mission was to understand, inform, and influence foreign publics in promotion of the national interest, to broaden the dialogue between Americans and U.S. institutions and their counterparts abroad, and to foster exchanges of students, professors, and diverse categories of citizens between the U.S. and foreign societies.

2. **Hubert Humphrey:** (May 27, 1911–January 13, 1978) Hubert Horatio Humphrey was the 38th vice president of the United States, serving under Lyndon Johnson. Humphrey twice served as a United States Senator from Minnesota, and served as Democratic Majority Whip. In 1968, Humphrey was the nominee of the Democratic Party in the U.S. presidential election but lost to Republican Richard M. Nixon. In one of the most renowned speeches in American political history, Humphrey told the 1948 Democratic National Convention: "The time has arrived in America for the Democratic Party to get out of the shadows of states' rights and walk forthrightly into the bright sunshine of human rights."

3. **muzzling the press in Vietnam:** The John F. Kennedy administration was accused of trying "to muzzle" the press by limiting its access to army helicopters and other means of transportation, thus preventing journalists from reporting on what was happening in the countryside. The controversy reached its peak when JFK unsuccessfully tried to get reporter—and later Pulitzer Prize winner—David Halberstam fired from the *New York Times*. The dispute carried over into the Johnson administration to a lesser degree. In retrospect, most observers believed that, while there was always tension between the government and journalists, the media were granted unprecedented freedom to report the war as they saw fit, and censorship was seldom an issue.

4. **Horace Busby:** (March 10, 1924–May 2000) Horace W. Busby Jr. was Lyndon B. Johnson's advisor, speechwriter, and confidant throughout his political career. Busby had a sometimes tumultuous relationship with Johnson but stayed on the job from the earliest days of LBJ's career as a congressman in Texas to the twilight of his presidency. Busby not only

articulated and refined Johnson's political thinking, he also helped shape the most ambitious, far-reaching legislative agenda since FDR's New Deal.

5. **Chevy Chase Club:** An exclusive country club and golf course in Chevy Chase, Maryland. Located just a few miles from Washington, D.C., the club is in Montgomery County which is one of the most affluent counties in the nation.

6. **Chester Bowles:** (April 5, 1901–May 25, 1986) Chester Bliss Bowles was a liberal Democrat, a diplomat, and a politician from Connecticut. He was appointed U.S. Ambassador to India and Nepal by President Truman, serving from 1951 to 1953. Under President John F. Kennedy, he was appointed undersecretary of state in 1961. In early December 1961 he was replaced by George Ball as undersecretary as a consequence of his perceived failure to fulfill his administrative duties at the State Department, and his earlier leaking to the press of his opposition to the Cuba Bay of Pigs Invasion. In July 1963 Bowles was again made Ambassador to India, a position he would hold through the remainder of the Kennedy administration, and for the duration of Lyndon B. Johnson's presidency. Bowles was known as a generous source for the media, to official Washington's chagrin.

7. **George Reedy:** (August 5, 1917–March 21, 1999) George Edward Reedy was White House press secretary from 1964 to 1965 under President Lyndon B. Johnson. He worked as an aide to Johnson during his presidential campaign in 1960, during his term as vice president and his early months as president. When Pierre Salinger resigned as press secretary in August of 1964, Reedy was named to the position. During the escalation of the American involvement in Vietnam beginning in March 1965, press questions over the veracity of the Johnson Administration's public assessments of the war led to charges of a so-called credibility gap. In 1965 Reedy took a leave of absence because of his disagreement with Johnson's Vietnam policies. In 1968 he returned to the White House to work as a special assistant shortly before Johnson's surprise announcement that he would not seek reelection. In 1970, Reedy published *The Twilight of the Presidency*. The book was a critical and influential look at the modern American presidency and, in particular, at the impact that war has had on the office. While the book was not specifically critical of Johnson, the former president was reportedly unhappy with its frank assessment of the presidency and refused to speak with Reedy ever again. Reedy said of Johnson: "He may have been a son of a bitch. But he was a colossal son of a bitch."

8. **Liz Carpenter:** (September 1, 1920–) Elizabeth "Liz" Sutherland Carpenter is a writer, feminist, former reporter, media advisor, speechwriter,

political humorist, and public relations expert. Carpenter stood at the forefront of the Women's Movement when it began and never wavered from her stand. In 1942 she began covering the White House and Congress for the *Austin* (Texas) *American-Statesman*. For the next eighteen years, she reported on presidents from Franklin D. Roosevelt to John F. Kennedy as a Washington reporter. She joined the staff of Lyndon Johnson in his campaign for vice president in 1961. After his election, she became the first woman executive assistant to the vice president. Mrs. Carpenter was in Dallas, Texas, on November 22, 1963, at the time of the assassination of John F. Kennedy. She drafted the fifty-eight words Johnson spoke on his return to Washington.

9. **Ev Dirksen:** (January 4, 1896–September 7, 1969) Everett McKinley Dirksen was a Republican U.S. Congressman and Senator from Illinois. He served as the Republican Senate leader. He helped write the Civil Rights Act of 1964 and played a decisive role in its passage. He was one of the Senate's strongest supporters of the Vietnam War. Lyndon Johnson and Everett Dirksen enjoyed the kind of close personal and working relationship that became rare in later years between Republicans and Democrats.

10. **Voting Rights Act:** The National Voting Rights Act of 1965 outlawed the requirement that would-be voters in the United States take literacy tests or pay a poll tax to qualify to register to vote. It provided for federal registration of voters instead of state or local voter registration, which had often been denied to minorities and poor voters, in areas that had less than 50 percent of eligible minority voters registered. It was signed into law by President Lyndon Johnson on August 6, 1965.

11. **Jack Valenti:** (September 5, 1921–) Jack Joseph Valenti co-founded Weekley & Valenti, an advertising/political consulting agency, in 1952. Valenti's agency was in charge of the press during the November 1963 visit of President John F. Kennedy and Vice President Lyndon Johnson to Dallas, Texas. Valenti then became the first "special assistant" to President Lyndon Johnson. After serving Johnson, he worked as the chief lobbyist and long-time president of the Motion Picture Association of America.

12. **Mary McGrory:** (August 22, 1918–April 20, 2004) Mary McGrory, a journalist and columnist, was a fierce opponent of the Vietnam War, which stirred the dislike of Lyndon Johnson and later landed her on Richard Nixon's enemies list. Mary McGrory was hired in 1947 by the *Washington Star* and began her career as a journalist, a path she was inspired to take by reading *Jane Arden* comic strips. She rose to prominence as the *Star's* reporter covering the McCarthy hearings in 1954. McGrory won the Pulitzer Prize in 1975 for her articles about the Watergate

scandal. After the *Star* went out of business in 1981, McGrory went to work for the *Washington Post*.

13. **Haldemans:** (October 27, 1926–November 12,1993) Harry Robbins Haldeman, publicly known as H. R. Haldeman, and informally as Bob Haldeman, was a U.S. political aide and businessman, best known for his service as White House chief of staff to President Richard Nixon and for his role in events leading to the Watergate scandal. Nixon named Haldeman as his first White House chief of staff. Together with John Ehrlichman they were called "The Berlin Wall" by other White House staffers because of their penchant for keeping others away from Nixon and serving as his "gatekeepers." Both were ruthless in protecting what they and Nixon saw as the president's best interests; Haldeman referred to himself as Nixon's "son of a bitch."

14. **Ehrlichmans:** John Daniel Ehrlichman (March 20, 1925–February 24, 1999) was counsel and assistant to the president for domestic affairs under President Richard Nixon and a key figure in events leading to the Watergate scandal. Ehrlichman created "The Plumbers," the group at the center of the Watergate scandal. After the start of the Watergate investigations in 1972, Ehrlichman lobbied for an intentional delay in the embattled confirmation of L. Patrick Gray as director of the F.B.I. He argued that the confirmation hearings were deflecting media attention from Watergate and that it would be better for Gray to be left "twisting, slowly, slowly in the wind." The quote served as the embodiment of one of Ehrlichman's main functions during his years in the White House, to seek and destroy Nixon's enemies at virtually any cost, a function that would overshadow his domestic efforts in a White House consumed with foreign policy.

15. **Stokely Carmichael:** (June 29, 1941–November 15, 1998) Stokely Carmichael, also known as Kwame Ture, was a Trinidadian–American black activist leader of the Student Nonviolent Coordinating Committee (SNCC) and the Black Panther Party. He later became a black separatist and a Pan-Africanist. After helping organize voting rights drives in Mississippi in 1964, in Selma in 1965, and in Lowndes County, Alabama, in 1966, he became chair of SNCC in 1966, taking over from John Lewis. A few weeks after Carmichael took over SNCC, James Meredith was shot by a sniper during his solitary "March Against Fear." Carmichael joined Dr. Martin Luther King Jr., Floyd McKissack, and others to continue Meredith's march. Arrested during the march, on his release he gave his "Black Power" speech, using that phrase to urge black pride and independence. Stokely Carmichael is credited with coining the phrase *institutional racism*.

16. **Rap Brown:** (October 4, 1943–) H. Rap Brown came to national attention in the 1960s as a civil rights worker, black activist, and as the justice

minister of the Black Panther Party. He is perhaps most famous for his proclamation during that period that "violence is as American as cherry pie." He once said, "If America don't come around, we're gonna burn it down." His activism in the civil rights movement included involvement in SNCC, of which he was named chairman in 1967. That same year, he was arrested in Cambridge, Maryland, and charged with "inciting to riot" as a result of a fiery speech he gave there. He left the SNCC and joined the Black Panther Party in 1968.

17. *Agronsky & Co.*: This weekly show featured a panel of prominent Washington journalists who discussed the week's political events. It was first titled *Martin Agronsky: Evening Edition* and appeared on a local PBS affiliate in Washington, WETA, in 1971. The retitled show went national in 1976 on PBS affiliates and was syndicated by the show's producer, the *Post-Newsweek Company*. The host, Martin Agronsky was a distinguished journalist who gained national prominence as the host of the long running CBS interview show *Face the Nation*.

18. marines to Lebanon: The 1983 Beirut barracks bombing was a major incident during the Lebanese Civil War. Two truck bombs struck buildings in Beirut housing U.S. and French members of the Multinational Force in Lebanon, killings hundreds of soldiers, the majority being U.S. Marines. The October 23, 1983, blasts led to the withdrawal of the international peacekeeping force from Lebanon, where it had been stationed since the Israeli invasion in 1982. The attack remains the deadliest post–World War II attack on Americans overseas.

Ethel Payne

19. Interstate Commerce Commission: The Interstate Commerce Commission (or ICC) was a regulatory body created by the Interstate Commerce Act of 1887, which was signed into law by President Grover Cleveland. The Freedom Rides were first conceived in 1947 when the Congress of Racial Equality (CORE) and the Fellowship of Reconciliation organized an interracial bus ride across state lines to test a Supreme Court decision that declared segregation on interstate buses unconstitutional. Called the Journey of Reconciliation, the ride only challenged segregation on buses and was limited to the upper South to avoid the more dangerous Deep South. The ride, however, failed to elicit much national attention or the results CORE had hoped for. Fourteen years later, in a new national context of sit-ins, boycotts, and the emergence of the Southern Christian Leadership Conference (SCLC) and the Student Nonviolent Coordinating Committee (SNCC), the Freedom Riders were able to harness enough national attention to force federal enforcement and policy change.

20. **Alex Wilson:** (1908–October 11, 1960) L. Alex Wilson was a black journalist, the editor and general manager of the *Tri-State Defender* of Memphis, Tennessee. The *Tri-State Defender* was the southern outpost of the *Chicago Defender*, one of the foremost black newspapers in the United States. Wilson was one of the black journalists assigned to cover the school desegregation attempts at Little Rock Arkansas in September of 1957. The situation had been brewing for three weeks until the morning of September 23, 1957, when the nine black students attempted to enter Central High School. Wilson was savagely kicked, beaten, and hit in the head with a brick by a white mob while the nine students safely entered the school building. Wilson sustained permanent physical damage and in 1959 began experiencing a "nervous ailment" which seems likely to have been Parkinson's Disease. According to the writer Hank Klibanoff, Wilson's wife and friends concluded that the condition had been brought on by the beating he took in Little Rock.

21. **Jimmy Hicks:** (May 9, 1915–January 19, 1986) James L. Hicks was a reporter for the *Amsterdam News* on the Emmett Till case and other cases involving civil rights. He was the first African American member of the State Department Correspondents Association and the first African American reporter to cover the United Nations. He served in World War II as a decorated army officer. See also Chapter 9: James Hicks.

22. **The *Daily Worker:*** The *Daily Worker* was a newspaper published in New York City by the Communist Party USA. Publication began in 1924. While the paper generally reflected the prevailing views of the Communist Party, it made attempts to cover the spectrum of left-wing opinion. At its peak, the newspaper achieved a circulation of 35,000. Richard Wright, author of *Native Son*, was one of the paper's notable contributors.

23. **CIO:** The American Federation of Labor and Congress of Industrial Organizations, commonly known as the AFL-CIO, is America's largest federation of unions, made up of 53 national and international (including Canada) unions, together representing over 9 million workers. The AFL-CIO was formed in 1955 when the AFL and the CIO merged after a long estrangement. From 1955 until 2005, the AFL-CIO's member unions represented virtually all unionized workers in the United States. Since 2005 several large unions have split with the federation.

24. **Drew Pearson:** (December 13, 1897–September 1, 1969) Drew Pearson was one of the most prominent American newspaper and radio journalists of his day. He was best known for his muckraking syndicated newspaper column *Washington Merry-Go-Round*. He was an early opponent of McCarthyism. His column helped bring about the firing of George

S. Patton from his command of the Seventh Army during World War II. Pearson's criticism of James V. Forrestal may have contributed to Forrestal's "mental breakdown" and resignation as U.S. secretary of defense.

25. **Biafra:** The Republic of Biafra was a short-lived secessionist state in southeastern Nigeria. It existed from May 30, 1967, to January 15, 1970. The military's chief of staff formally announced capitulation on January 12. The country was named after the Bight of Biafra, the bay of the Atlantic to its south.

26. **Winston Churchill III:** (1940–) The grandson and namesake of Britain's wartime prime minister, Winston S. Churchill III was for many years a journalist and war correspondent, reporting on conflicts around the world. Mr. Churchill entered Parliament in 1970 as the youngest conservative member. He served twenty-seven years in Parliament, was appointed spokesman on Defense by Margaret Thatcher, and served on the Defense Select Committee of the House of Commons until 1997 when he stood down as MP. He is the author of several books.

27. **Balkanizing:** Balkanization is a geopolitical term originally used to describe the process of fragmentation or division of a region into smaller areas that are often hostile or noncooperative with each other. The term arose from the conflicts in the twentieth-century Balkans. The first Balkanization was embodied in the Balkan Wars, and the term was reaffirmed in the Yugoslav Wars.

28. **Ibos:** The Igbo, often erroneously referred to as "Ibo" are one of the largest single ethnicities in Africa. Most Igbo speakers are based in southern Nigeria, where they constitute about 17 percent of the population; they can also be found in significant numbers in Cameroon and Equatorial Guinea. Their language is also called Igbo.

29. **Idi Amin:** (January 1, 1925?–August 16, 2003) Idi Amin Dada was an army officer and president of Uganda (1971–1979). Much sectarian violence took place during his rule, including the persecution of the Acholi, Lango, Indian, and other ethnic groups, as well as Hindus and Christians in Uganda. The death toll during Amin's reign will never be accurately known. The International Commission of Jurists estimates that not less than 80,000, and more likely around 300,000, people were killed. Another estimate, compiled by exile organizations with the help of Amnesty International, put the number killed at 500,000.

30. **Zhou Enlai:** (March 5, 1898–January 8, 1976). Zhou Enlai (spelled Chou En-lai in the Wade-Giles system of transliteration) was premier of the People's Republic of China from 1949 until his death, serving the ultimate leader, Mao Tse-Tung, with unflagging loyalty.

Joel Dreyfus

31. **Dahomey:** Dahomey was a kingdom in Africa, situated in what is now the nation of Benin. The kingdom was founded in the seventeenth century and survived until the late nineteenth century, when it was conquered by French troops from Senegal and incorporated into France's West African colonies. In 1958, Dahomey became an autonomous republic and gained full independence in 1960. The Republic of Dahomey changed its name to Benin in 1975.

32. **UNESCO:** The United Nations Educational, Scientific and Cultural Organization is a specialized agency of the United Nations established in 1945. Its stated purpose was to contribute to peace and security by promoting international collaboration through education, science, and culture in order to further universal respect for justice, the rule of law, and the human rights and fundamental freedoms proclaimed in the UN Charter.

33. **Leonard Boudin:** (July 20, 1912–November 25, 1989) Leonard Boudin was an attorney who represented such controversial clients as Judith Coplon, Fidel Castro, Paul Robeson, and was counsel to numerous left-wing organizations. His was the father of Kathy Boudin, a member of the Weather Underground, which described itself as a "fifth column" of the Viet Cong and the North Vietnamese Army. In 1984, she was convicted of felony murder for her 1981 involvement in a robbery of a Brinks armored car near Nyack, New York, in which three people were killed.

34. **"Jimmy" story:** Janet Cooke (July 23, 1954–) is an African American journalist who became infamous when she won a Pulitzer Prize for a fabricated story that she wrote for the *Washington Post*. In an article entitled "Jimmy's World," which appeared in the *Post* on September 29, 1980, Cooke wrote a gripping profile of the life of an eight-year-old heroin addict. Despite growing signs of problems, the *Post* defended the veracity of the story, and Assistant Managing Editor Bob Woodward nominated the story for the Pulitzer Prize. Cooke was named winner of the prize on April 13, 1981. Two days after the prize had been awarded, *Washington Post* publisher Donald Graham held a press conference and admitted that the story was fraudulent. Cooke resigned, and the prize was returned.

35. **Ed Bradley:** Edward Randolph Bradley Jr. (June 22, 1941–November 9, 2006) Ed Bradley was an American journalist who was best known for his award-winning work on the long-running CBS News television magazine *60 Minutes*. See also Chapter 19: Ed Bradley.

36. **Max Robinson:** Max Robinson (May 1, 1939–December 20, 1988) Max Robinson was a television journalist and the Chicago–based co-anchor of ABC News *World News Tonight* from 1978–1983. He was best

known for being the only African-American network news anchor in the country. He was also a founder of the National Association of Black Journalists (NABJ). See also Chapter 8: Max Robinson.

37. **Les Payne:** (July 12, 1941–) Les Payne is an African American journalist and author. He served six years in the U.S. Army and worked as an Army journalist and wrote speeches for General William Westmoreland. He joined *Newsday* in the late 1960s, serving as the associate managing editor for the paper's national, science, and international news. He covered the Black Panther Party and the assassination of Dr. Martin Luther King Jr. He won a Pulitzer Prize for "The Heroin Trail," which was a *Newsday* series in thirty-three parts that traced the international flow of heroin from the poppy fields of Turkey to the veins of drug addicts in New York City.

Ben Holman

38. **Gary Hart:** (November 28, 1936–) Gary Warren Hart (born Gary Warren Hartpence) is a politician and lawyer from the state of Colorado. He formerly served as a Democratic U.S. Senator representing Colorado (1975–1987), and ran in the U.S. presidential elections in 1984 and again in 1988, when he was considered a frontrunner for the Democratic nomination, until he withdrew from the race because of a scandal involving a woman who was not his wife.

39. **Bob Maynard:** (June 17, 1937–August 17, 1993) Robert C. Maynard was an African American newspaper editor, publisher, writer and social commentator. He attended Harvard on a Nieman fellowship in 1965–1966; eventually receiving eight honorary doctorates. He was editor-in-chief, publisher and owner of the *Oakland Tribune*.

40. **Louis Farrakhan:** Louis Farrakhan (born Louis Eugene Walcott, May 11, 1933) is the head of the Nation of Islam.

John Q. Jordan

41. **Speed Graphic:** There is a tendency for the name "Speed Graphic" to be used to denote any "press" style camera. The Speed Graphic was manufactured by Graflex, a camera producer based in Rochester, New York. It was the dominant portable professional camera from the 1930s through the end of the 1950s. The Speed Graphic has not been manufactured since 1973.

42. **Pillboxes:** Pillboxes are small brick or stone structures, which are designed entirely for defensive purposes. They are normally intended to hold from one to ten men armed with rifles, light or heavy machine guns or small antitank weapons, depending on the location.

43. **the Gothic Line:** The Gothic Line, known also as the Linea Gotica, formed Field Marshal Albert Kesserlring's last line of defense along the summits of the Apennines during the fighting retreat of Nazi Germany's forces from Italy in the final stages of World War II. The Gothic Line developed as a result of one of the Allies' missteps in the Anzio breakout.

Karen DeWitt

44. *Jet* **magazine:** *Jet* magazine is a popular African American publication founded in Chicago, Illinois, in 1951 by John H. Johnson of Johnson Publishing Company. *Jet* is notable for its small digest-sized format. Influential in the early days of the American civil rights movement, with its coverage of the murder of Emmett Till and the Montgomery Bus Boycott, *Jet* is part of Johnson Publishing's *Ebony* publishing empire.

Max Robinson

45. *Mohammad, Messenger of God: Messenger of God* is a film released in 1976 chronicling the life and times of the Prophet of Islam, Muhammad. Although the movie revolves around Muhammad, his image is not depicted in any way throughout the movie, out of respect for Muslim traditions. Nevertheless, some cinemas still received threatening telephone calls from those who thought that the film offended Islam by portraying the Prophet in a physical way, even though Muhammad is not shown on screen. On March 9, 1977, a group of Black Muslims (Hanafi Muslims), seized several buildings and took 134 hostages in Washington, D.C. Their actions were related to a sectarian dispute within the Black Muslim community. One of their demands was to prevent the release of the film. One of the terrorists specifically said "he wanted a guarantee from the whole world it will never be shown or they would execute some of the hostages." They held the hostages for more than 39 hours. They shot Washington, D.C., council member Marion Barry in the chest, and shot a radio reporter dead.

46. **Roone Arledge:** (July 8, 1931–December 5, 2002) Roone Arledge was an American sports broadcasting pioneer who became chairman of ABC News from 1977 until his death. He played a key role in raising ABC's status to a competitive level with the two other main broadcasting companies, NBC and CBS.

47. **American hostages in Iran:** The Iran hostage crisis was a 444-day period during which student proxies of the new Iranian regime, who were Muslim student followers of the Imam's line, held hostage 63 diplomats and three citizens of the United States inside the U.S. Embassy in

Tehran. The standoff lasted from November 4, 1979, until January 20, 1981, and was resolved when the hostages were freed.

48. **Earl Caldwell:** See Earl Caldwell chapter.

49. **DuPont Awards:** The purpose of the Alfred I. DuPont Columbia University Awards is to bring the best in television and radio journalism to professional and public attention and to honor those who produce it.

50. **Charlayne Hunter-Gault:** (February 27, 1942–) Charlayne Hunter is currently a foreign correspondent with National Public Radio. In 1961, she and Hamilton E. Holmes were the first African American students to attend the University of Georgia, ending racial segregation at that institution. Her dormitory, Myers Hall, became the center of racial riots early in her stay there. The academic building at the University of Georgia where she and Holmes registered for classes was renamed the Holmes-Hunter Academic Building in 2001.

James Hicks

51. **Charlie Diggs:** (December 2, 1922–August 24, 1998) Charles Coles Diggs Jr., was the first black U.S. congressman from Michigan. He served from January 3, 1954 until June 2, 1980. His career ended when he was charged with mail fraud and other offenses and sentenced to three years in prison.

52. **Ralph Matthews:** Ralph Matthews, Sr., was known as the *Baltimore Afro-American* newspaper's answer to H. L. Mencken. He became, as one web site says, "a power at the *Afro-American*, serving as the theatrical editor, city editor, managing editor, and editor of the *Washington Afro-American*. A witty and acerbic man, Matthews had one or two columns in the *Afro-American* from the 1920s onward. In them he lampooned sacred cows in the black community, such as the black church and its ministers, black politicians, black society and the institutions of marriage and family."

53. **White Citizens Council:** The White Citizens Council was a U.S. movement against racial desegregation. It began as a protest against federal court decisions that ordered racial desegregation, most notably *Brown v. Board of Education* (1954). Fourteen whites in the Delta town of Indianola, Mississippi, founded the first known chapter of the WCC on July 11, 1954. Within a few months, the WCC had spread beyond Mississippi into the rest of the Deep South. In most communities, there was little or no stigma associated with being a member of the WCC. Unlike the Klan, the WCC met openly and was seen by many as being "reputable." Also, unlike the Klan, its tactics did not often involve direct confrontation with violence, or terrorism, but rather economic ones.

54. **Murray Kempton:** (December 16, 1917–May 5, 1997) James Murray Kempton was a major American journalist who was a significant presence on the political left for many years. In 1939, he worked for a short time as a labor organizer, then joined the staff of the *New York Post* in 1949, where he was the labor editor and later a columnist. During 1960s he edited the *New Republic*. In 1981 he began writing a regular column for *Newsday*, and was also a regular contributor to *The New York Review of Books*. He won the Pulitzer Prize in 1985.

William Raspberry

55. **CORE:** The Congress of Racial Equality is a U.S. civil rights organization that played a pivotal role in the civil rights movement of the twentieth century. CORE membership is open to "anyone who believes that all people are created equal and is willing to work towards the ultimate goal of true equality throughout the world." CORE was founded in Chicago in 1942 by James L. Farmer, George Houser, and Bernice Fisher. The group's inspiration was Krishnalal Shridharani's book *War Without Violence* (1939), which outlined Gandhi's step-by-step procedures for organizing people and mounting a nonviolent campaign.

56. **SNCC:** The Student Nonviolent Coordinating Committee (or SNCC, pronounced "snick") was one of the primary institutions of the American civil rights movement in the 1960s. It emerged in April of 1960 from student meetings led by Ella Baker held at Shaw University in Raleigh, North Carolina. Its purpose then was to coordinate the use of nonviolent direct action to attack segregation and other forms of racism. SNCC played a leading role in the Freedom Rides, the 1963 March on Washington, the Mississippi Freedom Summer, and the Mississippi Freedom Democratic Party. In the later part of the 1960s, led by fiery leaders like Stokely Carmichael, SNCC focused on Black Power, and then fighting against the Vietnam War.

57. **Urban League:** The National Urban League grew out of the spontaneous grassroots movement for freedom and opportunity that came to be called the Black Migrations. After the Supreme Court declared its approval of segregation in the 1896 *Plessey v. Ferguson* decision, the white South quickly adopted oppressive measures that turned what had been a trickle of African Americans moving northward into a flood. To help blacks who fled the South adapt to urban life and fight discrimination they faced in the North, the Committee on Urban Conditions Among Negroes was established on September 29, 1910. The name was shortened to the National Urban League in 1920.

58. **Bob Jones University matter:** On January 19, 1976, the Internal Revenue Service notified the University that its tax exemption had been revoked

retroactively to December 1, 1970. The school appealed the IRS decision all the way to the U.S. Supreme Court, arguing that the University met all other criteria for tax-exempt status and that the school's racial discrimination was based on sincerely held religious beliefs that "God intended segregation of the races and that the Scriptures forbid interracial marriage." The University was not challenged about the origin if its interracial dating policy, and the District Court accepted "on the basis of a full evidentiary record" BJUs argument that the rule was a sincerely held religious conviction, a finding affirmed by all subsequent courts. In December 1978, the federal district court ruled in the University's favor; two years later, that decision was overturned by the Fourth Circuit of Appeals.

On January 8, 1982, just before the case was to be heard by the U.S. Supreme Court, President Ronald Reagan authorized his Treasury and Justice Departments to ask that the BJU case be dropped and that the previous court decisions be vacated. Political pressure quickly brought the Reagan administration to reverse itself and to ask the Court to reinstate the case. Then, in a virtually unprecedented move, the Court invited William T. Coleman Jr., to argue the government's position in an *amicus curiae* brief, thus insuring that the prosecution's position would be the one the Court wished to hear. The case was heard on October 12, 1982, and on May 24, 1983, the U.S. Supreme Court ruled against Bob Jones University in *Bob Jones University v. United States* (461 U.S. 574). The University refused to reverse its interracial dating policy and (with difficulty) paid a million dollars in back taxes.

59. **Yassir Arafat:** Yassir Arafat (August 4 or 24, 1929–November 11, 2004) was born in Cairo to Palestinian parents. Arafat was Chairman of the Palestinian Liberation Organization (PLO) 1969–2004). He was president of the Palestinian National Authority (PNA) (1993–2004); and a co-recipient of the 1994 Nobel Peace Prize, along with Shimon Peres and Yitzhak Rabin, for the successful negotiations of the 1993 Oslo Accords.

60. **Little Rock Nine:** The Little Rock Nine or the Little Rock Crisis refers to an incident in which nine African American students were prevented from attending Little Rock Central High in Little Rock, Arkansas, in 1957 during the civil rights movement.

Henry M. "Hank" Brown

61. **AFL-CIO:** The American Federation of Labor and Congress of Industrial Organizations is American's largest federation of unions, made up of 53 national and international (including Canada) unions, together

representing over 9 million workers. The AFL-CIO was formed in 1955 when the AFL and the CIO merged after a long estrangement. From 1955 until 2005, the AFL/CIO's member unions represented virtually all unionized workers in the United States. Since 2005 several large unions have split with the federation.

62. **the situation in Poland:** When the Polish government suppressed the Solidarity Movement under Lech Walesa in late 1981, President Ronald Reagan imposed economic sanctions on the People's Republic of Poland.

63. **Anwar al-Sadat:** (December 25, 1918–October 6, 1981) Mohammad Anwar Al-Sadat was an Egyptian soldier and politician who served as the third president of Egypt from October 15, 1970 until his assassination on October 6, 1981. He is considered in Egypt and in the West to be one of the most influential Egyptian and Middle Eastern figures in modern history.

Leon Dash

64. **Operation Crossroads Africa:** American's premier cross-cultural exchange program, Operation Crossroads Africa was established in 1957 by Dr. James H. Robinson, who foresaw a "clear, honest, hard-hitting program" in which young North Americans would work at the grassroots level with young Africans. He envisioned young people "building bridges of friendship to Africa."

65. **UNITA:** The National Union for the Total Independence of Angola, commonly known by its Portuguese acronym, UNITA is an Angolan political faction and a former rebel force. From its foundation until his death, UNITA was lead by its leader and founder, Jonas Savimbi.

66. **EEOC:** The Equal Employment Opportunity Commission, or EEOC, is a United States agency tasked with ending employment discrimination in the United States. Signed into law by President John F. Kennedy, it can bring suit on behalf of alleged victims of discrimination against private employers. It also serves as an adjudicatory for claims of discrimination brought against federal agencies. The EEOC's mandate is specified under Title VII of the Civil Rights Act of 1964.

67. **Mau-Mau-ing:** The Mau-Mau uprising was an insurgency by Kenyan rebels against the British colonial administration that lasted from 1952 to 1960. The core of the resistance was formed by members of the Kikuyu tribe. The uprising did not succeed militarily, but did create a rift between the white settler community in Kenya and the Home Office in London that set the stage for Kenyan independence in 1963. ("Mau-Mau," when used as a verb by black professionals, denotes forceful intellectual resistance against the white power structure.)

68. **Jimmy Hoffa:** (February 14, 1913–July 30, 1975?) James Riddle "Jimmy" Hoffa was a noted American labor leader with ties to the Mafia. As the president of the International Brotherhood of Teamsters from the mid-1950s to the mid–1960s, Hoffa wielded considerable influence. He is also well-known in popular culture for the mysterious circumstances surrounding his still-unexplained disappearance and presumed death.

69. **FNLA:** The National Front for the Liberation of Angola (FNLA) was one of the three national liberation movements that fought against Portuguese colonial rule in Angola. It was founded in 1957 by Holden Roberto. The other two were the Popular Movement for the Liberation of Angola (MPLA) and the National Union for the Total Independence of Angola (UNITA).

Barbara Reynolds

70. **Operation Breadbasket:** Operation Breadbasket was an organization dedicated to improving the economic conditions of black communities across the United States. It was founded as a department of Martin Luther King Jr.'s Southern Christian Leadership Conference (SCLC) in 1962. Nearly all the early activities were in Atlanta and other Southern cities. A key figure in the history of Operation Breadbasket was Jesse Jackson. Although King was suspicious of Jackson's intense personal ambition and hunger for attention, he gradually gave him greater responsibilities. When Jackson returned from Selma, he threw himself into King's effort to establish a beachhead in Chicago.

71. **Andy Young:** (March 12, 1932–) Andrew Jackson Young is an American civil rights activist and former mayor of Atlanta, Georgia. He was the United States' first African American ambassador to the United Nations. He received a Bachelor of Divinity degree from Hartford Seminary in Hartford, Connecticut in 1955. In 1960, he joined the Southern Christian Leadership Conference and in 1964 was named executive director of that organization. He became one of Dr. King's principal lieutenants. Young was with King in Memphis, Tennessee when he was assassinated in 1968.

72. **Ralph Abernathy:** (March 11, 1926 – April 17, 1990) Ralph David Abernathy was an American civil rights leader. He was Martin Luther King's number two in the Southern Christian Leadership Conference, and held the official title of secretary-treasurer. Abernathy was with Martin Luther King in Memphis when King was assassinated. In fact, they shared Room 307 at the Lorraine Motel the night before.

73. **Hosea Williams:** (January 5, 1926–November 16, 2000) Hosea Lorenzo Williams was a U.S. civil rights leader, ordained minister and later a

politician. He served with the U.S. Army during World War II, in an all African-American unit under General Patton. He first joined the NAACP and later became a leader in the SCLC along with Martin Luther King Jr., Joseph Lowery, and Andrew Young, among others. He also led the first 1965 march on Selma, Alabama and was beaten unconscious. He was left with a fractured skull and a severe concussion.

74. **Bernard Lee:** Bernard "Jelly" Lee was an early member of Dr. Martin Luther King Jr.'s Southern Christian Leadership Conference (SCLC) and an organizer and participant in the sit-ins in Montgomery, Alabama. He later became King's aide-de-camp.

75. **PUSH:** People United to Save Humanity (PUSH) was founded in 1971 through efforts led by the social activist Jesse Jackson and Operation Breadbasket, an organization that served as the economic foundation for the Southern Christian Leadership Conference. Jackson had previously been selected to lead Operation Breadbasket by Martin Luther King Jr.

76. **Ethel Payne:** (August 14, 1911–May 28, 1991) Ethel L. Payne was an award-winning African American journalist. Known as the "First Lady of the Black Press" she was a columnist, lecturer, and freelance writer. She combined advocacy with journalism as she reported on the civil rights movement during the 1950s and 1960s. She became the first female African American commentator employed by a national network when CBS hired her in 1972. In 2002, the US Postal Service honored Ethel Payne with a commemorative 37-cent stamp. See also Ethel Payne chapter.

77. **Dick Gregory:** (October 12, 1932–) Richard "Dick" Claxton Gregory is an American comedian, social activist, writer, entrepreneur, and nutritionist. After completing his military service, Gregory performed as a comedian in small, primarily black nightclubs while working for the U.S. Postal Service during the day. He soon began appearing nationally and on television, with his 1964 autobiography, *Nigger*, selling seven million copies. In time he became involved in civil rights struggles, the anti–Vietnam War movement and antidrug issues. He developed a reputation for going on hunger strikes to support his protests.

78. **Nieman Fellow:** The Nieman Fellowship is an award given to mid-career journalists by The Nieman Foundation for Journalism at Harvard University. This prestigious award allows winners time to reflect on their careers and focus on honing their skills. Twelve American and twelve international fellowships are awarded annually.

C. Sumner "Chuck" Stone

79. **Adam Clayton Powell Jr.:** (November 29, 1908–April 4, 1972) Adam Clayton Powell Jr. was the first African American to become a powerful

figure in the United States Congress. In 1937, he succeeded his father as pastor of the Abyssinian Baptist Church in Harlem, New York. He was elected to the U.S. House of Representatives from Harlem in 1944, and became chair of the Education and Labor Committee in 1961. As one of the great modern legislators, Powell steered some fifty bills through Congress. He passed legislation that made lynching a federal crime and bills that desegregated public schools and the U.S. military. He challenged the Southern practice of charging blacks a poll tax to vote, and stopped congressmen from saying the word "nigger" in sessions of Congress. After over two decades in Congress, Powell's career was ended by a corruption scandal.

80. **Educational Testing Service:** The Educational Testing Service or ETS is the world's largest private educational testing and measurement organization. ETS develops various standardized examinations primarily in the United Sates. Many of the assessments they develop are associated with entry to U.S. undergraduate and graduate institutions.

81. **Marcus Garvey:** (August 17, 1887–June 10, 1940) Marcus Mosiah Garvey, a national hero of Jamaica, was a publisher, journalist, entrepreneur, black nationalist, and founder of the Universal Improvement Association and African Communities League (UNIA-ACL). Garvey is best remembered as an important proponent of the Back to Africa movement, which encouraged those of African descent to return to their ancestral homelands. His movement later inspired other movements, ranging from the Nation of Islam to the Rastafari movement, which proclaimed him a prophet.

82. **Jaycees organization:** Jaycees or Junior Chamber of Commerce was founded in 1923 and has 300,000 members internationally. The goal of the organization is to provide members with management and leadership skills. The Jaycees try to help young professionals circumvent the Old Boy's Network and the glass ceiling that lead to unfairness in promotions, hiring, and job assignments.

Bernard Shaw

83. **Ralph Abernathy:** See note 72.

84. **Andy Young:** See note 71.

85. **Westinghouse:** The Westinghouse Electric Corporation was founded in 1886. In 1995, Westinghouse Electric Corporation acquired CBS for $5.4 billion. Having participated in commercial broadcasting since 1920, Westinghouse sought to transform itself into a major media company with its purchase of CBS. This was followed in 1997 with the $4.9 billion purchase of Infinity Broadcasting Corporation, owner of more

than 150 radio stations. Westinghouse was renamed CBS Corporation in 1997 until its acquisition by Viacom.

86. **Leonard Woodcock:** (February 15, 1911–January 16, 2001) Leonard Freel Woodcock was an American labor union leader and diplomat who was the president of the United Automobile Workers (UAW) from 1970 to 1977. He was United States Ambassador to the People's Republic of China from 1979–1981. Woodcock's name appeared on Nixon's enemies list.

87. **brothers Kalb, Roger Mudd, Dan Rather, Nelson Benton, George Herman, Eric Sevareid:**

Marvin Kalb (June 9, 1930–) Marvin Kalb is an American journalist. He spent thirty years as an award-winning reporter for CBS and NBC News, as chief diplomatic correspondent, Moscow bureau chief, and host of *Meet the Press*. His work landed him on the master list of Nixon political opponents. Marvin Kalb was the last newsman recruited by Edward R. Murrow to join CBS News, becoming part of the later generation of Murrow's Boys. During many years of Kalb's tenures at CBS and NBC, his brother Bernard was also part of the news staff.

Bernard Kalb (February 4, 1922–) Bernard Kalb is a veteran journalist, media critic, and author. Kalb has traveled the globe for more than three decades as a correspondent covering world affairs for CBS News, NBC News and the *New York Times*. He was the founding anchor and a panelist on the weekly CNN program *Reliable Sources* for a decade.

Roger Mudd (February 9, 1928–) Roger Mudd is an Emmy Award–winning U.S. television journalist and broadcaster, most recently the primary anchor for The History Channel. Previously, Mudd was weekend anchor of *CBS Evening News*, co-anchor of *NBC Nightly News*, and hosted NBC's *Meet the Press*.

Dan Rather (October 31, 1931–) Daniel Irvin Rather Jr., is the former longtime anchor for the *CBS Evening News*. Rather was anchor of the *CBS Evening News* for twenty-four years, from March 9, 1981 to March 9, 2005.

Nelson Benton (September 16, 1923–February 13, 1988) Nelson Benton joined CBS News in New York in 1960 as an assignment editor and reporter. He worked in Dallas when President John F. Kennedy was assassinated in 1963. He reported on the civil rights movement in the South and covered the Vietnam War from Saigon, Hue, and the Vietnamese countryside. He covered Watergate and the resignation of President Richard Nixon in 1974. He won an Emmy for a special broadcast about the Watergate tapes.

George Herman (January 14, 1920–February 8, 2005) George Edward Herman was a veteran CBS journalist. Herman was CBS's first correspondent to file sound-and-film reports from abroad, and he was also the first reporter to broadcast coverage of the break-in at the headquarters of the Democratic National Committee in 1972. Herman was a long-standing moderator for the *Face the Nation* program.

Eric Sevareid: (November 26, 1912–July 9, 1992) Arnold Eric Sevareid was a CBS News journalist from 1939 to 1977. He was one of a group of elite war correspondents—dubbed "Murrow's boys"—because they were hired by pioneering CBS newsman Edward R. Murrow. Sevareid's work during World War II, with Edward R. Murrow, was at the forefront of broadcasting. He was the first to report on the fall of France and the French surrender to Nazi Germany in 1940. Shortly afterward, he joined Murrow to report on the Battle of Britain.

88. **Tom Capra:** Tom Capra was named executive producer of NBC's *Today Show* on January 29, 1990. Capra had extensive local and network news experience. He was a senior news producer for both CBS and ABC News. He is the son of the film director Frank Capra.

Austin Scott

89. **Bob Maynard:** See note 39.
90. **Horace Mann Bond:** (November 8, 1904 – December 1972) Horace Mann Bond was a noted educator, writer, and the father of civil rights leader Julian Bond. Bond graduated from Lincoln University in Pennsylvania at 19, and would later become the first African American president of his *alma mater* from 1945–1957. Horace Mann Bond earned an M.S. and Ph.D degree from the University of Chicago where his dissertation won the Rosenberger Prize in 1936. Albert Einstein, who had a long-standing policy of not speaking or accepting honorary degrees, relented when Dr. Bond invited him, and Einstein spoke and received an honorary degree from Lincoln University in May 1946.
91. **EEOC complaint against the *Washington Post:*** From a November 28, 1972, article in the *Washington Post*, written by Staff Writer Stephen Green— Headline: POST REBUTS CHARGE OF RACIAL BIAS.

The *Washington Post* has told the federal Equal Employment Opportunity Commission (EEOC) that its local office acted irresponsibly by accusing the newspaper of practicing discrimination against blacks without citing a single case of racial bias. Calling for the charges to be withdrawn, the *Post* said the EEOC accusations, made Nov. 1, contain 'serious errors of fact and unsupportable inference on virtually every page.'

The EEOC letter, which said the Washington office found "reasonable cause to believe" that the newspaper unlawfully discriminates against blacks in firing and promotion practices, followed a formal complaint by seven black reporters last April."

"We believe that for an agency of the United States government to have transmitted such a document based on so obviously inadequate an investigation with no effort made to verify the accuracy of the statements made was irresponsible," said the *Post* reply to EEOC. "We stand by our original charges," said Richard Prince, one of the Metro Seven reporters. The answer is directed toward EEOC, not us. In its reply, the *Post* asked that the accusations of discrimination made by the Metro Seven be dismissed as "obviously baseless."

The EEOC letter said *Post* payroll figures show that disproportionately small numbers of blacks work in the various departments of the newspaper plant and that few are assigned to management and other higher-paying positions.

Earl Caldwell

92. **Ivanhoe Donaldson:** Ivanhoe Donaldson worked with the Student Nonviolent Coordinating Committee (SNCC). During that time, he corresponded with Thomas Merton, a Trappist monk and acclaimed Catholic theologian, poet, author, and social activist. He worked alongside another Merton correspondent from this time, Marion Barry, who would later become mayor of Washington, D.C. He served as advisor to Barry from the 60s to the 80s and was involved in Jesse Jackson's 1984 presidential campaign.

93. **Scotty Reston:** (November 3, 1909–December 6, 1995) James Barrett Reston (nicknamed "Scotty") was a prominent American journalist whose career spanned the mid-1930s to the early 1990s. Associated for many years with the *New York Times*, he became perhaps the most powerful, influential and widely-read journalist of his era.

94. **David Hilliard:** David Hilliard was one of the first members of the Black Panther Party (BPP) and became chief of staff of the organization. Hilliard was arrested in January, 1968 for passing out leaflets at Oakland Technical High School. When Huey Newton was arrested in September 1968, Hilliard took over the command of the Black Panther Party. On April 6, 1968, eight BPP members including Hilliard, Eldridge Cleaver,

and Bobby Hutton were traveling in two cars when they were ambushed by the Oakland police. Cleaver and Hutton ran for cover and found themselves in a basement surrounded by police. The building was fired upon for over an hour. When a tear-gas canister was thrown into the basement, the two men decided to surrender. Cleaver was wounded in the leg so Hutton said he would go first. When he left the building with his hands in the air, he was shot twelve times by the police and was killed instantly.

95. **Tom Wicker:** (June 18, 1926–) Tom Wicker is an American journalist, one of the lead reporters on the *New York Times*' coverage of the assassination of President Kennedy. His 1975 book *A Time to Die: The Attica Prison Revolt*, which recounted events at the Attica Correctional Facility in Attica, New York during September 1971, received an Edgar Award from the Mystery Writers of America for the Best Fact Crime Book. He was a longtime columnist for the *Times* and the author of several books about U.S. presidents.

96. **Anthony Amsterdam:** (September 12, 1935–) Anthony G. Amsterdam is a professor of law at the New York University School of Law. In 1962, he took his first teaching position at the University of Pennsylvania, moving to Stanford in 1969. Throughout his career, Amsterdam has engaged in an extensive pro bono practice. Serving a wide variety of civil rights organizations, legal aid organizations, and public defender organizations, he has appeared in courtrooms, as well as (several times) in the Supreme Court of the United States with the NAACP Legal Defense and Educational Fund. In *Furman v. Georgia*, he persuaded the Court, which later reversed itself, that the death penalty was unconstitutional.

97. **Axis Sally:** (November 29, 1900–June 25, 1988) Axis Sally was a female radio personality during World War II. Born Mildred Elizabeth Sisk, she took the name Mildred Gillars. Gillars studied drama at Ohio Wesleyan University but dropped out before graduating. She found employment in Europe, working at the Berlitz School of Languages in Berlin, Germany. Later, she accepted a job as an announcer with Radio Berlin where she remained until Nazi Germany fell in 1945. With her sultry voice, Gillars was a well-known propagandist to Allied troops who gave her the name "Axis Sally." Her most infamous broadcast was made on May 11, 1944, prior to the D-Day invasion of Normandy, France. Gillars portrayed an American mother who dreamed that her son had been killed in the English Channel. After the war, Gillars was captured and eventually flown back to the United States in 1948. She was charged with ten counts of treason, although she was actually only tried for eight. The sensational, six-week trial ended on March 8, 1949. After long deliberations, the jury convicted Gillars on only one count of treason. She was sentenced to ten to thirty years. She became eligible

for parole in 1959, but did not pursue it until two years later when she applied for parole and received it.

98. **two other cases involving journalists:** *Branzburg v. Hayes*, 408 U.S. 665 (1972) was a landmark United States Supreme Court decision invalidating the use of the First Amendment as a defense for reporters summoned to testify before a grand jury. The case was argued February 23, 1972, and decided on June 29 of the same year. The case was decided on a vote of 5–4. It remains the only time the Supreme Court has considered the use of reportorial privilege. The case involved three reporters, all of whom had been called to testify before grand juries. Paul Branzburg of the *(Louisville) Courier Journal* in the course of his reporting duties had witnessed people manufacturing and using hashish. Earl Caldwell, a reporter for the *New York Times*, had conducted extensive interviews with the leaders of the Black Panthers. Paul Pappas, a Massachusetts television reporter, had also reported on the Black Panthers, spending several hours in their headquarters. All three reporters were called to testify before grand juries about illegal actions they might have witnessed. All three refused, citing privilege under the Press Clause, and were held in contempt. The Court ruled against the journalists as stated above.

Carole Simpson

99. **Voice of America:** Voice of America (VOA) is the official international radio and television broadcasting service of the United States federal government. It is vaguely similar to other international broadcasters such as the *BBC World*, *Radio France Internationale*, and *Radio Canada Internationale*, although these other agencies are not fully government-controlled.

100. **Mayor Daley:** (May 15, 1902–December 20, 1976) Richard Joseph Daley was the longest-serving mayor of Chicago. He served for twenty-one years as the undisputed Democratic boss of Chicago and is considered by historians to be the "last of the big city bosses." The year 1968 was a momentous year for Daley. In April, Daley was castigated for his sharp rhetoric in the aftermath of rioting that took place after Martin Luther King Jr.'s assassination. In August, the 1968 Democratic National Convention was held in Chicago. Intended to showcase Daley's achievements to national Democrats and the media, the proceedings during the convention instead garnered notoriety for the mayor and city. With the nation divided by the Vietnam War and with the assassinations of King and Robert F. Kennedy earlier that year serving as backdrop, the city became a battleground for antiwar protesters who vowed to shut down

the convention. In some cases, confrontations between protesters and police turned violent, with images of this violence broadcast on national television. Later, radical activists Abbie Hoffman, Jerry Rubin, and three other members of the "Chicago Seven" were convicted of crossing state lines with the intent of inciting a riot as a result of these confrontations, although the convictions were overturned on appeal.

101. **Lesley Stahl:** (December 16, 1941–) Lesley R. Stahl is an American television journalist. As of 2005, she had reported for CBS on *60 Minutes* for almost fifteen seasons.

102. **Yippies:** The Youth International Party (whose adherents were known as Yippies, a variant on "Hippies" that is also used to designate the surviving circles of activists who came out of the now-defunct YIP) was a highly theatrical political party established in the United States in 1966. An offshoot of the free speech and antiwar movements of the 1960s, the Yippies presented a more radically youth-oriented and countercultural alternative to those movements. Since they were better known for street theatre and politically-themed pranks, many of the "old school" political Left either ignored or denounced them.

103. **Bobby Seale:** (October 22, 1936–) Bobby Seale is an American civil rights activist, who along with Huey P. Newton, co-founded the Black Panther Party in 1966. He was one of the original Chicago Eight defendants charged with conspiracy and inciting to riot, in the wake of the 1968 Democratic National Convention, in Chicago, Illinois. Judge Julius Hoffman sentenced him to four years of imprisonment for contempt of court because of his outbursts, and eventually ordered Seale severed from the case, hence the "Chicago Seven." During one of the court trials, Bobby Seale's many outbursts led the judge to have him bound and gagged.

104. **Dave Dellinger:** (August 22, 1915 – May 25, 2004) David Dellinger was a renowned pacifist and activist for nonviolent social change and one of the most influential American radicals in the twentieth century. He was most famous for being one of the "Chicago Seven," a group of protesters whose disruption of the 1968 Democratic National Convention in Chicago led to charges of conspiracy and crossing state lines with the intention of inciting a riot. The ensuing court case was turned by Dellinger and his co-defendants into a nationally-publicized platform for putting the Vietnam War on trial. On February 18, 1970, they were found guilty of conspiring to incite riots, but the charges were eventually dismissed by an appeals court due to errors by U.S. District Judge Julius Hoffman.

Ed Bradley

105. boat people: In the years following the Vietnam War, over one million refugees fled the war-ravaged countries of Vietnam, Cambodia, and Laos. Those Vietnamese who took to the ocean in tiny overcrowded ships were dubbed the "boat people." The survivors sometimes languished for years in refugee camps in Asia. The luckier ones were taken in by countries like Canada.

106. APC: Armored Personnel Carrier. The M113 is an armored personnel carrier family of vehicles in use with the U.S. military and many other nations. It is a tracked vehicle capable of limited amphibious operation in lakes and streams, extended cross-country travel over rough terrain, and high-speed operation of improved roads. Although not a tank or even designed as a fighting vehicle, the M113 was the most effective armored vehicle of the Vietnam war, and remains in service and production in the twenty-first century.

107. eve of the collapse: The Khmer Rouge initiated their dry-season offensive to capture the beleaguered capital on January 1, 1975. Their troops controlled the banks of the Mekong River and were able to rig ingenious mines to sink convoys bringing relief supplies food, fuel, and ammunition to the slowly starving city. After the river was effectively blocked in early February, the United States began airlifts of supplies. This was extremely risky because of Khmer Rouge rockets. The communists also fired rockets and shells into the city, causing many civilian deaths. Doomed units of republican soldiers dug in around the capital; many of them had run out of ammunition, and they were overrun as the Khmer Rouge advanced.

108. Neil Davis: (February 14, 1934–September 9, 1985) Neil Brian Davis was an Australian combat cameraman who achieved worldwide recognition for his work as a photojournalist during the Vietnam War and other Indochinese conflicts. He was famed for his courage, professionalism, and sheer pigheadedness in the face of danger. He was the only cameraman who remained filming as tank 834 famously broke through the gates to the Presidential Palace in Saigon in 1975, and this image has long remained a symbol of the American failure to stop Communism in Vietnam. After many dangerous assignments on the battle fronts, "charmed" Neil Davis met an incongruous death by shrapnel in Bangkok while filming a minor Thai coup attempt that ended after only a few hours. Both Davis and his American soundman were killed when a coup faction tank opened fire on them without warning.

109. Year Zero: The term "Year Zero" applied to the takeover of Cambodia in 1975 by the Khmer Rouge, in an analogy to the Year One of the French Revolutionary Calendar. During the French Revolution after the abolition of the French monarchy (September 20, 1792), the National Convention instituted a new calendar and declared the beginning of Year One. The Khmer Rouge takeover of Phnom Penh was rapidly followed by a series of drastic revolutionary policies vastly exceeding those of the French Reign of Terror.

110. **Nguyen Cao Ky:** (1930–) Nguyen Cao Ky was premier (1965–1967) and vice president (1967–1971) of the former Republic of South Vietnam. Flight trained by the French, he returned to Vietnam (1954) and held a series of commands in the South Vietnamese air force. Ky's involvement in President Diem's overthrow (1963) led to his appointment to the air force command. Following a military coup led by Nguyen Van Thieu in 1965, Ky became premier, and was Thieu's vice-presidential running mate in the 1967 election. After the Communist takeover in 1975, he settled in the U.S. where he published a book, *Twenty Years and Twenty Days* (1976) and lectured at various universities.

WALLACE TERRY

111. Wallace Houston Terry, II (April 21, 1938–May 29, 2003) The contribution by Wallace Terry was adapted from a July 1, 1990 article in *Parade* magazine entitled "A Friendship Forged in Danger" by Wallace Terry.

INDEX

ABOUT THE AUTHOR

WALLACE TERRY WAS BORN IN New York City and raised in Indianapolis, Indiana where he was an editor of the *Shortridge Daily Echo*, one of the few high school dailies in America. As a reporter for the *Brown University Daily Herald*, he gained national attention when a photograph of him shaking hands with Orval Faubus, the outspoken segregationist governor of Arkansas, appeared on the front pages of the *New York Times* on September 14, 1957 and in newspapers around the world. Later, at Brown, Terry became the first black editor-in-chief of an Ivy League newspaper. He did graduate studies in theology as a Rockefeller Fellow at the University of Chicago, and in international relations as a Nieman Fellow at Harvard University.

When he was only 19, he was hired by the *Washington Post* and he later worked for *Time* magazine. Wallace ("Wally") Terry has been a Washington reporter, war correspondent, radio and television commentator, public lecturer, university professor, advertising executive, ordained minister and advisor to the Air Force, Marine Corps and Veterans Administrations.

Terry covered the civil rights March on Washington for the *Washington Post* on August 28, 1963. He wrote the first series on the Black Muslims, followed demonstrations in Danville, Jackson, Birmingham, and Selma and was the first to report the rise of the Black Power movement. When Terry joined *Time* magazine in 1963, he became the first black Washington correspondent for the mainstream media and the first black news magazine reporter. For *Time*, he covered urban upheavals in Harlem, Watts, Detroit and Newark, as well as the 1964 presidential campaign.

In 1967, Terry left for Vietnam where he became deputy bureau chief for *Time* in Saigon and the first black war correspondent on permanent duty for the mainstream media. For two years, he covered the Tet Offensive, flew scores of combat missions with American and South Vietnamese pilots, and joined assault troops in the Ashau Valley and on Hamburger Hill. His fellow reporters cheered his daring rescue with *New Republic* correspondent, Zalin Grant, of the bodies of four reporters killed by the Viet Cong during the May 1968 Offensive.

At *Time* Terry had exclusive interviews with Adlai Stevenson, Lyndon Johnson, Jimmy Hoffa, Malcolm X, Adam Clayton Powell, and Medgar Evers. As a member of the founding staff of *USA Today*, Terry originated the op-ed page and counted among those he interviewed Jimmy Carter, Edward Teller, Howard Baker, Marian Wright Edelman, Walter Mondale, Terry Bradshaw and Jerry Falwell. At *Parade* magazine, he profiled Dick Clark, Stevie Wonder, Quincy Jones, Lionel Hampton, Don Johnson, Christopher Walken, Gregory Hines and James Earl Jones. As a news analyst, he appeared on *Meet the Press, Face the Nation, The Lehrer News Hour, Agronsky & Co.,* and the *CBS Evening News.*

Published in 1984, his widely acclaimed book, *Bloods: An Oral History of the Vietnam War by Black Veterans* was named one of the five best nonfiction books of the year by *Time* magazine and was nominated for the Pulitzer Prize. *Bloods* has been honored by fifty-two cities and states and by the U.S. Congress and Vietnam Veterans of America.

Terry's one-man show, *Bloods: An Evening with Wallace Terry* was performed at more than 200 high schools, colleges, museums and libraries. He wrote and narrated the only documentary recording from the Vietnam battlefields, *Guess Who's Coming Home: Black Fighting Men Recorded Live in Vietnam,* which was released by Motown in 1972 and released independently in 2006. He wrote and narrated the PBS *Frontline* show, *The Bloods of Nam,* and the Mutual Broadcasting show, *Marching to Freedom* which won an NEA citation and the Edward R. Murrow Brotherhood Award from B'nai B'rith.

In 1991, Terry received the Medal of Honor for Distinguished Contributions to Journalism from the University of Missouri. In 1992, he became the first J. Saunders Redding Visiting Fellow at Brown University. And in 2000, the *Brown Alumni Monthly* named Terry one of a hundred graduates who made the greatest contributions to the twentieth century.

In 2003, Wallace Terry developed a rare vascular disease called Wegener's granulomatosis, which strikes about one in a million people. The disease can be treated with drugs, but in his case it was diagnosed too late. He died under treatment at a Reston, Virginia hospital on May 29, 2003.

He is survived by his wife of forty years, Janice Terry (née Jessup), who served during his career as his editorial assistant and researcher; also by three children—Tai, Lisa, and David—and two grandchildren, Noah and Sophia.